MW00630248

RIDIN' FREE

For Knuckles —

a songwriter, guitar-
picker and ex-hobo.
I salute you.

Whitey

RIDIN' FREE

GUITAR WHITEY

Edited by

Duffy Littlejohn

ZEPHYR RHOADES PRESS

Ridin' Free. Copyright © 2002 by Zephyr Rhoades Press.

All rights reserved. Printed in the United States of America.

No part of this book may be used or reproduced in any manner whatsoever without written permission of Zephyr Rhoades Press, except in the case of brief quotations embodied in critical articles and reviews.

For further information or to order a copy of this publication, please send $12.95 plus $5.00 shipping and handling, total: $17.95, addressed to: Zephyr Rhoades Press, Post Office Box 1999, Silver City, New Mexico, USA 88062-1999. Telephone: (505) 534-1888.

Please also visit our website for additional publications and credit card purchases at:

www.zrpress.com

-Edited by Duffy Littlejohn.

-Cover design by Ann Lowe.

-Cover photo courtesy Southern Methodist University, Dallas, Texas.

-Back cover photo courtesy Fran DeLorenzo, "The Hobo Minstrel."

-Printed in USA by Thomson-Shore, Inc., Dexter, Michigan.

ISBN   0-9723856-0-6

Library of Congress Card Catalogue Number: **2002114388**.

TABLE OF CONTENTS

Table of Contents – Cont'd

Table of Contents – Cont'd

* * * * *

Proclaimer

If you've ever wanted to do the daring thing, the exact opposite of what your parents and friends warned you against; maybe you owe it to yourself to break out and be the rebel you've long suspected was the real you. I've heard it all my life from well-meaning friends and family; don't ride those awful freight trains – you could get yourself killed. Besides, it's against the law. Same with hitch-hiking. It's forbidden in several states. Why accept rides with strangers? Don't you realize you might possibly be kidnapped, robbed or harmed?

I started doing all these things, and more, when I was about ten years old. I found it to be a thrill, a gas, a groovy way to go, and I refused to listen to all the prudent advice given to me by persons who, of themselves, would never dream of taking a chance, of running a risk, of bending the law, of living the daring life, and never mind the consequences. A rolling stone gathers no moss, that's true, but it picks up a high polish.

If it's true that you only go around once, then maybe you'd best get at it and do it – while you still can. You can always go back to school at any age. If you are of the adventurous spirit and feel you should test yourself – then GO FOR IT – get out there and adventure on life. Go for broke. Go ahead and do it. I would urge you to hop a freight train while you still can. Never mind where it's going or where you'll end up. Get that first ride under your belt and see how you like it. Get out on the highway, stick your thumb out and see what happens. Forget about a destination, just travel. Hike down some railroad track to the far horizon. Test yourself to see how far you can walk. Try spending a cold night out somewhere without blankets. Peace Pilgrim crisscrossed this country on foot for 23 years, as an older lady, with no sleeping gear. She didn't even wear a coat.

Take a vagabond trip carrying a bedroll, but take no money, and take no credit cards. Not even a quarter for the phone. See how long you can hold out. You may be surprised to find out who your friends are. Try floating down some river on a homemade raft, Huck Finn style. Take a job on a boat, any kind of boat or ship as a workaway, never mind where it's going. Try some hellishingly hard job of work (physically demanding). See how long you can tough it out.

Hike the Pacific Crest Trail. Beat your way through Canada on up to Alaska and try for a job – any job, with no concern for the pay. Canada and Alaska come about as close as you'll ever get to a "last frontier."

Find your own adventure. Take the risk. Be a dare-devil. Try something new and scary. Try giving your money away. Go for it. Express yourself.

My Way

This is going to be MY book – so it's going to be done MY way. This is the story of parts of MY life, what I've seen and done and what I believe. It's not a diary. It is, rather a collection of anecdotes, experiences and conclusions arrived at. It is to be anything but "politically correct." It is to be a free-flowing, high-spirited saga of miscellaneous events. An un-structured, un-improved, un-edited, un-corrected, un-grammatical, loosely bound set of stories, with the whole idea being to present an outlet for my thoughts. I make no pretense toward journalism. There will be no struggle, striving or attempt made to write scholarly or properly as I am entirely innocent of any training or schooling in writing, syntax or grammar. (You say this is already obvious?)

I am not even composing, thinking up or creating this material. The ego-deflating truth is that I am only the recorder or stenographer hammering out on an ancient typewriter, whatever comes through from the "silence" or "within." I am, therefore, unconcerned if these stories don't make sense or square with the "real" happenings of my day. Most of the really good, fine and worthwhile incidents of my life came from out of nowhere, by surprise and without being deserved or earned. Truth sometimes doesn't make sense or square with known facts but is recognized intuitively as truth by those attuned and receptive.

Abraham Lincoln said "Most people are about as happy as they make up their minds to be." This theme in many variations will be the thread running throughout these pages. I am trying to write pretty much the same way as I talk. Same complexion, flavor, color and style – and, as though the reader is sitting here beside me while I am telling a story.

It is conversation and that is the general effect I am striving for. Not a single yarn has been edited, polished or improved – just as our conversation would have to stand exactly as spoken – with no chance of revision. I do not want to sound like the Reader's Digest. I hope to sound like Whitey – out along the tracks.

This whole thing has been dredged from memory's vault, consulting no notes, maps, diaries and so is subject to possible minor errors of dates and places. In the main, however, it is true as I recall it and as I lived it.

Henry Thoreau said "Those authors are successful who do not write <u>down</u> to others, but make their own taste and judgment their audience . . . . It is enough if I please myself with writing; I am sure of an audience."

Those are my sentiments exactly. Here is a quote by George H. Sheehan, "If you are doing something you would do for nothing, then you are on your way to salvation. And, if you could drop it in a minute and forget the outcome, you are even further along. And, if while you are doing it you are transported into another existence, there is no need for you to worry about the future."

"Don't push the river – it flows by itself."

"Let us not take ourselves too seriously, life is a short assignment."

"I wold rather be tried by twelve than carried by six."

"The destination is of only minor importance, the journey itself is <u>all</u>."

"Poverty plus obscurity plus un-accountability plus anonymity equals PRIVACY – something we could all use more of."

"Unless you are the lead dog – the scenery never changes."

4

The Last Free Adventure

Is there a free adventure left? Only one. Riding the rails. On freight trains, in North America. Specifically the U.S. including Alaska and Canada. Not in Mexico. Yes, it's still free and hasn't changed all that much since the Civil War. This challenge is available to all age groups and both genders. It requires practically no money, hardly any equipment, no lessons or training. You need no license, you are not required to buy a ticket and you need ask no one for permission.

You do need a craving for adventure, a daring and independent attitude plus a liking for travel and the gall of a burglar. If you are not in optimum physical condition, even that won't hold you back, but you should be able to walk carrying a pack and be nimble enough to climb the short ladder to the rear platform of a grain hopper car.

It's essentially a mental attitude that's most needed. If you are terrified to pass a no-trespassing sign or would be devastated to answer a railroad detective's questioning, or wouldn't consider boarding a slow-moving train not knowing where it was going or could not stand the thought of getting filthy dirty – then you better pass.

On the other hand if the prospect of seeing new country excites your imagination especially if it's all for free, and you can see yourself as a train-rider standing in the doorway of a boxcar doing 65 miles an hour and waving nonchalantly at passing motorists, and enjoying it, then you might seriously consider giving it a whirl. Are you a risk-taker? Does a little danger spice your life? Would being called a "Bum" put a crimp in your image? Would you enjoy beating the system? In short, are you an off-beat, underground adventurer? Then go for it, man.

I'm constantly being asked, "Why would you ever want to ride a freight?" There's really no answer except maybe Santa Fe Bo's classic: "If you've never rode. . . then, you'll never know." If you're a geography hound like me, and like to pour over maps you'll discover myriad rail lines all over the U.S. and Canada on which no passenger trains ever go. These are some of the most scenic and intriguing runs known. Only by riding freight trains will you ever have the opportunity to experience the little-known delights. Then, too, there are still some "short lines" operating today but only marginally profitable, which will be closed down and abandoned before long. If you'd like to ride these, you'd best get a wiggle on, as they might not be around too much longer. I notice we are losing one or two each year. I had a chance to ride the Oregon, California & Eastern a few years ago but passed, thinking I could still do it next year. By the time I got around to it, not only had the line folded, but even the tracks had been torn up. It was like losing an old friend.

Why do I call it the "last, free adventure?" Because it's just about the only non-structured adventure left. All the standard well-known thrills sought after by the red-blooded adventurers either cost money, require special equipment, or training, or they are seasonal or for "elitists" only. I'm talking about Downhill skiing, mountain-climbing, rock-climbing, hang-gliding, para-sailing, ocean sailing, river-rafting, sky-diving etc. The list is endless. Even canoeing, tour-biking and even just plain hiking are pretty restricted to those with money. I'm talking about a bare-bones escapade!

I'll admit that jumping freight trains is at best only second – for that true satisfaction; The first, by a thousand miles, has always been "go out West and be a cowboy." I can see the indulgent smile creasing some faces at this bit of sophomoric nonsense, but consider this, " I want to be a cowboy" syndrome has captivated the imagination of generations of restless youngsters since about 1850 – and is still around today, even though the chances now, of some green city kid coming West to ranching country and being given a job in order to learn the cowboy art are practically non-existent. Nowadays this aspirant would have to pay for the privilege.

If, as I'm told, Muhammad Ali is the one most recognized persons world-wide, then the world's most easily-recognizable figure has to be the slim, lean character wearing the big hat, jeans and boots – either on or off a horse – the Western cowboy! Anybody doubt that?

Okay, so that's the top! But it's just not viable anymore – unless you are up to financing your own cowboy career. I gave this matter a whole lot of thought when I was a kid, even going so far as to order myself a "rope" from the Stockman-Farmer catalog and practice with it endlessly, in front of our 3-story house on Queen Ann Hill in Seattle. I had the insight to abandon this venture, realizing I was just not tough or rugged enough to compete. I studied the cowboys I saw at fairs and rodeos after careful comparison I knew I just didn't measure up. In retrospect I see now it was a wise and prudent decision.

But I loved trains and hobo-ing almost as much, and did finally become one, and, looking back I wouldn't trade my travel experiences on the trains for anybody's college education. I still wake up some morning with the old irresistible urge to catch out. I become restless and dissatisfied if I don't indulge this whim as I admit to being an addict, and, when asked by railroad police (while being I.D.'d), "What's a man of you're age doing out here on these trains?" I often confess, "I got the fever so bad I just can't help myself!" Sometimes this brings a sympathetic grin to the special agent's face and then again some are turned off – considering it a flippant answer. But it's not. It's the truth.

You might object to meeting up with some of the less-than-wholesome characters out doing the same thing as you. Relax, these guys are not out to do you harm – most of them anyway. It doesn't take long to spot the troublemakers. Just mind your own business, don't ride in the same car with someone you don't know or trust, avoid loud, boisterous, rowdy persons, don't travel in large groups – that is more than four. Stick to twos and threes. Gals should be with guys. Two or three gals by themselves – that's not good – too much of a strain on temptation – it's like asking for trouble. Wear dull, dark, drab durable clothing, keep out of sight and remember not to drink while on or around the trains. Always have a good-sized water jug, a decent pair of leather boots and a cheap sleeping bag (not an expensive mummy bag) and keep it unzipped while sleeping on the train. You might need to slip out of it quickly. It's also a good idea to wear your boots all laced up while sleeping – to expedite a sudden move.

You'll pick up your know-how as you go along by watching how the pros operate – how they dress, how they pack, how they seem to know how to build a fire, make coffee, how and where to ride – on which car and on which end of the car. They'll be happy to show you how to get train information, where to find water, where to jungle up, which way is the mission and where the closest all-night convenience store is located.

In the Navy an old Boatswain's Mate told a bunch of us green recruits, "Never call a shipmate a son-of-a-bitch. He might prove to be the very one who pulls you out of the water." This might also apply to some of the grungie guys seen out along the rails – they might be the very ones who would slide open the stuck boxcar door in the event of your being trapped inside! I guess you've figured out by now that the railroads don't want you on their trains. You represent a hazard and a liability. Technically once you've set foot on any freight train you are guilty of trespassing and illegal train riding, or as they put it "stealing services." What they are trying to avoid are lawsuits in the event you are killed or maimed.

Up until about 1940 the railroads could care less about accidents to persons on their trains. Even rail employees were seldom compensated if injured. Danger to life and limb came with the territory and it was considered just one of the hazards of the job. Any illegal rider had no clout at all, the companies taking no responsibility whatsoever for what might happen to him. After WW2 everything changed with a growing public awareness that everybody had "rights" and could sue the carriers for injuries sustained even when they were riding illegally.

Before this the railroads still didn't want you riding their trains, but it was for a different reason. They were losing "revenue," and were incensed that hobos, tramps and harvest workers were stealing rides – that is – riding for free. This went against their grain and became downright intolerable. Jack London tells in his "The Road" of one Midwestern railroad refusing to run their train because hundreds of "Coxey's Army" demanded space in their boxcars on their journey to Washington D.C. Rather than give in to the outrageous demands of these "Hooligans" – the railroad halted their train movements.

Nowadays with no private passenger trains (Amtrak having taken over completely) the roads could care less about lost ticket sales. They found out years ago that running passenger trains was a pain in the behind, whereas freight was the only lucrative way to go – but they have never been totally successful at keeping the riders off their trains. Only Union Pacific and Santa Fe have come anywhere near it, and only by "automatic 30 Days" supposedly dealt out to hapless riders caught on their property and a reputation for tough, uncompromising punishment have they kept their trains and yards off-limits to the fool-hardy.

All this represents just a minor inconvenience to you daring souls who <u>still</u> insist that this "last free adventure" is after all, the way to go and prepared to face the Bull on his home ground. Yes, you will be "carded," ordered off the property and warned that "If I catch you in the yard again, you'll do jail time." If you are clean and sober, speak civilly and pose no threat you will be allowed to go and – can wait till later, then return and find your train.

A day ride out in the sunshine and fresh air would be a taste. Then, an overnight jaunt (in the summertime) would further confirm your pleasure. The real convincer should be a two or three week apprenticeship run - serious train riding, following which you will find yourself a confirmed "BO" or – heaving a sigh of relief, saying "Never again."

Wanderlust

When I was 12 years old I bought my first guitar, a Sears, Roebuck & Co. Silvertone which cost $3.89 prepaid from Chicago. It was a mail order guitar. Then, when I was 13 I rode my first freight train, a Great Northern fast merchandise express known as a hot-shot, from Seattle to Portland, Oregon. These two things pointed the direction my life would take. Today, 60 years later, I still play guitar and still ride certain freight trains. Here's how it all started.

Instead of staying after school to join the other boys playing baseball, touch football or soccer I would usually cut out and head for the docks and railroad yards at Smith's Cove, now known as Interbay, or Balmer yards. There I would roam the docks talking to the sailors and longshoremen and try to sneak aboard the cargo vessels or try to hitch rides on railroad cars as the switch engines shunted them around the various tracks. This was my excitement. I might hang around for two or three hours rain or shine (always lots of rain in Seattle) before heading back up Queen Ann Hill where we lived.

My father worked in an office downtown where I would some-times show up hoping for a ride home. It seemed strange, this business world, where everyone wore suits and ties and shined shoes. It was sometimes difficult to get my Dad's attention as he and his associates were always going out to lunch, or in conference, or in a meeting. Oh, they were all cordial to me but seemed preoccupied and too busy to talk. I felt uncomfortable and ill at ease in these lavishly appointed offices and much preferred the company of overall-clad laborers, sailors and long-shoremen who seemed friendly and took an interest in me. They had time for me. I liked most all of the rough sort of men but my favorites were the guys I'd run into in the train yards, sitting around a fire. My heroes have always been hobos. Their style of talk, the way they dress-ed, their whole outlook on life impressed me tremendously. While not accepted as one of them, I was tolerated and often offered food which I politely declined.

One June evening in 1934 a boy name Eugene Weaver and I showed up at the Northern Pacific yards just South of the King Street station (exactly where the Kingdome Stadium is now), where we joined the already considerable bank of would-be freight-hoppers assembled in the jungles and all along the mainline. Yes, we were out to jump a train.

About 6:30 here she came out of the tunnel, headlight gleaming, smoke and steam pouring out, connecting rods flashing – a perfect pic-ture of power, incarnate. The train, mostly boxcars, thundered down the track braking to a screeching stop, whereupon the bums, tramps, hobos, transients (that's what the press called all rail-riders those days – "transients") descended on the cars en mass – climbing the side-ladder to the "deck" or roof, or trying to find room in the one, lone empty.

Not knowing just what to do, me and Weaver ran up to the empty where we were immediately accepted and hauled up inside by friendly, willing Bo's. Some 20 or so people inside, there was no room to sit down, but we wanted to stand up and look out anyway. We weren't about to miss anything. Wasn't this our first ride?

As we pulled out of town gathering speed, standing spread-legged so we wouldn't be jerked off our feet, we gradually became accustomed to the motion and started to enjoy the ride. A feeling of euphoria descended as we flashed through the towns of Kent, Auburn, Puyallup and Tacoma, waving to the people at the crossings. This was big-time stuff. A couple of kids out beating a railroad train, seeing the country, and what's more – loving every minute.

I recall we stopped to take on water at Centralia – a town about half way between Seattle and Portland – where, 59 years later, in the same Depot men's room, Roadhog and I discovered the logo of A-No. 1 – the Rambler, carved in the marble partition and dated 1934 – same year! We made no other stops till we got to Vancouver where most everybody got off. We asked why they didn't stay on till Portland, the last stop? The answer was, "Better get off here, kid, and walk across the bridge. The Portland yards are 'Hot'!"

So we got off too, about 3:00 in the morning and headed for downtown Vancouver to catch an early morning streetcar. The fare was a dime. The surprising thing to me was the number of people we saw wandering around the train yard and streets in the gray dawn. Nowhere to go, and carried bedrolls tied with rope. These, I was to learn, were the working hobos who were called "bindle-stiffs." A bedroll was a bindle. A man was a stiff.

We spent all day in Portland wearily walking the streets, then another streetcar ride and here we were again, back in Vancouver, tired and disillusioned, a bit homesick and looking for a train back home.

We met a young, cheerful-talking black man sitting by the tracks who was playing some kind of card game. "Betcha can't find the queen!" he offered. We stopped to watch him. He had three playing cards spread out on the sod, two were numbered cards, the third being a queen. He would turn them over face down, then switch them around and ask us to pick the queen. It looked simple enough. I told him I knew which one was the queen. He said "Betcha a nickel you don't!" I pulled out a nickel, put it down and pointed to the middle card – "there." He laughed "You sure enough picked the right one." He paid me my nickel plus another. "Let's try again – betcha a quarter this time." He re-arranged the cards again, this time quite a bit faster, but I was sure I'd spotted the queen again. "Okay, here's my quarter." About this time my buddy decided he knew where the queen was, too and said, "I got a quarter, and I'm betting this card is the queen – this here card on the end." I nodded, that's where I thought it was, too. We both layed our quarters down, watching the smiling-faced black man expectantly; He turned over our choice; it was <u>not</u> the queen, instead it was the 7 of clubs. He pocketed the .50 cents, got to his feet and ambled away. That was our introduction to 3-card monte. It costs you to learn life's lessons – but you learn them <u>well</u>.

Out along the tracks you seldom get more than one chance. Our next lesson was a crash course on HOW NOT TO RIDE A FREIGHT TRAIN. We came very close to paying for this lesson with our lives.

That same evening our train, originating in Portland, crossed the Columbia River bridge but failed to stop in the Vancouver yards. We were not sure just how to handle this emergency but decided we could climb on even though it was moving. It didn't look to be rolling too fast so we just jogged along with it until a tank car came by. We could see that it had a wooden running board along the side with a little ladder we could climb on by. Just the ticket, a place to sit down, and it would be all ours – no sharing with 20 other riders. We made it okay and scooted to the middle where there was a grab-iron to hang on to. We sat down on the 2 x 12 running board, looked at each other triumphantly and proceeded to check out the scenery. At 20 or 30 miles an hour the ride seemed safe enough but when she got up to 40, 50 and even 60 miles an hour, our weight on the running board produced a sympathetic vibration, acting just like a springboard. We began bouncing up and down, ever higher and more violently, trying desperately to hang on to the single grab-iron.

We looked at each other, terror-stricken, understanding all too well what our predicament was. If we were bounced off we would most certainly land on the tracks and be decapitated or hit the edge of the ties and suffer a broken neck or broken bones. Our speed was somewhere around 60. We kept one hand on the grab with the other gripping the running board, trying to control the bounce. How long could we hang on? We were sick with fear and wishing oh, so bad that we'd never gone near a train.

I could picture visions of my dear mother when she got the news of her precious little boy dead and mangled along a railroad track. I thought, "I <u>must</u> hang on. I've just <u>got</u> to hang on. Dear God, please don't let me fall!"

It seemed an eternity; I was in a trance. I couldn't think. Then suddenly I became aware that the train was slowing down. What! Slowing down! Yes, we were coming into a town – it looked like Centralia – for another water stop. Sure enough we gradually ground down to a stop. Saved! Oh Hallelujah! We were going to be all right!

We jumped down so weak we could hardly walk. Reprieve! We got up enough strength finally to make it back to the rear of the train, where there was an empty boxcar we hadn't seen. It was full of riders but we climbed in anyway.

My thoughts all the way to Seattle were; your first train ride was almost your LAST!

The Rebel

There is some rebel in most of us, quite a bit in me. Looking back now I realize I've been a rebel my whole life, restless, dissatisfied, longing for new places, new jobs, new interests, and never really knowing why. Why have I always been a job-jumper, a gypsy, a dreamer, a hopeless romantic, a risk-taker, loving travel, adventure, throwing away security – following the illusion, the will-o-the-wisp with no regrets and no remorse? It could be in that I am a 7th-generation American whose forebearers deserted the farms, factories along with the religion of the staid, structured East and struck out for new lands and new chances with hardly a backward glance. I guess the word is pioneer. Our country has always had hordes of drifters, possibly more now than ever – even back in covered-wagon days. Seems like even the hobo is proliferating, his numbers increasing, though the breed doesn't resemble the old-timers except in the glint in their eyes, their determination to remain free and uncommitted and their unquenchable appetite for travel.

As a boy I wanted to be a cowboy, then a merchant sailor, then a mountain climber, then a trapper and hunter up north. Whatever job or occupation could be done out of doors, on the sea, in the woods, along the open road – that was for me. None of this inside office stuff, no indoor factory job, no desk-sitting and no wearing a suit and tie. I was serious about it too.

I admired the work of the "pond-monkey," a sawmill worker, wearing stagged pants, corked boots, walking carelessly from one floating log to another on the log booms in the front of any waterfront sawmill. He carried a 20 foot pike pole for balance and was responsible for steering the logs up to the entrance-chute where each was fed into the mill. Now, there was a job a man could get his teeth into and be proud of his day's work, actually getting paid for having fun out on the water, all day in the sun or rain, and the occasional ducking (even the best fell in sometimes) was part of the job.

I learned, early on, to keep my dreams to myself. In euphoric moments I'd sometimes let it slip out that I'd sure like to be a hobo or a railroad engineer or a logger – whatever was big on my list at the time. This would invariably bring on a protest or an outburst of parental reprimand about how silly that all sounded and that I didn't really know my own mind, and that when I got a little older I would realize how foolish these pipedreams sounded, and that I should put my feet on the ground, get a good education and amount to something!

My father, ever the play-it-safer, always seeking security, suggested I should get in with the government – get a civil-service job, while my mother wanted me in some clean, genteel, upstanding white-collar role – just what, I never knew.

So there I was, bursting with energy, enthusiasm, dreaming ever wilder, more fantastic dreams and not about to settle for some crummy, citified job! Not me! No sir! Not wanting to fight nor liking to argue, I developed my own passive resistance, pretending to go along with the status-quo – but secretly, with no fanfare, I'd just go ahead with my own plans and dreams, gradually wrapping myself in a cloak of quiet unaccountability. I became a loner, attending school and outwardly conforming to what was expected of boys my age, but meanwhile, after school and on weekends, hitch-hiking to the docks and railroad yards, stealing rides on streetcars, riding the ferries and making friends with the transients found in the famous Northern Pacific jungle (one of many such "Hoovervilles" depression era shack-towns) found in most big cities of that day. I picked up their lingo and soaked up their philosophy. The casualness and quiet self-reliance of these men intrigued me. I was drawn like a magnet by their stories and friendly attitude. These guys were not in a hurry, not too <u>busy</u>, they had <u>time</u> for me. I loved their disappearing act. Every evening, when the trains left the yards, they'd be on them, hopping on the fly. Where were they going? I was fascinated by the mystery and romance and could see myself doing it too.

My father took me aside to consult with me what classes I had opted for upon entering high school. We were given considerable leeway on the electives even back then (1935), so I told him I wanted to enroll in auto mechanics, woodshop and beginning electricity. He frowned and thought a moment. He seemed to sense I was not turning out exactly as he had hoped for, and was troubled about it. He had me hold out my hands, palms down. "Look at those hands, Bob. See the long, tapered fingers, the long, narrow fingernails, the slender wrists, your slight, somewhat delicate frame? You see, you're not cut out to be a rough-tough working man, doing all those hard, physical jobs. No, you are built to be in some refined, intellectual profession – such as school teaching, or business or selling. Don't you understand, Son, you'd never be able to keep up with those big, burly roughnecks. You must accept your own talents, revamp your thinking and substitute those shop classes for a college-prep course." What he told me was right for him – and dead wrong for me. He was convinced he'd done the right thing and that it was all for my own good. He'd under-estimated his son's natural bent.

It seemed terribly unfair. Why should I scrap all my hopes and dreams of a life of adventure just to knuckle under and go with the stream, accept the workhorse role of white collar mediocrity just because my forbearers had saddled me with the physical attributes of a bank clerk? Must I accept this trip which had been laid on me? Did I have nothing to say about what I could do with my own life?

Deferring to parental pressure I ended up taking algebra, geometry, Spanish, Civics and Literature. Oh yes, and typing. The only subject that I can ever recall as being helpful in later life was typing!

I've always been grateful for that. How many, many times have I wished I had insisted on auto mechanics, wood-working and electricity! I could use all three to this very day! My father meant well but didn't understand what motivated me. You see, I was the only boy of the family. Boys were always at a premium in our family – both sides. You could almost say that we were a matriarchy with lots of sisters, girl-cousins, aunts etc., with hardly any boys around at all. No one among my relatives seemed to understand boys or how to deal with them. I craved some man around to teach me how to use tools and show me how to build things. Alas, my poor dear Dad was hopeless in that department but did attempt to ease my frustrations by buying me a set of wood-working tools for Christmas one year.

Ironically my dear Dad lived to see that whole syndrome reversed, when, following a business adversity, he lost everything (financially) which left me with the role of breadwinner at age 17. No, it wasn't cruel nor unfortunate, nor did I resent it. It was, in fact the making of me and I shall be forever grateful for the chance to learn, at an early age, how to get out there and "make it" rain or shine – sick or well.

Our family situation changed overnight from upper-middle class gentility to scrabble-assed poor. My dear aunt generously provided us with a little cabin way back in the Oregon forest country. Us kids loved it! My parents felt humiliated. No running water, a well. No indoor plumbing, an outhouse. No electricity, kerosene lamps. No automobile, we walked.

I dropped out of school, working at anything I could find, doing the strangest assortment of rural jobs such as cutting wood, building fences, picking fruit, hoeing strawberry fields, weeding onions, driving tractors, until eventually falling into the routine of traveling fruit picker – riding freight trains and hitch-hiking to various "fruit-tramp jobs" like digging spuds in Tulelake CA, picking beans in West Stayton, OR, knocking applies in Naches and Wenatchee, WA, picking hops in Yakima, WA and on and on. Winters I'd spend with the family and try to hire on with the local sawmills as "dogger" on the carriage, or pulling lumber on the greenchain. My favorite job as a "Pond Monkey" was an indication of how far I'd come. I was happy around the saw mills and learned many of the skills, such as loading lumber in freight cars, riding the carriage as dogger, then ratchet-setter. In spite of my small size, I was able to "cut" it and hold my own.

As you can see these are all strong back and weak mind occupations, but it was all an unskilled person like me could get and I was glad of the chance. This constant exertion at hard, dirty, physical jobs – instead of breaking me – worked wonders for my physique, enlarging my arms and shoulders and giving me strength and resilience. That was, to me, flat out amazing! I could have gotten this type of education and job training nowhere else. The determination to succeed where failure had been predicted seemed to turn my life around. I began to discover I could do most anything I turned my hand to. What a lesson.

There I was, a backwoods hillbilly, working at all the menial jobs and picking a little guitar too. I fell into that life like a natural and possibly would have continued on for years – except for an unforeseen happening that changed everything – Pearl Harbor.

I Get My Eyes Opened

In the summer of 1933 when I was 12, I went to stay with my cousin Joe and my uncle George who lived in a tiny cabin on a small hill farm in the forest country of northwestern Oregon. This move became one of the turning points of my life.

I learned about cigarettes, how to roll them and smoke them. I saw my first guitar, close up. It was love at first sight. Before the summer was over I had mastered the C, F and G7 chords and was well away towards a lifetime of picking guitar and singing cowboy songs. My cousin Joe, who owned the guitar, knew only these three chords – so that's what he taught me. He was 18, and, I thought, really grown up.

Joe used the guitar as a hiding place for his sack of Bull Durham, as my uncle George, though a smoker himself, didn't want his son to do it, so we had to sneak our puffs. We would disappear at odd times during the day into the woods where we would find a sunny spot, break out the tobacco and brown colored, wheatstraw papers, carefully roll us each a smoke, then sit back and puff and enjoy with infinite satisfaction. It took me a while but I learned to like it, too. After more than 60 years I can still recall with a certain fondness the actual smell and taste, and even feel the texture of that home-rolled cigarette.

Having been city-bred I was in for an eye-opening new way of life. Country boys did things different than city kids. You were expected to carry a gun with you for shooting varmints. I had to buy one – a Stevens .22 single shot lever action. Cost me $3.00. I wasn't sure just what a varmint was, as we killed nothing but "Grey-diggers," a type of ground squirrel found everywhere, but I fell right in with that habit too and was seldom without my trusty rifle.

My uncle George was a beer drinker. He made his own, called it homebrew. Joe and I stumbled upon his cache one day out under some fir trees. It was a wooden box set down in the ground covered with a gunny sack and brushy fir boughs. When full it contained 24 brown-colored bottles of homemade beer. We swiped a couple one day and proceeded to "get drunk." I could hardly down the foul-tasting stuff, so Joe had to finish off both.

That was the first time I discovered I didn't like to drink. I realize now what a God send that proved to be – as, even to this day I still don't care for it. I never picked up the booze habit, so that's one I didn't have to quit. I've been known to enjoy the odd glass of wine with dinner in my later years, but it's never grabbed a hold of me.

So there I was, a reckless, eager and wild little kid, learning how to saw logs, fell small trees, chop firewood for the stove, play guitar a little, smoke the occasional roll-your-own and developing a growing love for woods-lore and firearms. This hill farm life style had opened up new and ever grander vistas – all delightfully new and interesting to a sheltered city kid from a middleclass family of school teachers and businessmen. I loved it.

One day Joe and I hiked into town just for a kick. Gaston was a little burg of 200 souls but a thriving community at that time. It was a walk of about 3 miles. What I saw there has remained sharp and indelible to this day.

A railroad paralleled the highway on the eastern edge of town with the most prominent feature being a huge, black, wooden watertank. Sitting in its shade were two men. I was instantly curious as they didn't look like farmers or, for that matter, any other kind of men I'd ever seen. Joe and I walked closer to get a better look. They looked us kids over, extending a greeting. This was a surprise as I wasn't used to having grown men take any notice of me. We sat down near them as they asked us where we lived, what our names were and so on, just relaxed and friendly.

I was totally fascinated, wondering at their clothes and boots and bedrolls. They wore black pants held up by large suspenders, hickory shirts, old, battered felt hats and workboots that had iron horseshoes embedded in the heels. It finally dawned on me that these two fabulous, colorful-talking, interestingly clothed men were wanderers, hobos, the sort my parents called tramps.

They offered us the "makings" which we accepted. I proudly showed off my newly-learned skill at twisting a cig. Yes, that was a grand moment, I felt accepted, I was one of them, I knew it in my heart. There were no words formulated, no conclusions arrived at and I didn't even realize it myself at the time, but the die was cast, the seed had been planted. I was hooked for life. The age-old question – "What do you want to be when you grow up?" had been irrevocably answered. Not in so many words, but the desire was crystal clear; I wanted to be a hobo, a tramp, a wanderer of the world, someone marching along in the sunshine in the big outdoors, seeing the sights, searching the out-of-the-way places, exploring the backwaters of the world – enjoying myself!

A life on the rails seemed the perfect answer. To complete the picture a freight train chugged into the station stopping with the tender right by the tank. As the giant engine stood wheezing and panting, the fireman climbed up onto the tender, opened a chute, then jockeyed the enormous teakettle-like spout over the opening, then pulled on a chain that sent a large stream of water pouring down into the bowels of the water-tender.

This was the signal for our two heroes to arise to their feet, yawn and stretch and remark to Joe and me, "Well, time for us to be going. See ya later." Strolling unhurried down along the train's length they disappeared into an empty boxcar. We waited as the crew finished taking on water, then watched as the train crawled slowly out of town.

Our hobo friends waved one last farewell standing in the door-way looking larger than life. We watched the train clear out of sight, then headed for home – subdued and lost in thought.

I never knew if my cousin was <u>that</u> impressed, but I'm sure he was, as neither of us said hardly a word all the way back. For me it had been a profound awakening – a moving experience. I couldn't get it out of my mind for days.

Several years later in a civics class at Queen Ann High school, each pupil was required to get up before the class to report on, "What would you like to be when you grow up?" I gave a lot of thought to what I would say and nearly told this very story. I had second thoughts as a premonition came to me that my inner longing might be misunder-stood and possibly condemned (a premonition that has since been veri-fied many, many times).

At the last minute I chickened out and, instead of my heart's desire, I made up some garbage about "owning my own business." I was too shy to speak out, spill my guts and tell the <u>truth</u>.

I Learn About Hobos

We've all heard about hobo signs and hobo marks or drawings mysteriously placed in inconspicuous places by previous wayfarers intended to inform the newly arrived tramp as to where to get food or water, which house to avoid, what to expect in a certain town – all kinds of tips, suggestions and warnings intended to help make his stay a pleasant one.

I've seldom been able to locate these markings. I suspect they are not being used today and possibly haven't been in vogue since maybe the 1920's. Few people are at home in the daytime anymore, besides, a wandering hobo going door to door in today's world would bring the Law down on him before he'd gone half a block.

I am inclined to believe that our house in Seattle was so marked. a small boy I saw an endless trickle of hungry men stop at my)ther's door for a handout. They were never refused. My Mother s the personification of an easy touch. She was kind-hearted, sympauictic and always eager to help these unfortunates with huge plates of sandwiches, fruit, cookies and milk. They unfailingly called at our door, yet I don't recall ever seeing them at our neighbor's, which is why I suspect our house was marked. Somehow the word had been spread that this was the place where you would be well-treated and could expect not only food, but also the odd pair of shoes, pants or even an old suit. Today's vagabonds would probably not thank you for a suit but in the 20's and 30's these men were still trying to "fit in" not "drop out" and many wore suits and sometimes neckties, if you can believe that!

Sometimes if a hungry man appeared at mealtime my mother would invite him in for a "sit down" but mostly she fed them outside on the porch. This was called a "knee-shaker." They were always polite and seemed grateful. I studied them intently, fascinated by their mysterious lifestyle, never dreaming that I would, one day, be joining their ranks.

I loved to sit on the porch steps while they ate, plying them with questions such as where they were from, where were they going, where did they sleep, did they have any kids my age? and all sorts of personal queries. These men sensed my sincerity, tolerating my eager prying without any provocation, often opening up with deeply personal disclosures. They seemed to trust me. Unknowingly I was being conditioned, absorbing a knowledge and forming an attitude that would appear full-blown a few years later – an attitude of sympathy, understanding – almost of belonging. I felt underneath that I was one of them. These were the most interesting men I had ever seen.

One day an enormous black man stood, hat in hand, quietly inquiring if my mother could give him something to eat. In short order a huge stack of sandwiches with milk was being made up while the man waited on the porch, thoughtfully smoking a long, black pipe. When the platter of food was set down he put the pipe down at his side and proceeded to wolf down the sandwiches, not stopping till every single one was gone. I sat beside him wondering amazed how <u>any</u>one could eat that much!

Finished, finally the man sighed, stretched contentedly, then felt around for his pipe. It was gone. He looked around murmuring to me, "Did you notice where I layed my pipe, Son?" I was just as mystified. Then, looking up, out on the street I saw my little white mongrel, LOBO, a happy dog with a tail that curled up over his back. I had been petting him there on the porch where he had, evidently, sniffed out the man's pipe, grabbed it between his teeth (right side up) and was now strutting along the sidewalk with the pipe jutting out of his mouth for all the world as if he were smoking it. It was an instant cartoon-like picture — one of the most comical things I have ever seen. LOBO seemed to sense how cute he was, hamming it up shamelessly, and by now, refusing to let me catch him. I noticed my mother looking out the kitchen window laughing uncontrollably.

The black man, on his feet now was also chuckling but not as enthusiastically as me and mom. I finally retrieved the pipe, wiped off the stem on my pants and returned it to the man, who, saying nothing, stuck it in his pocket and moved off.

The Apple Knocker

At age 18 I finished up the apple season in Naches, Washington, caught the local into Yakima, converted my dollar bills into one $50 bill that I slipped into a money belt around my waist. The remaining few bucks I stuck into my shoe. I'd read about money belts in the detective magazines I'd been reading, so when I saw one in a pawnshop window, I bought it – $2.00. I was really grown up now.

The season was about over, it was November with the nights grow-ing chilly. Now it was time to head back to Oregon where I was pretty sure I could find a winter's job cutting cordwood. My apple-knocking partner and I were headed for the Northern Pacific yards hoping to catch a ride over to Auburn that evening.

The orchard owner, Mr. Whitney, had told me six weeks earlier, "We are paying three and a half cents a box. At that rate, if you hustle, you can make yourself three dollars or more a day."

I nodded. I was happy to get it – I'd have taken anything. I never did manage to pick a hundred boxes a day, though. Between 65 and 85 boxes was the best I ever did – and that in a ten hour day with only a lunch break. But no matter, I'd stuck it out and now I had some spending money for myself – plus $50 to give to my Mom, which would be enough to get her and my two younger sisters through the winter. At that time (1939) you couldn't carry in your two arms all the groceries $3.00 would buy.

Apple picking wasn't all that easy, as I'd soon found out. First there was the big, heavy orchard ladder you had to lug around, and set it up just right or over you'd go, sprawling into the soft dirt, bruising your sack of apples and feeling stupid and inexperienced. If you set up too close to your work, you had no room to pick; too far would force you to reach, thus losing your balance, and over you'd go. It was a ticklish, precarious compromise but eventually I got on to it.

Then (and this was tricky), you had to learn to twist each apple in such a way that the stem remained in the apple. That took a lot of prac-tice. If you just pulled – the stem would stay on the tree, instead of the apple, and that particular one would not stay nice and fresh. No, with the stem gone it would rot. The owner was quick to let me know if he found very many of these in my stack of boxes.

You wore a canvas sack, like a packsack, only it was at your front and not your back. It held exactly one box full. When you had filled your pouch you'd climb carefully down, kneeling low over an empty box and gently unfasten the bottom part, allowing the apples to transfer from your pack into the box – without getting bruised. This was important as these were fancy prime Washington Delicious targeted for worldwide markets.

Six solid weeks of that and I was overjoyed to be done and gone and couldn't wait to ride another good old freight train.

Somewhere in mid-season, on a day when we couldn't work, I'd hitched into Yakima in a discouraged, disgusted and disgruntled frame of mind. I was tired of sleeping out, never having cooked meals and working like a mindless Zombie for low pay. I'd heard that saying, "If you pay peanuts, you get monkeys." So . . . did that mean I was a monkey? Well?

I decided I wanted something else – like security, maybe. So, in this mood I walked into the office of the United States Army Recruiting Station. They paid you $30 a month, board and room, a uniform and even gave you (so the recruiting poster said) Adventure and Travel! Sounded pretty good to me. Like a lamb to the slaughter I went – right up to the desk and told the man, "I want to see about joining the Army!"

The sergeant behind the desk, a youngish-looking, well-built guy wearing immaculately clean and pressed khakis, looked me over good. He didn't say anything right away – just kept staring at me. Nervously I said, "Do I have to fill out a form or anything?"

"How old are you, son?"

"Eighteen."

"You don't look it. Why do you think you want to join the Army?"

I mumbled something about being tired of working the fruit tramp and was looking for Adventure! And Travel! – like the posters advertised. There was no one else in the office, just him and me. He rose from his desk, came over to where I was standing looking me straight in the eye, "You don't want to join the Army." Flat out. Just like that! I was dumbfounded! He'd caught me by surprise! It was the last thing I expected to hear! It was like walking into a barbershop only to have the barber say, "You don't want a haircut!"

I could only stammer – "I don't?"

Pearl Harbor was still more than two years away, it was peacetime and I knew that at age 18 I didn't require my parents' permission to join. So why would he say a thing like that? Didn't he want any new recruits? "Kid, you're too young to know what you'd be getting your-self into. Besides, you'd be signing for a four year hitch – and that's just too long. Think it over, long and hard – and then – come back and talk to me."

He turned and went back to his desk. Interview over. I stood there, feeling silly, then walked slowly out. I had mixed feelings. I felt like I'd been rejected – and at the same time I felt a sense of tremendous relief – like I'd just had a narrow escape.

Since then I've silently thanked that man a hundred times. He could read me like a book. Knew intuitively I was just not soldier material. I wasn't tough enough, too small of build, too easily discouraged – I was the kind who belonged in a library, not on a drill field. I suspect he felt sorry for me – my sniveling about "Adventure and Travel." He knew I'd be eaten alive in the barracks rough and tumble. The peace-time Army was a hard, tough, brutal career. In his mind he knew he couldn't allow it.

Looking back I realize how lucky I've been. Seems like I've always had a Guardian Angel hovering close.

My apple-picking buddy, Warren, and I were lazing around in the jungle at the edge of the NP train yard. A switch-engine was kicking some cars around. I noticed these NP engines all burned coal instead of oil like the Great Northern ones did. Warren told me it was because the NP owned lots of coal mines here in Washington and in Montana. Coal smelled good but was dirtier to work around and got you really filthy with the smoke and cinders during a ride.

A brakeman stood on the top of a boxcar that had been sent drifting by itself down the track. I hollered up at him, "What time does the Northbound come through tonight?"

He studied me pityingly, taking his time answering, "Trains don't go North or South around here. They go East and West." Stupid, green kid that I was, I hated to show my ignorance so I shut up.

Warren, who had helped me get this apple job was only a couple of years older but was sharp on his train lore and had had plenty of rid-ing time. From Ames, Iowa he came West every spring to work the crops in Washington and Oregon. Then along about November he'd head back to this same little town where he had a winter's job in a hard-ware store. The owner paid him a dollar a day for sweeping out in the morning and keeping the big potbellied stove going all day.

He'd gone to Business School for two years, Warren had, and was always practicing on his shorthand. None of the things he'd learned at this college made much sense to me, but he insisted that, someday, when the depression was over (this was its tenth year with no end in sight) he'd be able to get a real good job and command a big salary because of it. Like me, all he'd ever done was hard, dreary, low-paying jobs in the fruit harvest, having to ride freight trains in between, but he kept his ambitions and enthusiasm high.

It had turned cool in the Yakima Valley. Warren suggested we sleep in the sand house if no train came through. I looked at him ques-tioningly, "The sand house? What's the sand house?"

He never put me down when I'd ask stupid questions. He patiently explained, "They've got 'em in every yard, usually near the roundhouse. It's a place where they keep the sand for sanding the tracks, and it's usually warm inside, 'cause it's gotta be kept real dry."

"Why do they need it?" None of this was making much sense.

"Oh, it's for when the rails get slippery and the engine can't make it up the hill. You know – when it's icy or snowing in the winter."

"Do the guys have to get out and shovel it onto the tracks?"

"Oh, no, you see the engines carry it right with them and when the engineer feels his drivers start to spin, he just moves a little lever in the cab and a little trickle of sand funnels down through a tube and drops right on top of the track. Then the driver-wheels can get a good grip on the rails, and away they go."

Warren had an amazing grasp of what went on along the railroad. It struck me he'd make a better crew member than a "male secretary," but I never told him that. He had his heart set on a place in the business world.

We got our train that evening, rode her slowly up the Yakima River Canyon, transited the stampede tunnel about midnight, breathing coal smoke, fumes and all and pulled into the Auburn yards at daybreak. It had been a miserable, shivering night, but came morning, everything began to look better.

We had to leave the NP we'd come in on and switch over to the Great Northern to head south towards Portland. There were some 15 or 20 Bo's milling around waiting for the same train, so it was no problem. There were so many men traveling the rails in 1939 you usually could get all the train info you needed without having to bother the "rails." Some of these "transients" as they were called in the papers, had been on the bum nearly ten years now, and knew the roads, trains and connections all too well.

When the Southbound came in about 20 guys, me and Warren included, all crammed into the only empty, and waited. Along hobbled a huge black man carrying a bedroll, the largest bundle of blankets I'd seen yet, and had – of all things (and they very first one I'd ever seen) a PEG-Leg! Just a wooden stick attached at the knee. He was real cheerful, laughing and chuckling at the remarks being made, "Hey there, POPS, ain't that bedroll a whole lot of bother to pack around?" He answered, laughing, "Yes sir! It sure is – 'specially in the daytime. But it's sure sweet at night!"

In Tacoma, Warren and I switched to a flatcar so we could see the scenery better. In those days the GN right-of-way led smack-dab right up the main drag of the city. We got to wave at all the people along the sidewalks – something I've enjoyed doing all my life. Tacoma is a good-sized city but never-ever have I seen or been stopped by a bull in that town. Yet it's got it's share of tramps. This was the Western Terminus of the Milwaukee Road which ran their trains with electricity for 656 miles through the mountainous portions of Washington, Idaho and Montana and boasted of a clean and quiet ride!

The Northern Pacific had an interesting and delightfully scenic route leaving Tacoma. It ran right along the shores of Puget Sound for about 30 miles, giving us free-riders a panoramic sight-seeing trip past the parks, beaches, boat marinas and ferry slips clear along this beautiful inland sea all the way to Olympia. A knock-out of a trip!

But this time we were riding the good old "Big G" which takes an inland cut-off through the town of Tenino where we stopped shortly. We got off, ran over to a little store where we each bought some penny candy – little individually wrapped caramels, five for a penny! What a deal for a hungry kid craving sweets!

Later we made another stop to take a siding to allow a passenger train to go by. A farmer had a field of carrots growing out there. We jumped off, grabbed a few handfuls and got back on. What a life! Living off the fat of the land.

This was our last day together and we knew it. Warren would be catching the Union Pacific out of Portland tomorrow, while I would be thumbing West, the 40 miles to our mountain cabin – coming home like a conquering hero after six months out on the fruit tramp – and with money in my pocket, too. We were enjoying and relishing every minute of this day out in the Autumn sunshine, as we both secretly knew we'd, in all likelihood, never meet again. We made the most of it.

In Portland we shared a $2.00 room in the Essex Hotel on 3rd street, bathroom down the hall. We were lucky – no bedbugs and no roaches! We could have flopped for 35 cents a piece at any number of chicken-wire hotels, but we'd just come off the apple circuit. We were professionals – apple knockers – and had money in our jeans. We went for the best!

We parted next morning after a 20 cent breakfast at the Seattle Cafe. Two enormous hotcakes and all the coffee you wanted. We paused, momentarily on the sidewalk, shook hand one last time – and went our separate ways.

No, I never saw him again. Adios, Warren!

Nailing a Passenger Train

I saw this man hunkered down behind a stack of railroad ties closely observing the activity around the Union Pacific crack train that was about to depart. She left out at 4:20 pm right on the dot to Portland, Oregon. I'd often catch the streetcar after school to the Union Station in Seattle just to watch this train pull out. Trains intrigued me. I never got enough of them. Sometimes I'd sneak my way right down to the platform, mingling with the throng of boarding passengers and walk on up to the front to see the big gleaming engine.

The engineer was a large heavy man who smoked cigars and wore spotless white overalls. He had a big gold watch on a chain that he consulted every minute or so. He'd climb leisurely down from the cab, then take a long-spouted oil can and proceed to squirt oil around the giant wheels and connecting rods. When it got close to departure time he'd climb back up then sit looking out the window, keeping close watch on the conductor back towards the rear. Then at exactly 4:20 I'd see the conductor make a motion with his right arm, whereupon the engineer would grasp the throttle (which I could plainly see) with his left hand and move it slightly forward. Like a mammoth oceanliner that marvelous engine would spring to life, the rods would start to move as bursts of steam jetted out at each stroke, the wheels would turn slowly at first, then faster and faster and in a matter of seconds the train would be gone and down the track. What a thrill. I never got tired of seeing it.

This time I was standing up on the street level looking down on the train and about even with the locomotive. This guy, crouched behind a pile of railroad ties and dressed in an old suit and gray felt hat kept watching the train like he was up to something. I was immediately interested. I judged he was thinking of trying to hop on and take a ride and was just waiting for the right time to make his move. If he tried to climb on too soon before she had any momentum, and was seen, it would be an easy matter to stop the train and take him off. If he waited too long the train would be going too fast for him to climb on, so the timing was critical. This guy must have been an experienced train hopper as he pulled it off to perfection. He had no gear or luggage of any kind. Just as the conductor gave the highball the wheels began to roll, then the engineer "spun" the big driver wheels a turn or two to sort of show off the enormous power his hand controlled (a definite no-no I later found out), the sparks would fly as the train glided quietly out of the station.

As if on signal the train hopper sprang to his feet, made a mad sprint to the engine-tender, caught a hand-hold, stuck his foot in the lower rung (stirrup) and swung easily and gracefully up onto a ledge of the oil-tender and sat down. He'd done it! No problems. No one saw him but me. It was as slick a job of train-catching as I'd ever seen. I felt proud of this man, envious of his skill and determined to go and do likewise some day.

This ledge was on the rear-end of the tender – just forward of the first baggage car, so until the train stopped at the next station this fellow was un-assailable and secure. No one could get at him. He was safe until the next stop, where he would be obliged to repeat his boarding move all over again. Obviously this was a nighttime activity as he would be too visible by day, although it was only about 4:30 in the afternoon the time I saw him do it. It was a dangerous and daring maneuver and a person would have to want a ride real bad to try it, but with me it was "hats off" to this bold adventurer. I thrived on excitement.

As I was only 12 years old and not quite up to "nailing" a passenger train (that was to come later) I did the next best thing – I walked up to 2nd Avenue and "Hooked" a ride on the back end of a #24 streetcar that dropped me off a block from our house on Taylor Ave. To make it stop at my street, all I had to do was to pull the rope that connected to the trolley wheel (pantograph), thereby preventing the electricity from being fed to the motors, and of course the streetcar would stop. I'd jump off and run like mad before the irate conductor could catch me. Nice kids didn't do things like that. I was not a nice kid. I was a wild and crazy thrillseeker – a black sheep of a boy; As Merle Haggard sings,

"One and only rebel child from a family meek and mild"

In those days (1933) the freight train was synonymous with the word hobo, as every train it seemed was loaded with them. You'd see guys riding the tops (deck) of boxcars holding onto the upright brake wheels, see the faces peering over the tops of gons (gondola or coal-car) sitting in open boxcar doorways like a row of birds with their legs hanging down (a terribly dangerous practice), riding on top of piles of lumber on flatcars – in fact you could see these "transients" (as the newspapers called them) all over the trains – any place a man could find to ride.

So as an impressionable kid I picked up on all these tricks, biding my time and secretly planning to join these colorful characters. This was THE bona fide adventure available to a youth of that day and secretly dreaded and feared by so many loving mothers and fathers who lost their sons to the lure of the "road." Again Merle,

"First thing I remember knowin' was a lonesome whistle blowing and a young-uns dream of growing up to ride On a freight train leavin' town, not knowing where I'm bound and no one could change my mind – but Mama tried."

The summer I turned 12 I decided to hop a freight. The Northern Pacific ran a switching local to the South end of Lake Union every day about 4:00 in the afternoon. It fooled around humping and shunting the cars until it had a string of a dozen or so, then headed along Westlake on a trestle, down the length of the Lake Washington Ship Canal, ending up in the big yards called Interbay – a total distance of possibly seven miles. I studied the situation carefully and without telling anyone decided to try it. Walking three miles to the end of the lake, I hung around till it looked like the train was made up and ready. Finding an open door of a boxcar, I managed to somehow struggle up and into the car. Looking back I can't recall exactly how I accomplished this, as a small boy cannot even reach the floor they are so high, but I did get up there without help, and hid in the corner until the magical moment when that little teakettle of a coal-burning switch-engine made her move and we were off! On an honest-to-God freight train (sort of) and I had finally gotten up enough nerve to jump one! Hanging tightly to the door jam, I feasted my eyes on the boathouses, steamers, sailing schooners and assorted craft operating in those days on the lake. Golly! What a ride! This was better than I'd even hoped for! We trundled along the Lake Union trestle about 15 miles an hour, breathing coal-smoke all the way. To this day I love the smell of coal smoke – it's as delicious as the smell you get opening a fresh can of coffee. This was my very first catch-out. I was deliriously happy. That day probably set the tone and established the precedent I was to follow all my life. There was something so satisfying about standing on the wood floor of a boxcar watching the scenery slide by, sniffing the pungent smells of creosote and tar and fresh lumber (Douglas Fir is best) plus the secret sense of delight that I, a small kid had, all by himself challenged and beat the system – stolen a ride and gotten away with it! It was a feeling akin to ecstasy. I felt like a conqueror, as I jumped down at Smith's Cove, the ride all too soon over and started the three mile walk home. I'd be late for supper and would have to explain my tardiness. Never mind, I'd think of something. Where things like this were concerned, I was an accomplished liar. Nobody ever understood, so you learned to keep it to yourself.

That happened 70 years ago. I'd do it all over again.

I'd Do It For Free

     One September morning I boarded a passenger train at the King Street Station in Seattle bound for Puyallup. I was going to the fair. It was the first time I'd ever bought a ticket and rode all by myself. I was about 12 and filled with excitement, anticipating having a wonderful time gawking at the displays, farm animals and horses and stuff. The ads said there was to be a rodeo. That interested me. I'd never seen one. I'd never been to the Western Washington Fair, either. It was a big one.

     I'd bought a round trip ticket on the day coach and still had plenty of cash to see me through. I'd have a hamburger and pop for lunch and maybe some cotton candy too. Pretty soon a man in a black uniform came along asking for tickets. I said. "Sir, what's the name of this train?" He seemed amused. "Well, it don't have a name. We call it number 71."

     I was disappointed. Having collected a bunch of railroad time-tables, I knew that most trains had names. The Great Northern had the Empire Builder and the Oriental Limited. The Northern Pacific ran the North Coast Limited; also the Mainstreeter. Milwaukee boasted of the Olympian and the Hiawatha while the Union Pacific's famous trains were the Portland Rose and Challenger. So, here I was on a train that didn't have a name. Seemed like a train with just a number couldn't be really important.

     I decided to examine this train. I walked through three coaches and abruptly came to the end. What? Only three cars? I felt cheated. The man who'd collected my ticket was sitting at a little desk in the last car. He didn't appear too busy so I got my nerve up and approached him asking, "Excuse me sir, could you tell me if there are any sleeping cars or dining cars on this train?"

     He laughed, "No, son, nothing like that. This train's just a stubby – a local." I asked him what that was. "Well, kid, we're only three cars long, so we call it a stubby, meaning it's not very long." I nodded, then asked him what a local was. "Oh, well, a local is a train that stops at <u>every</u> station – even stops in all the jerk-water towns?" Boy I was learning a lot!

     "What's a jerk-water town?"

     "That's a town that's real small. It might not have hardly any stores or people, but it <u>would</u> have a water tank. You've seen 'em – those big black-looking towers where a train stops when its engine needs to take on water? The fireman turns on the water by jerking on a chain – so they call them jerk-water towns. See?" I understood.

     "Do you always ride on this train?" My curiosity knew no limits.

"About half the time. My regular job is conductor on freight trains."

"Which do you like best; passenger or freight trains?"

"I'd have to say freight. You see, it's more casual and relaxed and I don't have to wear this monkey suit."

"What's a monkey suit?" I was afraid he might consider me a pest and tell me to get lost, but instead he kind of enjoyed it.

"Oh, that's what we call this conductor's uniform I wear."

It was a shiny black suit with gold buttons. His hat was flat on the top and said "Conductor." I thought it looked pretty neat. It was years before I realized that the term "Monkey Suit" was derived from the similar-looking costume worn by Organ-Grinder Monkeys who circulated through the crowd collecting coins. I can only recall seeing an Organ-Grinder with a monkey once in my life – in New York City.

Before I knew it we'd arrived in Puyallup and I reluctantly had to get off. I loved riding a train, any train. It was still early and the main gate at the fairgrounds wasn't open yet. I waited around and was among the first customers, as the place started to get busy. I circulated around till I came to an area where the horses and stagecoaches were kept and the cowboys were getting ready. This was as far as I got. You could have spent all day wandering around this giant fairgrounds but it was all to be lost on me. I found something fascinating and didn't budge. I discovered a strange and wonderful breed of men like I'd never seen before. COWBOYS.

Oh, sure I'd seen lots of them in the movies – all dressed up, sitting on white horses and kissing the girl, but these were different, these were real, honest-to-God <u>working</u> cowboys. I recognized the genuine article and couldn't tear myself away. There was something familiar here, like I'd known these guys in some past life. I loved watching them and especially the way they talked. They appeared to be having such a marvelously good time, enjoying it all so.

I was surprised to see how small they were. Not tall, rangy, statuesque men like Tom Mix, who I'd seen at his circus, but rather short, thin, wiry little guys all about the same size and, it seemed – about the same age. I would have guessed them to be 40 or more, but realized now, they were probably closer to 30. It's a tough life and they age rapidly. They were dressed pretty much alike in jeans and blue chambray shirts but wore different colored hats and boots. Some wore chaps. They were getting ready for the rodeo part of the show, brushing the horses, coiling ropes, fooling around with their saddles, all the while making a huge joke of the way a bunch of women operating a lunch stand nearby were hawking their wares. One good-natured old gal would call out in a high, long drawn-out voice, "Red hot coffee!" Some cowboy would mimic, "Ice-cold coffee!" The girls would laugh, then one would holler, "Ice-cold sody pop!" Another cowboy would mock, "Red-hot sodeee-pop! Ice-cold coffee!" This good-natured banter went on all morning. These guys were so fun-loving, everything was a big joke. They were enjoying themselves so.

Along about early afternoon the rodeo started and it was then that I got to see firsthand just how skilled these working cowboys were. One stood out on the track spinning a rope, building the loop bigger and bigger and as the stagecoach came by pulled by six galloping horses he deftly flipped his rope and encircled the entire stagecoach, something I'd never seen before. There was the usual bronc-riding and bull-riding and calf-roping (all so new to me then) plus I got to see a couple of acts that later became famous. One was Monte Montana on his white horse (he has since become a legend and a fixture in the Rosebowl Parade) and Buff Brady and his son, Buff Brady, Jr., who could jump off a horse backwards while riding at full speed – and then grab the horse's tail and vault right back up in the saddle again. Wow!

I was in a daze. Never have I been so caught up. I was witnessing at close up something so new, so revealing, so inspiring that it took me years to sort out my thoughts and pinpoint just exactly what I'd learned. These cowboys had turned my life around, but I was at a loss to grasp the full import of what I'd seen. That would come later.

I had to drag myself away from that fairground and walk slowly and thoughtfully back to the train depot, catching another coal-burning old local back home to Seattle. I had no questions for the trainmen but sat quietly trying to digest the import of what I'd seen that day.

It had to do with attitude. I'd always considered going to work sort of like going to school. You didn't like it all that much but it was something you had to do. It was expected of a man to go out to work and bring home the bacon. Never mind if the job was pleasant or back-breaking – just get out there and do it. I'd taken notice of all sorts of tradesmen who came regularly to our door, the cleaners, the milkman, the laundryman, painters, carpenters and landscape gardeners – none appeared too pleased with their occupations. They took on more of a stoic, grit-your-teeth and bear it attitude. It was their job – and they acted like it was more of a burden than a privilege – at least it looked that way to me. These guys weren't all that happy with their work. No complaining, mind you, but no enchantment either.

Now these cowboys I had spent the day observing were a different breed. They loved their work. That was obvious. In fact it didn't seem like they considered it work. They enjoyed doing what they did so much they could hardly wait to get to it. There was a total absence of worried looks, tense faces, sullen attitudes, or negative talk. Instead they were bright, cheerful, breezy, smiling, laughing and looking for fun. Health and high-spirited energy exuded from their every move.

Were they worried about their "future"? Would they consider going out on strike? Were they "interested in saving money? Were they concerned about getting hurt? Did they have or want insurance of any kind? They were careless and carefree to an unbelievable extent.

They probably earned about $30 a month plus board and room and got a chance to augment that by entering the saddle-bronc riding contest, etc., and possibly win the odd $25 purse. Rodeo had not yet become big-time, nor had the day arrived when elitist, "Name" cowboys would fly their own planes – thereby allowing them to enter two or three different "shows" on the same day. In that day (1933) all that was unheard of. What we hear so much about today of stress, anxiety, worry, nervous breakdowns – all those work-related problems seemed not to exist for the carefree cowboy. He loved his job, probably would-n't consider doing anything else and if it came down to cases – might even work for nothing – just to be a cowboy.

It occurred to me that <u>this</u> attitude, this feeling, this love and lik-ing for his lifestyle should be the determining factor guiding <u>every</u> man's choice of a lifetime occupation and <u>not</u> settling for some play-it-safe, money-grubbing, people-pleasing, security-minded, personality-stifling, pension-attaining dull and deadly round of daily duties.

I still look for this indefinable, peaceful air found in persons who are doing their life's desire, following their dreams. If you look for it you will find it and it's not just cowboys, either who are so lucky. No, there are lots of them around. You could even say that anyone who <u>means</u> it when he says, "Do you mean we get <u>paid</u> for doing this?" – he has found it.

Cardboard, the legendary hobo and I were sitting around the jungle up in North Dakota one summer day sipping our coffee. He surprised me with, "Ya know Whitey, I'd live like this even if I had a million dollars!"

You know what? I believed him.

The Fruit Tramp

My very first job picking fruit and vegetables was in 1938 in the bean fields of West Stayton, Oregon. The pay was a cent a pound. Actually it was only nine-tenths of a cent a pound, but if you stayed the whole picking season they gave us a bonus – one-tenth of a cent – thus making it an even cent a pound.

I slept on the ground in an old sleeping bag, which was no hardship as it only rained once in the six weeks I was there. Oh yes, most of us hung in for the entire season, as we not only wanted the bonus but we were told we could come back the following year and be assured of a job. This was important as it was not all that easy to find a job, even fruit-tramping. The money was so important. To be able to earn a grubstake (say $50 to 100) in the summer time would guarantee that a family could survive the long winter months (when there were no jobs at all) and be able to buy groceries, kerosene (for the lamps) and gas for the car – if you had one.

My first day on the job I worked 10 hours, picked 39 pounds of string beans and made myself 39 cents. As the summer wore on the beans grew faster and larger and I was able to make as much as $2.00 in one day. If you can picture a pile of beans weighing 200 lbs you'd have an idea of what a hustling picker could produce in a ten-hour day.

As always my main interest and real reward was in the people I met. Most of the pickers were family people, migrants mostly who got around in old Fords and Chevys and camped out in makeshift tents. There was a single guy there the first two weeks they called the "California Kid" because he was continually telling stories of what he'd done and where he'd been in the San Joaquin Valley of California – considered a fruit-picker's paradise. He was an interesting cuss, my first introduction to a real old-time fruit-tramp. He'd come in by freight train. I respected that. He said he'd worked with lots of Chinese people down around Fresno. Claimed he'd heard one say, "Chinaman come California, stay, ten years. No speaka very good English. Oklahoman come California, stay three weeks. Speak pretty good English!"

The California Kid made it through the first pay day, but came the second Saturday night "Draw," he got drunk and failed to show on Monday morning. I asked the boss what happened to the Kid? His terse reply, "He bunched it."

They say a year out on the road is the equivalent of a college education. Could be true. I learned plenty. You become street-smart in a hurry. There were hundreds of people working the bean harvest that year, all jammed up in a vacant field in tents, packing water in buckets from one overworked tap and cooking outside over makeshift grills. There were two men who kept their camp somewhat removed from the rest. I used to go over in the evening (when I wasn't playing "horseshoes") just to listen to them talk. They seemed friendly to me but I noticed after a while that most people shunned them. I didn't know why. They spoke and dressed a little different than the run of the mill workers and one had a really high-pitched voice. I thought nothing of it at the time, after all I was only 17 and green as a gourd. It didn't even dawn on me what was going on until, a few years later, when I was waiting for a ship in San Francisco, and I ran onto quite a number of guys who reminded me of my two bean pickers. I'm not stupid but possibly was guilty of being a little slow. Education is a gradual process especially with me.

Living free and easy, traveling light (all I carried was a bedroll and water jug) it was a good feeling to finish out the season, collect your pay (always in cash), head for the post office, convert most of it into a Postal Money-Order, send it on home to your family, then wait around for the noon train. The SP ran a three times a week freight into Salem and then down to Albany where you could diverge off in several directions. I loved this part best – this hoboing from one job to the next.

My next stop was in a place called Yamhill, Oregon, where I worked by the hour (25 cents) in a prune dryer. After a month of this I find I can hardly face a dried prune to this day. By now September had rolled around and it was time to head north for the apples. I'd met a young guy named Warren from Ames, Iowa who picked apples each year for the same grower up in Naches, Washington. He invited me to show up about September 15th and he'd get me on, too. This involved about a 350 mile jaunt; Southern Pacific into Brooklyn Yard, Portland; then a streetcar ride across the Columbia to Vancouver, Washington; then catch the Great Northern into Auburn, switch over to the Northern Pacific all the way into Yakima, then a short hitch-hike up the valley to Naches. Nothing to it. Didn't cost us but a dime.

Late October, after apple season, one more trip down to Tule Lake, California where I got a job driving truck in the potato harvest, then back home to the little cabin in Northwestern Oregon for a possible winter's work cutting cordwood for the pulp mill.

Welcome to life on the fruit tramp!

I Quit Cigarettes in Albuquerque

I'd been dying for a smoke all the way from Grand Junction but I'd fought it all night. Riding the Big Red into Albuquerque I thought I'd won the battle. That was till I'd finished breakfast at Tony's Cafe, then, all at once I could stand it no longer, bought a pack of Camels and went outside on the sunny side of the street where I lit up – marveling at how good it tasted. This was more than 30 years ago but I can still taste that delicious cigarette. I smoked with infinite satisfaction – relishing every puff. Now why did they have to discover they were bad for you?

That was when I noticed I'd lost my glasses. Must have slipped out of my pocket when I was sleeping on the bus. This was not good. I had hours to wait for the Santa Fe Chief to take me into L.A. and I'd planned on doing some reading at the city park.

I found a cut-rate drug store on the main drag where they sold reading glasses – which were simply magnifying glasses of varying strength. Trying them out I settled for the #9's – the strongest pair they had. Cost $13.95. High, but so what? I had to have them if I expected to read a book.

Armed with my new glasses I hunted down a used book store where I made a real find! For $2.00 I bought an old dog-eared copy of Jack London's "The Road." Written 1894, it was an account of his two years as a wandering hobo. It's a classic and is still pertinent to this day. What a deal!

Walking the eight blocks to the park armed with my new glasses, fresh pack of cigs and a good book – I was set for the day. To my discomfiture I soon discovered that these glasses were way too strong and were "pulling" my eyes, giving me a headache to boot. Deciding to return them for a refund I walked back towards the store, but on the way I decided to check at the bus station to see if by chance my regular glasses had been found and possibly turned in.

Imagine my delight as the dispatcher fished around in a box, bringing out my very own bifocals, holding them out, "Are these yours?"

I replied jubilantly, "Yes, they are! Come home to Papa." I felt so relieved at having them back I could have kissed him.

Passing by the railroad station I had another brainstorm; I would quit smoking. Again? Yes, again – and I'd stay quit this time! Feeling brave I deposited the nearly full pack in the trashcan by the depot door and went swinging happily on my way. I had that same good feeling you get when church lets out.

Arriving at the drugstore I presented the reading glasses to the clerk, saying I couldn't use them as they hurt my eyes. His firm reply, "Sorry, sir, we don't make any refunds." Period. Just like that! Whoa! Hey, what goes on here? I didn't expect this. What to do? I kept bugging the man but he didn't want to listen to me, just kept repeating himself like a stuck record, "No refunds, sorry!"

I decided to try intimidation. Rubbing my eyes, all the while holding the unwanted glasses, I loudly complained, "But sir! These glasses you sold me have made my eyes water and they've given me a headache, and I only used them a half-hour! What if they've damaged my optic nerves? What if my eyesight has been irreparably ruined? I'd hate to think what would happen if these glasses were found to be the cause!"

He was beginning to take notice of me, eyeing me suspiciously. I sensed that I had struck oil. I continued on, now even louder, "What if I reported this incident to the authorities and they decided to take action. They'd ask me where I bought them – these harmful glasses, and I'd have to tell them . . . ." I stopped in the middle of a word. The clerk had opened his cash register, proffered me my $13.95, snarling "Here! Take your money. Give me back those glasses – and – don't bother me again!" I pocketed my dough feeling a definite sense of victory and headed for the park. As East Coast Charles says, "And so it goes."

I read every story in Jack's book – some of the best-told tramp yarns I've ever read, lolled around on the park bench soaking up the sun till nearly train time.

On the way back to the Santa Fe Depot I started craving a cigarette. What, again? Would they never get off my back? Oh well, that's life. By this time quite a crowd had gathered. Must be a bunch heading West tonight. There were also a lot of Navajo sales ladies with their jewelry spread out on blankets. I rummaged around in the same trash can – all eyes on me – finally retrieving my cigs – held the pack up triumphantly as the ladies laughed, then walked up to the train platform where I lit up once more, inhaling contentedly, feeling that deep-down satisfaction only a cigarette can provide.

Just then the Chief roared in and as I stepped aboard I realized, "Hell, I'm only human."

Is It Dangerous Out There?

Alan Curl was a cowboy who'd turned to herding sheep. A fall from a horse had crippled him a bit; could no longer ride, but could still walk. I first met him in Spokane where he was staying at the old Great Northern Hotel. He'd come off the sheep range every fall and head for Spokane to have a pair of boots made to order at White's Boot Factory. He'd hang around town till his boots were ready, then go hobo-ing down along the Mexican border until the spring sheep herding jobs came up. Then he'd return to his home state of Wyoming to hire back on with the well-known Warren Livestock Co.

Over six feet tall, well set-up, startlingly blue-eyed, the clearest complexion on any man I've ever seen, he was a stand out. Stepping along Trent Avenue in his new White's boots and gray Stetson hat, he'd stick out of any crowd like a man from Mars. He was then over 60 and looked 40. I met him in a skid row restaurant on Main Street called Stan's Coney Island where we both ordered a hamburger and got to talking. I spotted him for an adventurer right away. He took to <u>me</u> because I appreciated <u>him</u>. In a half-hour we became lifelong friends. I used to visit him at his sheep camps and stay a few days. He'd explain all about the cowboy and sheep herding life; I'd do my best to teach him to play the five-string. He never did get the hang of it but he didn't give up, and used to haul his banjo around with him, even on freight trains. One of those guys who was given no ear and no aptitude for playing stringed instruments – but was SADDLED with a desire to play that amounted to almost a passion. One of life's minor tragedies!

We were looking out over his band of sheep one day near the little town of Tie Siding, Wyoming, (pop. 7), watching the UP trains start up the grade. When I first arrived, Alan would point out these trains, but I couldn't see them. After a couple of days in that high, clear air, my eyesight would improve so that I could make them out easily and even tell how many units were in the lead. This was the main line from Laramie to Cheyenne and about a dozen miles distant. Alan told me this story.

He'd been camping out up in Montana and had drifted south and into the town of Yuma, Arizona. Too many tramps around to suit him, so one evening he got his gear together and headed for the SP. Strong as a bull, he packed not only the aforementioned banjo, but complete camping gear including a tent and even an axe. A pair of STREAMLINERS (strong-arm thieves) spotted him and couldn't believe their own eyes! What pickings! This was not your usual Bo with worn-out, faded gear and a few food stamps, oh, no! This was a real PILGRIM, a pigeon, just ASKING to be jackrolled! Wow! Irresistible!

Alan walked along all innocence, unaware that he'd been targeted; found a nice cozy boxcar, climbed in, arranged his mountain of gear, then stood in the doorway. He could tell the train was about to leave.

About then along came the two jolly swag-men, peeked in; one said, "This looks like a good car; I think we'll ride along with you!"

Alan said later, "Bells started going off in my head. These guys had no gear at all and were a pair of unsavory characters if ever I saw any." He told them, "No, you're not riding with me; there's plenty more empties up ahead, go get one of them."

The first man replied, "What do ya <u>mean</u>, I can't ride with you? We'll just <u>see</u> about that!" With that, he swung nimbly up into the car and made for Alan, pulling a sheath knife as he came. He took a vicious swipe at Alan's chest, Alan countered by bringing his arm and hand up to stave off the weapon, getting his little finger cut. The blood started spurting out, he'd severed an artery, and before the jackroller could make another lunge, Alan stepped over to the side of the car, where moments before he'd set out his short-handled cruiser axe, grabbed it with both hands, whirled and swung, catching his assailant on the side of his face with the flat part of the axe. If he'd turned it blade-side to it would have taken the man's head off. As it was the blow caved in the cheekbone, knocking him screaming and writhing to the floor. His partner, who was in the act of climbing up to his buddy's aid, seeing the result, lost all the fight in him and was now running down the track. Just then, the train lurched to a start. Alan pulled the unconscious streamliner to the edge of the doorway and booted him off onto the ground. Alan tied a bandage around his finger and wiped off the axe-handle, which was covered with blood. He stood and watched Yuma fade into the night.

Next morning the train was stopped in Gila Bend, surrounded with police. They came straight to Alan's car, told him someone had called the cops and ambulance back in Yuma, and told a story about some WILD COWBOY who'd tried to murder his buddy with an axe.

Alan told his side simply and straight-forward, showed them his cut finger and bloody axe-handle. The situation was so clear-cut and believable, that they let him go – didn't even make him get off the train.

Moral of this story is: NEVER TRAVEL STICKING OUT!

Hobo Alarm Clock

I'd been riding the "Wobbly" (Western Pacific), had slept right on through a set-out and woke to find myself abandoned in the heart of the Sierras – a prettier place you would seldom see. The stillness of the mountains, the big trees, the rushing river down a deep gorge all combined to complete the picture of total tranquillity. I sat by the tracks lost in a muse, wondering if some higher power had conspired to teach me some obscure lesson by side-tracking me in this fairyland.

Later that day I'd layed down by the tracks to take a little nap, pretty sure I'd wake up when the train came. I'd run on to the gandy crew and the foreman told me there was a Southbound due from Beiber somewhere around noon, which, he said, slowed down just before crossing the Feather River Bridge.

It was hot that July day. I found a shady place to lay down almost directly underneath a sign that said "Keddie Wye." There was another sign painted on the face of a rock in neat white block letters; "Harold the Hobo" and the date, 1969. Reminded me of the neatly done signs seen all over the West – some still legible today of "Tex K. T." with an arrow indicating direction of travel. I have never learned just who this Tex, King of Tramps was. No matter. He was a good sign-writer.

This spot where I was lying was the place where the trains from the North (Nu-Beiber) would be switched off to the West for Oroville, or continue on straight, thru the tunnel to Portola and East. I was looking for the Oroville Man, so was stretched out right alongside of where the tracks diverged.

A half hour later I was abruptly awakened by a strange sound, a noise I was not at all familiar with . . . a spasmodic series of clicks, quite loud. It almost reminded me of the sound a rattlesnake makes – a sort of "chk chk chk chk chk." I sat up, immediately alert to see what was making this strange noise. It was coming from a silver painted switch-box opposite the switch, and, as I watched, the rail points were moving in short jerks to their new position. This took perhaps five seconds and I knew instantly just what had happened. This track was controlled by CTC (Centralized Traffic Control) and someone at the board, possibly in Stockton, had pressed a button activating this remote-controlled electric switch-motor, thereby "throwing" the switch over to the Oroville track. Which meant? . . . why, of course, a train was approaching! Simple, when you have the picture. Then, I reasoned, after this oncoming train had passed and gone – another button pressed, another electrical impulse would "line" the switch back to its normal "through" position.

Hmmmmmm. Very interesting I thought. This could be used most anywhere. I must remember to use this new wrinkle.

Sure enough, in 15 minutes I heard the sound of flanges screaming on the curve as the Oroville Man dropped down out of the mountain and headed down the Feather River Canyon.

Slowing at the bridge like the foreman had promised, I swung on the rear end of a lumber load, climbing way up high to ride the top for safety and the 360 degree view of the magnificent scenery of the Sierras.

The next time I had a chance to try out this "Alarm Clock" idea was in Wishram, Washington a few weeks later. I'd held down (ridden) a grainer from Vancouver and was looking for the California Man to take me to Bend. A helpful "rail" back at the crew shack told me,

"There's something due through here at about midnight heading across the river and south, but I couldn't tell you the exact time." It was about 7:00 pm, so I asked, "Will it be coming from Pasco – or from the Portland end?"

"Oh, it's out of Portland/Vancouver."

With hours to spare I had me a cheeseburger and coffee at the Beanery, then mosey'd slowly down river for about a mile, past the YTR to where the track splits off towards the bridge. There it was – just as I knew it would be – the remote switchbox just like the setup at Keddie. I made sure the track was "lined" straight, then spread out my bedroll and waited. After the hot day the black rocks were still retaining the warmth, so I lazily watched the mighty Columbia roll silently by, noting the occasional towboat and barge movements. By 9:00 I was asleep, hoping no rattlers were out.

I was jolted upright by the clicking sound of the switch mechanism, only this time even louder and more pronounced. My alarm clock worked! Oh happy day! Looking down river I saw the headlight of the approaching train. Fifteen minutes later she took the switch and ran on up to the wooden apron of the YTR.

I took my time rolling up and finding myself a good car to ride as I knew the train had to wait 13 minutes for the bridge to lower.

Welcome to life on the road!

I Never Pick Anybody Up

Hitch-hiking, once a noble, bold and venturesome undertaking, has fallen upon sorry times. I started doing it when I was 10 years old in the days when a three mile ride was considered real fine. Hardly a year has passed but I have reverted to my old ways on occasion, to see if the old magic would still work. Yes it does, but only to a limited degree. Today most drivers are mortally afraid to invite strangers into their cars. With good reason. It's a touchy situation but still possible. Hitch-hikers are known today as "Thumb-bums" or "Ramp-tramps," indicating their lowered status. They are remotely related to the freight-hopping clan only in that they, too, are traveling "free."

The main difference is one of concept and attitude. The hitch-hiker is essentially a beggar. He is standing out there along the highway pleading with the motorist to stop and give him a lift. The freight hopper on the other hand asks for nothing. He merely finds himself a train and TAKES his ride. When you are "riding your thumb" it is more times than not a temporary way to get from point A to point B; not something a person does regularly. With the rail-rider, it's a way of life. He pursues his dangerous and illegal traveling because he likes it. He does it for pleasure.

Never one to consider the philosophic differences, I loved to hitch-hike. It would allow me to visit places far removed from railroads. In a never-ending attempt to hone my skills and refine my methods, I found that I was very good at it, partly because of my clean-cut and harmless appearance, and partly due to my technique. I studied the subject closely. Watching other persons and noting their mistakes, I worked out my own system.

There are several categories of cars and drivers from which you will very likely NEVER get a ride. You learn to spot these quickly and ignore. The family car loaded and going for a Sunday drive. An elderly lady, of genteel appearance in a fancy auto; a motor home containing two "Dried Prunes." A "hot" car full of teenagers; most sports cars (no room). Most franchise-owned trucks; add one more; ANY driver who is "uptight" and shows his hostility by his glance or who looks straight ahead and veers way over to give you a wide berth.

Okay, now, what's left? Good question. At your very luckiest, you can only choose from the spectrum less than ten per cent of all the cars that pass. Which are they? They are people like you. They are the daring, the risk-takers, the adventurers, the lonely; salesmen looking for company; independent truckers needing someone to talk to; blue-collar working men are excellent; people who have had a rough life or who have done some hitching themselves and know the feeling. In short, anyone who is open to meeting people and who, seeing your predicament, want to help you – these are your potential rides. The others are all afraid of you.

I always carried gear, but not too much. I found out having a guitar along was helpful, but a real drag to carry if I was forced to walk a lot. I tried to keep my personal appearance clean, neat and avoided long hair. It is always important to be standing in a spot where the driver could pull over out of the lane of travel. Stand straight and tall and look the driver right in the eye. For some reason this eye-contact is impor-tant. A smile helps. In order to achieve a fighting chance for a ride I found I had to look "interesting" and never show a hang-dog attitude. Never play "Poor Me," your best results come when you can give the impression that you could care less whether they stop or not. Above all I tried to appear innocent and harmless – allay their fears. I learned NOT to extend my thumb, but rather to just stand there facing traffic. Of late I find it helps to hold up a sign indicating destination.

All these fine points I developed over the years. In this way I have been able to travel fairly easily all over the lower 48, large sections of Canada and several times up to Alaska and back. I've never hitched in Europe or Asia.

All my life I have had short hair. It seems to suit me, plus it is the easiest way I know to take care of it. Sometimes it has made a difference. On the way back from Alaska I left Fairbanks heading down the Alcan Highway heading for Seattle. This was around 1970 as I recall. At that time only the section through Alaska was paved. The blacktop ended at the Yukon border at the town of Beaver Creek. From there for its entire length to just north of Fort St. John the Alcan was a two-lane gravel road. Large, coarse gravel. Prudent travelers rigged temporary wire screens on their front bumpers to take the brunt of the storm of rocks encountered, thrown by the wheels of oncoming and passing vehicles, thereby reducing the breakage of headlights and windshields. Alaskans, wishing to drive down to the lower 48 (they called it going "Outside") preferred to make the run in mid-winter. Then the road was at its best. FROZEN!

The handsome Canadian who picked me up in Whitehorse, Yukon, dropped me off at a remote crossroads village known as Johnson's Crossing. A rickety plank bridge crossed a tributary of the Yukon River, flowing north out of Teslin Lake. The town was a combi-nation bar, restaurant and truck stop stuck all by itself way out in the Canadian Bush county, with the dusty highway its only link to the outside world.

I noticed a guy sitting by the edge of the road in a huge over-stuffed sofa. We greeted each other. He was a hitch-hiker himself who informed me he'd been "there" three days. Seemed hitching was pretty poor around these parts. I commiserated with him, wished him luck, then headed down the road. He, being #1 was entitled to "Front spot,"

which gave him first crack at oncoming traffic. What there was of it.
He told me it averaged about three cars an hour. Slim pickings.

I continued on down the road and saw there were more hitchers
– several more, spaced out about a hundred yards apart, sitting on their
packs or reading, resigned to waiting their turn and realizing it could
develop into a rather long wait, the traffic being so light. It was like running a gauntlet passing by each and stopping a minute to exchange plea-
santries like "how long have you been waiting?" Where had they come
from and where were they hoping to get to, stuff like that. Proper hitch-
hiking protocol demanded that I pass by to finally arrive at the tail end,
possibly a mile down the road past the lead man reclining in his sofa. I
found a shady spot, took an apple out of my pack and prepared to wait it
out. Two of the thumbers I'd spoken to told me they were from France
– a guy and gal traveling together. All the rest were singles.

You could see an approaching vehicle a long way off as it raised
a cloud of dust, and hurtling past, left us gasping in more dust. I'd
settled down with a book to read, after counting four cars passing, none
of which stopped. Then an extra big cloud of dust appeared. I saw all
my competitors spring to their feet in anticipation. Something was up.
Then I knew. The oncoming cloud was stirred up by a Truck. A huge
diesel truck was bearing down on us hopefuls, roaring along at a good
speed and showing no inclination to stop. Good Heavens, this was what
everyone was hoping and praying for. A truck was the best ride you got
on this forlorn highway. It meant a through ride. A long and comfortable through ride – maybe to Calgary or Vancouver or Seattle. Glory
be . . . Mr. Truckdriver . . . please stop and pick me up. The hitchers
were fairly jumping up and down with excitement. Was this to be their
ride? The thumbs were being held high. The feeling was contagious.

With me, I reasoned that someone up ahead just MIGHT get
lucky and be picked up – but me, I felt I had little chance, as I was
sucking the hind tit and so expected little consideration.   I didn't even
stand up, just kept sitting relaxed and watching the show the others put
on. On came the big rig barreling on through, not even slowing down
despite the arm-waving antics of the travelers.

Then a funny thing happened. This dusty juggernaut came
charging past me. I looked up at the cab and saw that the driver was
checking me out. Suddenly the sound of the big diesel changed, the air
brakes and the Jake-brake all being applied. The truck slowed, the
gravel flew and she came to a screeching halt about two hundred feet
past me.

Could this be true? Had he stopped for me? Had he passed
over all the others and selected me? I gathered my stuff together and
made a run for it, climbed up and opened the door. Then, as I slipped
down into the big black leather seat, I glanced back down the road. All
the unlucky ones were standing and looking in shocked amazement –

arms akimbo – not believing their eyes. I recalled that verse from a certain book – "And the first shall be last – and the last, first."

As we roared out of Johnson's Crossing heading for Seattle (yes, it did turn out to be a <u>through</u> ride) I thanked the driver for stopping. A big, burly man about 50 years old, dressed in overalls and wearing his hair really short – like a crew cut, said, "That's okay, glad to have someone I can talk to. You got a ride all the way to Seattle if you want." I told him, "That's great, I can use it."

Then after a while I inquired. "I sure do appreciate the ride, but I'm curious about one thing."

He turned, "What's that?"

"How come you passed all those other hitch-hikers up and then stop for me?"

He looked me square in the eye. "You were the only one of the bunch who had SHORT HAIR."

Riding Inside

Are the railroad men friendly towards the hobo? Do train crews resent tramps being on their trains? For the most part it seems to me that they not only tolerate the riders, they secretly enjoy seeing the Bo's ride their trains. Some are hostile, some are non-committal, but most are affable and cheerful when asked, "where's this train headed?" or "what time is she called for?" or "what's going out Eastbound up the river today?" Sometimes they'll even call up the dispatcher for you on their hand-helds and come up with, "There's an Eastbound already made up in the "B" yard due out early afternoon." Sometimes their helpfulness is overwhelming.

I'd caught a piggyback out of Wenatchee bound for Seattle. Riding backwards with my back resting against the trailer tires to help cut down the wind, the ride was fine until we stopped at East Portal in a siding to allow an Eastbound to clear the tunnel. I decided right quick that this stop gave me a chance to find a ride inside, as I really didn't relish going through the 7.9-mile Cascade Tunnel breathing all those diesel fumes. I hurried up forward a few cars to the rear-most unit where I saw a guy sitting by the open window. I hollered up, "Can I ride inside going through the tunnel?" He shook his head, replying, "Sorry, there's no room – we've already got guys in all the units." So, back I went to re-board my car, feeling a little disappointed but knowing I could survive the smoke by breathing through a dampened bandanna and pulling my wool sweater over my head. Which is just what I did and made it through okay.

A couple of hours later we pulled into Balmer Yards where I got ready to bail off, but this time for some reason the train didn't stop – just cruised on through, then along the Seattle waterfront, through the tunnel and kept right on going. We hadn't changed crews so I was pretty sure we wouldn't plow on through to Portland. Here I'd planned to get off in Interbay, catch a bus up to my daughter's house and enjoy a shower and a hot dinner.

Every turn of the wheels was taking me farther out of town. Would she never stop? Down through Georgetown, past the Boeing Field, and then I realized where she was going. About 10 miles south, at a place near Tukwila Junction, was a large inter-modal receiving yard where the trailer trains and stack trains were unloaded. Sure enough, we took a siding into this yard, which was surrounded by a high chain link fence. I piled off the minute she stopped and started hoofing it to a road I'd seen. Bad situation! Here I was, afoot, ten miles from town, evening coming on and tired and hungry to boot. What a predicament; but all in the day's work, I assumed a philosophical attitude and plodded down the right-of-way. Now comes the surprise!

The three big, green Burlington Northern locomotives came cruising back after having dropped their string off, heading for the roundhouse and day's end. They stopped right alongside of me. The same guys I'd spoken to back at East Portal hollered out the window, "Come on up, we've got room now, we'll give you a ride back to town."

Could I believe my ears? "Well, that's great," I said and lost no time crawling up into that unit. There were already three men there, but I sat on the floor, so grateful to be picked up. "We hated to turn you down back there at the tunnel, so I asked the engineer to stop for you this time. Just keep down out of sight and we'll have you back in Interbay in no time."

Could anyone have treated me nicer? That was only one of the many, many time I've been invited to "RIDE INSIDE."

When Springtime Does Come . . .

Andy Ewenson was a tramp who traveled with me a few times. I learned so <u>much</u> from him, such as showing me the advantage of carrying an air mattress, especially in the winter months. Instead of blowing it up to full capacity, you inflate it only about half-full – or until, when your weight settles down on it, you sink down till you almost, but not quite, touch the bottom. This makes the train's shocks and bumps go unnoticed, plus if you are sleeping on a metal-floored car, there is an air space between you and the cold steel. It is really the difference between having a comfortable night's sleep and laying awake, freezing, shivering and banging your hip.

Another thing, he loved to drink coffee. It seemed like every time you turned around he was heating up water for a fresh cup. In the car, he would heat the water on a Sterno stove that he carried with him. Outside on the ground he preferred to use an old wine bottle he'd find laying around; fill it about a third full of fresh water (rinsing out the residue first), set it on the ground, place wood shavings all around the base, then light it off. As the fire heated the water he'd watch it closely, then just as it started to boil over, he'd take his gloved hand, pick up the bottle and fill both cups which had coffee crystals already in. Occasionally, the bottom of the bottle would drop off just as he picked it out of the fire, but mainly it worked well.

One November morning Andy and I caught an empty boxcar on the fly just as she left southbound out of Brooklyn Yard, Portland. We were heading for Phoenix where the climate suits your clothes and were hoping for a daylight ride over the Cascade hump. Instead of following the mainline south, she took a diverging track across the Willamette River and headed west. We exchanged disparaging looks, "Now where? Are we bound for Hillsboro and on to the Coast, or what?" When you have to board a train that's already moving, you never get a chance to learn whither she's bound, so you just take your chances and hope. This time, we soon learned, we'd caught the McMinnville Man, a small town 40 miles west of Portland.

Half way there, in Newberg, our car got set off. We had such a scramble to get our gear together and jump off and then run to catch the rest of the train, then, for some reason, the train stopped, a brakeman walked up to where we were sitting on a flat car and said, "Come on back to the caboose; the conductor wants you guys to ride inside."

Well! How thoughtful! Yes, we'd like that, too! So back we go, enter the caboose, shake hands with the old-time conductor and settle down for a comfortable ride clear in to McMinnville riding the cushions, so to speak. We wondered about this royal treatment. The old timer answered it with a story.

Seems this was his last run; he was retiring soon as he returned to Portland; up till now, he had a perfect, accident-free record and didn't want to take a chance on either of us getting hurt – he wanted very much to be able to retire with his record intact. Said he was most concerned because several years before, while he was a brakeman, he'd broke both legs in a fall off a boxcar. Seems he was riding the top in a switching maneuver when the hogger jerked the train, sending him toppling between cars. As he was falling he had the presence of mind to remember to bounce clear of the wheels if that was at all possible. He said he landed on the outside rail, breaking both legs, but was still able at the last second to roll himself away from the train with his last conscious move – just inches ahead of the slow-rolling wheel. He lost consciousness after that, but did survive.

Said he was months in the hospital and had to learn to walk all over again, but still went back to railroading and eventually worked up to conductor. He was still highly accident-conscious. Said we were welcome to ride back with him to Portland. Andy and I thanked him, wished him well and headed down the track. I never get over some of the great people you meet out along the "Shining Ribbon."

I was hitch-hiking one time in the state of Wyoming and got picked up by a train. Here's what happened. In the little town of Greybull I was standing by the freight station one summer morning, soaking up the sunshine, when four guys got out of a van and walked past me towards the yards, carrying shoulder bags, with lanterns and stuff. I recognized them right off as being a road crew. There was a short string of cattle-cars coupled up behind two CB&Q (Chicago, Burlington & Quincy), engines toward which these guys were making their way.

I walked up and asked them if I could ride along. "No, we've got no room," the oldest one said. "Besides we're only going as far as Thermop." I thanked them and headed back to the highway out of town, wondering why the man had said there was no room when I could plainly see about 40 empty cattle cars.

I trudged on up to where a highway overpass went up and over the "Q"'s mainline. There I stood with thumb extended. A few minutes passed, no one stopped. Looking back I could see the train had started up and was heading my way. I turned and watched it approach. It would pass directly below me. For some inexplicable reason the train stopped. Somebody in the lead engine hollered up, "Still want a ride?" I heard him all-right, but couldn't hardly believe my ears. I stared down in disbelief. Then he repeated his question, "If you want a ride with us, better get on down here and take the back unit, we can't wait all day!"

That was all I needed to hear. Dashing down the embankment I hurried up the steps, opened the door, went inside and took a seat on the fireman's side, and sat there marveling at the strange ways of that wonderful, big-hearted clan known as railroad men. Why they stopped for me, I'll never know, but the probable reason was that they had felt bad about turning me down the first time, and wanted to make it up to me.

Up in North Central Ontario at a tiny little town called Hearst, I woke up to find myself in a crummy frontier-type hotel. I'd hitched in late the night before and needed a place to flop. I had no bedroll so I was directed to this place where I got a room for $4.00. Seems the hotel catered to single men who kept me up all night hollering, cursing and fighting. I have always pondered on why people take rooms in hotels, then raise Hell all night instead of sleeping. Shows how old-fashioned I am, I guess. Today, these guys would probably be referred to as "Native Canadians" but I recognized them right off as drunk Indians.

Next morning after a good whopping big breakfast, I explored the town, discovering that a train (passenger) was scheduled to leave southbound at 9:00 am headed eventually for Saulte St. Marie. I bought a ticket for the first stop, a place called Oba, where I hoped to hop a freight westbound. I'm not sure what the name of this road was, but I think it was called the Algona Central. The consist was one tired diesel-electric unit, one baggage car and three old-time day coaches. I was one of three passengers. We stopped several times way out in the woods, away from any town or house that I could see, to pick up people. In other words you could flag this train down any place along the right-of-way by simply standing out there and waving your hand. Seems there were almost no roads in this area and that's how the natives commuted to town and back.

A couple of hours put us into Oba (population about 30), where this railroad crossed the CN (Canadian National) mainline. I got off, checked out the crossing "diamond" and walked over to the tiny freight station. The sky darkened up and pretty soon a good rain was falling. Having no rain gear and no place to get under, I stood disconsolately by the track, feeling sorry for myself and wondering why I was always getting myself in these crazy situations. Here I was, alone and afoot, stuck way out in the middle of Canada's "Bush" country, nearly 3,000 miles away from home and for no earthly reason than just the urge to roam and to see some new country. Okay, I was seeing it.

I could see no railroad yard anywhere around, so had no idea of just where to go to catch a westbound. There I stood, wondering what to do. Pretty soon, way down the line I saw a light, a headlight, coming through the woods. My interest quickened; was it a freight? Was it a passenger? In any case it was heading the right direction. But, how to catch it? As she thundered towards me I saw it was a long mixed drag, pulled by two big, black-and-red CN lokies doing about 30 miles an hour. Just before she reached the place where I was standing, the train suddenly slowed way down and as she passed, the engineer leaned out and cupped his hands, shouting, "Are you looking for a ride?" I screamed back, "Yes, can I ride to Hornepayne?" (That was the next division, about 50 miles west).

He nodded, "Yes, catch the second unit." Maybe he thought I was a "rail" deadheading home or maybe he saw a forlorn, rain-soaked vagabond on whom he took pity. It was an easy matter to swing in, climb the steps, enter the cab, turn on the electric heater and relax in the engineer's chair. My faith in my fellow man once more resurrected, I leaned back, enjoying the ride through some of the most lonesome, dreary yet fascinating bush country I've ever seen. Not a town, village or hamlet did we pass – nothing but swamps and trees until late that afternoon, arriving in the bustling little town of Hornepayne. I waved to the generous-hearted engineer as I climbed down and made my way to a cafe, telling myself, once more, the wonderful people you run onto along the rails.

Wandering around the yards in Fremont, Nebraska, looking for a double-stack going west, the three of us, myself, Santa Fe Bo and Uncle Freddie had just come in on a coal-train from Boone, Iowa. It was about midnight and we were exploring some loaded stack cars but could find nothing to ride; all those we'd seen had no wells to ride. Wells, but no bottoms. We were psyched up to ride, were hoping for a fast trip back to California but saw no chance here. Fremont is where C&NW (Chicago & NorthWestern) hands over their trains to Union Pacific, so we knew we were in the right place.

About then, a man climbed down from a big UP locomotive, spotted us and came over to check us out. Asked where we were going, he told us he was the engineer on a UP hotshot, leaving out westbound momentarily and that we would be welcome to ride the third (unoccupied) unit. What a stroke of luck! Said to wait until we heard him sound his whistle, then to scramble on and to keep down until we cleared the yards. Said his train was a "70." Which meant he would do 70 miles an hour all the way to North Platte. How lucky can you get? Where could you find a nicer guy?

Sure enough, the whistle blew and we scurried on, taking our places on the floor. I unrolled and dropped off to sleep as we departed. Minutes before this and just before getting underway, this helpful man had come back into our unit to see if we were okay. Said he'd give us a wake-up call in plenty of time to alert us to arriving in North Platte, so we could get our gear together and leave the engine, as it was going to the fuel dock, and we'd better not be found on it. Every one knew that this division point was one of the hottest in the nation for bulls. We told him we'd be ready.

Four hours later, still pitch dark outside, a bell rang in our cab – our "wake-up call." We got ready and as we approached the outer yard of North Platte, we saw where two extra-bright lights straddled the double-track, illuminating each car as she passed. We'd heard this was a new thing – a camera, like television, taking pictures of each car, its number, plus indicating if any riders were aboard. What a tell-tale!

We kept down, out of sight, and departed that engine the minute she stopped, not wanting to compromise that engineer in case we were apprehended. We made a bee-line out of the yard and almost made it, when we noticed a pickup truck following us, and stopped, wondering what was up.

A young guy, a rookie bull, got out, asked us didn't we know we were trespassing? Demanded our I.D., took down all the particulars, then ordered us into the back of his truck. Curses! Jail for sure! It was common knowledge in the hobo fraternity that the standard punishment for getting caught in a UP yard was usually 30 days. The bull locked up the truck bed, started off and in a few minutes let us out, not at the city jail, but at an all-night convenience store, with the warning "If I catch you in the yard again, you'll do jail time."

The three of us, Santa Fe, Uncle Freddie and me, sat down at a table inside, drank coffee, ate maple bars and congratulated ourselves on our unbelievable good fortune. We shook hands all around – bonded for life.

Who's Out There?

People are always asking me, "Who do you see out there? What kind of men are following this life?" Well, mostly it's men who have sort of dropped out of society, who no longer feel that they BELONG. I guess there's some women, too, but I haven't run onto many – just a few, and they seem to always be with a guy. They're not out there by themselves, no, they're just with <u>him</u>, so I don't feel knowledgeable enough to speak for the gals.

Occasionally, you run onto someone who has let himself go to where he can't come back. These guys are like wild animals, foraging a living by dumpster diving, maybe collecting food stamps or whatever. They avoid people of all kinds. Some won't even say hello to another tramp. You see them out West around the smaller division towns like White Fish, Mt. Dillon or Havre – places where there's still a lot of wide-open spaces near the town and jungle. You might see one crouched over a fire in the wooded part of the Whitefish yard. He may be cooking up some grub, or maybe just keeping warm. If you approach him, he might not even look at you, much less speak. He's been exposed to so much diesel smoke from the engines plus campfire smoke, plus the fact that he has long since given up washing his hands and face, and now his skin is dark, his hands are black, with this ingrained dirt, his clothes are stiff with grease and filth. He has the over-all look of a WILDMAN. Keeps strictly to himself. If he spots you first, then you won't see him at all. Shy and spooked. He's abandoned all pretense of being sociable. Wants to be left alone. Won't answer questions. Yet these guys are usually harmless and are not out to steal, rob or harm anyone. They're just terribly shy dropouts, who have accepted their role. They fit no particular pattern, are composed of all and sundry ages, stay out of big cities and follow the railroads exclusively.

Then, there's the drinker. This is probably the largest group (in numbers) of all in this nomadic following. These are men (used to be years ago they were mostly OLDER types, but now there's as many <u>young</u> ones) who have given up trying to pretend that they can live without booze. They know they can't, and so have given in peacefully, and now EMBRACE their addiction. The boozing fraternity lives mostly for booze. They often are robust, strong and willing workers, but can't seem to get it together to hold down a job for more than a day or so. They'll do orchard work in a pinch, but, given a couple of days' pay they'll BUNCH it and move on.

On the road the chosen drink is WINE. Cheap fortified wine. The price is within reach and the alcoholic content high. They may not drink a large amount at any one time, but they're continually nipping, and are rarely stone sober. Another thing, they can't tolerate the company of a tramp who doesn't drink! They want <u>only</u> drinking buddies.

On cold nights, especially on trains going over the "Hump," this wine is known as a "TOKAY BLANKET," and with a goodly amount under your belt, you can pass out and sleep like a child.

To the average drinking tramp, the ever-recurring problem of how to buy booze is overcome in some astonishingly novel and ingenious ways. If he is "in between checks" but still has food stamps, he might visit several small stores, buying a candy bar or any item less than a dollar, receiving change at each purchase, then use the accumulated money to buy a "jug." Or he might take the grocery or food items out on the street and "sell" the whole bagful, cheap, for enough cash for the jug. If he gets desperate and is beginning to feel the "shakes" coming on, he will "stem it" or "hit the main stem" or "spare change it," in short – panhandle. It's a last ditch effort, and he hates like poison to demean himself – but if there's nothing else? He already knows . . . the bottom line . . . gotta have that drink! One quick way to raise money is to donate blood - $10 a pint – if they'll take it. Last time I tried, I was rejected – said I had "Iron Deficiency."

Then there's always the scam artists. Of late there's been a swelling tide of these – easily identified by the tool of their trade – the cardboard sign. Talk about originality! These guys are so creative! Known as SIGN-FLYERS, THEY ARE SEEN EVERYWHERE, but mostly stick to the most lucrative spots – Freeway off ramps and shopping mall exits. Signs used to say, STRANDED, from CANADA, need to return home! Please Help! Or the next one, HOMELESS, WILL WORK FOR FOOD! Or maybe, "DESPERATE – Mother ill – need to get to Salt Lake City!" This variety has gradually changed to a common ploy now accepted as the ultimate BUZZ word; it is simple, powerful, and hits home to the human heart, HUNGRY! – PLEASE HELP!

Some of these guys (and gals) should be on Madison Avenue, they are so creative! Of course, it was seldom that any of them would really ACCEPT work, so now they have grown much more honest and have omitted that word, plus, in most cities and towns nowadays, there are lots of "People Kitchen" and other food handouts, so this accent on the word "hungry" is sort of ridiculous.

I heard my daughter say she saw a sign-flyer in Tucson, AZ at the mall holding a sign that said, WHY LIE? I NEED A DRINK! So truth in advertising has come full circle. All that ANY of them EVER wanted was MONEY! – So why not say it?

In front of the Post Office in my town I saw a young, husky pleasant-faced fellow of about 23, slumped down on the grass holding a sign that said, "Injured my leg, unable to walk or work, PLEASE HELP!" He was wearing a sort of removable cast on his left leg. It occurred to me – after seeing him there every day during the Christmas rush – "I wonder who he gets to help him arrive at his 'post' each morning? Maybe he has a bicycle stashed in the shrubbery." Oh, come on, Whitey, give me a break!

The pickings are so good in this line of work, that you seldom see these artists out along the track much. Sometimes, but not often. Hobo-ing is just too tough, and you get so <u>dirty</u> riding these trains!

Now we come to the RECREATIONAL RAIL RIDERS. These are sometimes referred to as YUPPIE HOBOS. Believe it or not, in today's money-grubbing world where the whole syndrome is SUCCESS and BE SOMEBODY and GET YOURS, where our culture worships gold chains, big muscles, big wallets, big boobs, big cars and houses and the watchword is, "Never mind how you get it – but DO YOU HAVE IT?", there still lives and breathes a surprisingly large number of guys and gals who crave ADVENTURE. Wistfully hoping to find a real, red-blooded activity spiced with danger, slightly nefarious, and demanding a DARING quality – and – it <u>must</u> be non-structured, and off-beat – even an UNDERGROUND type of sport; they have found out, to their life-long delight, that this scene DOES, in fact, exist! Oh Yeah! It's been there, right under their noses for generations. You guessed it! RIDING THE RAILS!

I read, a few years ago, about a club of lawyers whose members doffed their three-piece suits, got into their grubbies (in Sacramento) and took off on an occasional weekend of freight-hopping. And loved it! I know personally quite a few well-positioned young men and gals who do this sort of thing on a regular basis. They've got this yen to travel and they flat out get with it! This is normally a planned trip. They stay out a few days or weeks, mostly in the summer, ride the trains to a certain destination and return to their work-a-day worlds, refreshed and invigorated. They have studied the fine points, have picked up the gear and know what they are doing. Some carry scanners to monitor the "rails'" communications, and they all have that one certain quality – they delight in beating the system, and they feel a real pride and sense of having DONE something. And it's not a subject they bring up to their stay-at-home friends. They keep it to themselves. This group includes a whole lot of RAIL BUFFS – who are really knowledgeable about trains and railroads matters. These comprise some of the top rail-riders in the nation, who have been doing it all their lives.

Yes, there're still a few OLD TIMERS out there. Not many, as their numbers are dwindling fast, but a hundred or so – maybe more – are still left. These are guys who started on the road in the 20's or 30's, lived the life a few years, until World War Two changed it all. Most everyone, including myself, came in off the tracks to take Defense or War-related jobs, and were either gobbled up into the service (I enlisted in the Navy) or learned job skills. Most never returned to the hobo life. I took a thirty-year hiatus to get married and raise a family, then, unable to resist the lure of the iron rail, went back to it.

So these guys are know as Bridgers (they bridged from Steam to Diesel), "Retreads" or "Crossovers." There seems to be a strong pull that a guy never gets out of his system that keeps dragging him back to the freedom or irresponsibility of this carefree vagabonding life, so after a lifetime – here they are, a few lonesome, bewildered and disillusioned old men wandering the wastelands of the American rail – land – hoping to recover their lost youth!

They bemoan the fact that nobody cooks out anymore; that they're not allowed to build fires in the yards; they point to the disgraceful litter of modern jungles, reminding you that in THEIR day each man respected the jungle and helped keep it clean. They deplore today's connivance for "welfare" and refer contemptuously to "Food-stamps" and simply cannot understand why no one wants to listen to them and "Learn something." Their day has long since passed them by, but they haven't realized it. I've seen these rugged old men up on the highline during the bleakest of winters, wearing a mountain of clothes, still "living out" and getting by in zero weather – still reveling in being able to "tough it out." For the most part, these are men who have left their homes. They resent anyone calling them "homeless." Their day is about over.

In the past twenty years a new rail riding fraternity has made an appearance. They're out there in goodly number; MEXICANS. These guys are the closest thing to what a hobo was a generation ago. Denied most of the freebies available to the citizen-tramp, they have to scrounge and hustle just to keep body and soul together, working mostly at farm labor jobs like tractor driving, chopping lettuce, changing irrigation pipes, squat-labor and all kinds of assorted back-breaking, unfulfilling work that the whites won't do anymore. Not speaking much English, and minus the proper I.D., they avoid the highway and do just what the old crop-working Bindle-stiffs did – ride the freights all over the West and the Sunbelt Southwest, traveling in two's, three's and more.

I've seen them on the Santa Fe, huddled in boxcars, and wearing tee shirts in cold weather, many with no money, no coat, no gear – just a pride in themselves and a lot of faith that there may be yet an opportunity for them in this vast land to the North. At first, being green, you see them making all kinds of mistakes, taking frightful chances like standing on the couplings between cars while the train is moving fast, or trying to nail an empty at too high a speed, but it doesn't take them long to figure out the finer points. Not only do these men have to keep an eye out for Railroad Bulls and city police – they are faced with an even tougher adversary – the IMMIGRATION! Our Border Patrol, driving their pale green vans, big, strong guys who speak Spanish like a native, and who are so skilled that they can board a moving boxcar and arrive STAND-ING UP – now that is what the poor wetbacks fear the most!

They are here in force, doing the orchard and field work as well or better than us fruit-tramps used to do, and I fully expect them to stay.

You Can't Teach An Old Dog

I'd no sooner started walking up the long hill out of town than a well-dressed man driving a big blue Buick stopped. Said he was going as far as Fort McCleod and the next day would be driving to Calgary. He was a salesman on the road. We chatted a while as he tooled expertly down the highway. Then he abruptly changed to questions.

"Are you a Christian?" I told him I was pretty close to that.

"What church do you belong to?" I said I didn't go to any.

"Do you read the bible?" I admitted I had.

"Do you expect to go to heaven when you die?" I told him I hoped to.

"How do you ever hope to go to heaven if you haven't been saved?"

I told him I hadn't given it much thought.

"Well, would you consider accepting Jesus as your personal savior?"

All of a sudden I remembered why I disliked hitch-hiking. Here I was, a captive audience, getting a free ride in a beautiful car when I might have had to stand out on that windswept highway for hours. Only, the price I was being asked to pay was, to me, way too high. This well meaning gent was sure, in his mind, that he had a live one and was bound and determined to land his fish. It looked to me like I was in for a long, stressful day.

Then it happened – I saw my salvation!

That same morning I'd piled off a westbound Canadian Pacific in the yards of Medicine Hat, Alberta. This train, after a crew change, would be heading farther west through Calgary, Banff, Golden and eventually Vancouver. But it would be taking the mainline. I'd been that way before and like many dedicated rail-riders, I wanted to see new country; I had the boomer mentality – "every trip – a different ship."

The CP ran another line to Kamloops, B.C. that paralleled their mainline, but was farther south and nearer to the U.S. border. It was not so well known and much less used – but it crossed the Rocky Mountains over the Crow's Nest Pass. This, I wanted to see.

So, I was feeling disappointed when I found out the only train going that way had already left an hour or more ago. Figured I could maybe catch it in Lethbridge, or even Fort McCleod if I could catch me a fast ride on the highway. Which is exactly what had happened. So far, so good.

Thinking back a few days, and to give you an idea of how loose my plans were, I'd missed a train in Glasgow, Montana, and rather than wait around for another I'd done my usual trip of trying to hitch on the road. Preferred to keep moving rather than jungle up and wait. Caught a ride too, but instead of going on west, this guy turned off on a secondary road – said he was going on up to a little wheat-growing town called Opheim, and did I want to ride along? Okay, that was Jake with me. I ended up spending a quiet night in an empty boxcar on a little used spur-line, in the town of Opheim.

Next morning I caught a short ride with a jolly person who said, "I'm just goin' a short ways; I'm building a grain storage elevator, you've seen 'em, y'know, those little round silver-colored things. There's thousands of 'em around here."

He let me out in the middle of a vast sea of wheat fields, no farms or people around anywhere. "If you're goin' up to Canada, the border's just a few miles ahead. You'll easy get another ride."

I started walking. I kept on walking. I continued walking. No cars in either direction. It must have been noon when hot, tired and thirsty, I limped into the tiny border station called West Poplar. I was traveling streamlined – no bedroll, no pack, not even a water jug. I do that on purpose sometimes just to test my fortitude. So far I'd managed to do nothing but SUFFER!

At most U.S./Canada border crossings I'd seen a line of demarcation where they'd left a cleared strip in the forest, about 30 feet wide and straight as a string as far as you could see. Here on the prairie it was only a strip of land left fallow between the two country's wheat farms, stretching limitlessly into the distance.

Hoping for a drink of water I opened the door.

"Where did YOU come from?" Two uniformed Canadian border men stared at me.

"I just walked in from near Opheim."

"You WALKED in?"

"All the way. I wonder if I could have some water, I'm sure dry?"

One of them indicated a fountain. "Here, help yourself."

I'd caught them by surprise, they hadn't heard a car drive up, kept staring, "You know, you're the very first WALKER we've ever had through here!"

Within an hour these two obliging Canadians had secured a ride for me from a hippy going all the way to Moose Jaw. From there I caught me a Westbound to Medicine Hat.

Then the Salesman picked me up. My benefactor, he of the fancy clothes and Buick automobile, warming to his subject, now shifted into high gear in his efforts to sell me on the merits – no the urgent NECESSITY of my accepting HIS brand of churchianity. I forget just what he claimed to be; either a LDS – or was it LSD? – or maybe the Lord's witnesses, or maybe even the Generous Assembly. In any case, it was one of those groups who are constantly proselytizing and real big on recruiting new members.

What he didn't then realize was that I had been preached at by EXPERTS and had successfully resisted all ear batterings. I was IM-

MUNE to having my soul saved. But still, I answered politely and gave him no trouble. It could be a long afternoon. He was a decent man and I hated to hurt his feelings or seem too callous. I bided my time.

We entered the small town of Taber, Alberta – that's when I saw it! My salvation! Now what do you suppose it was? A freight train! Of course! Yes, there it stood, a caboose and several cars. Down the track a good ways I spotted the power, doing some switching. I knew I had time.

My mind was set. Here I sat, in this warm and snug car, with a promised ride of many more miles, while all the time my black-hearted, ungrateful soul peered out at that dirty old freight train like it was a long-lost friend, welcoming me with open arms, and beckoning, smilingly, tempting me with an open-doored boxcar. If there'd been a large banner stretched the length of the car proclaiming "Welcome Back, Whitey – We've Missed You!" I couldn't have been more delighted. God, forgive me, but now you can see where my heart of hearts lies!

I asked the startled driver, "Would you please pull over and let me off? That's the very train I told you about, the one I missed this morning in Medicine Hat. It's going exactly where I want to go. I'm going to catch it."

He looked pained; disappointed, like I'd somehow betrayed him. With a sad heart, he stopped, wished me a pleasant day, then, with a puzzled note in his voice, said, "There's just one more thing; why would an intelligent person like you want to get on a freight train?"

The lyrics to an old Bob Dylan song rang in my ear,

> "It ain't no use to sit & wonder why, Babe,
> If'n you don't know by now,
> And it ain't no use to sit & wonder why, Babe,
> It don't matter anyhow . . . ."

Is there an answer?

The Power of the Stick

I usually travel alone, and like most travelers, I always enjoyed my own company. But sometimes it works out good to have companions. Uncle Freddie, Santa Fe Bo and myself arrived in Pueblo, CO one evening, looking for something headed west up the Royal Gorge. I'm a little guy, myself, but Freddie and Bo are both big, strong, well set-up guys who have a wealth of Road smarts and cheerful dispositions, so the three of us made for a fun relationship. Besides, I like having someone along who could watch my back and help me out in ticklish situations. We all enjoyed each other.

We found a place to keep out of sight by the newly renovated and restored D&RGW (Denver & Rio Grande Western) depot – a stately old time building made of sandstone. As usual I was detailed the job of watching the gear while my two buddies went uptown to hoist a few. The sky was threatening, big clouds scudding overhead – a storm was headed our way. As I was nibbling on peanuts a long mixed freight pulled in and stopped on the far track. Pretty soon here came a rail just off that train. I stepped up and asked him if it was leaving out soon. "Yes, she's going west later tonight and there are some empties on her, but be careful. The Bull is really on the prowl around here and he'll be watching this one. He drives a silver Blazer." I thanked him and got back out of sight.

When Bo and Freddie returned, the first thing I told them was the info on the train and what the rail said about the Bull; they laughed, saying the main subject at the bar where they'd just came from was this same Bull. Seems an article in the paper just the past week had embarrassed him and made it appear like he wasn't doing his job. The article quoted some train-riders who spouted and bragged that it was dead-easy to catch out of Pueblo, and that the hobo fraternity were coming and going as they pleased, paying scant attention to existing "security" – meaning this particular cop. The upshot was that he was sparing no efforts to crack down and try to redeem his reputation, and furthermore, that he was "going hard" on any trespassers he could collar, which meant he'd try for jail time if he could.

Well! Now that makes for even more fun, so we decided to try and nail this Westbound, right under his nose. With three buddies it's more like playing, "I dare you," or "I wonder if this jail feeds good?" or "Well, we don't have any place to stay tonight, anyway."

We waited as it grew dark, until we saw the Bull in his silver blazer drive off, then split fast for an open boxcar, one of five in a row towards the rear of the train. We picked the last one with both doors open, crawled in and squeezed into the forward corner, keeping low. The sky was black, the wind came up; it smelled like rain. This empty would prove heaven-sent if a storm came up, which appeared likely.

Bo and I sat down to watch Uncle Freddie, who was putting on his own show and was in great form; strutting around the boxcar with his brand new walking stick in hand showing off its magical qualities. "I hold in my hand this magical stick, and by the power of the stick I can command the elements!" We laughed and told him to shut up and get some sleep.

Freddie had been presented with this "stick" just the past week in Britt, Iowa at the hobo convention, where "hobo walking sticks" were a really big item. Seems like most everybody there was whittling these things, to sell to the tourists or give away to deserving Bo's like Freddie.

Seems there existed a huge and secret mystique that the stick mysteriously possessed – or at least certain people let on like it did. It was all news to me, as it was my first visit to Britt and frankly, I'd never set eyes on a hobo stick before. It seemed to me that a guy out riding the rails would be hampered and hindered carrying something like that around – it would flat out be in the way. It was already tough enough to grab out on a train while carrying your bedroll, much less to have to hold on to some stick!

But then, what do I know? These guys at Britt were old-timers and seemed to have all the answers. So I just kept my mouth shut. It was sort of like that old cartoon or caricature of the hobo that's been around for generations, the greasy looking, fat-bellied old tramp walking along carrying over his shoulder a stick, with a bandanna handkerchief tied on the back end holding his worldly belongings. Now we've all seen that so many times – in the funny-papers – but has anyone _ever_ seen that anywhere, _any_ time out along the tracks? Not me – but then, I haven't been everywhere, either.

Soon, Freddie, who was keeping watch, whispered, "The Bull's back; he's got his spotlight on our train!" Rats! Here we figured we could sack out and catch some ZZZ's while waiting for departure, and now we've got to stay alert to hopefully dodge the Bull! Freddie kept us informed; watching and whispering the scenario, "He's getting out of his car; he's carrying a big flashlight; he's checking out all these emp-ties; he's working his way down towards this one we're in; oh Jesus, we got to do something; he's getting closer all the time!"

We all looked at each other – questioning what to do. Nobody said a word. Bo suggested, tongue-in-cheek, "Well, Freddie, you might try the power of the stick again – Hell it can't do no harm!"

"Okay," says Freddie, grabbing the stick with both hands and pointing it skyward. "By the mighty powers vested in this stick," he whispered, "I hereby command the heavens to open up and give us RAIN! Yes, let the rains commence! I demand it right now!"

The words had no sooner left his lips than a brilliant steak of lightning illumined the entire scene, followed immediately by a majestic clap of thunder – and then – followed by a deluge – a cloudburst of rain such as you seldom ever see.

We stood in that boxcar awestruck, not quite believing what had happened. Like in a trance we peeked out the door just in time to see the Bull running like mad for the shelter of his truck. We watched him start up, turn and tear out of there, disappearing into the rain-swept night.

Hallelujah! We were saved! We hollered and screamed and hugged each other, dancing around the car like a bunch of idiots. We realized it would be highly unlikely the Bull would be back – not that night. We couldn't hardly get over the feeling of having been snatched out of the jaws of the Law by such a dramatic and timely natural phenomenon, but we reveled in our deliverance.

Shortly thereafter we heard the hissing of air and the groanings and creakings so dear to every train-rider's heart, then the drag got slowly underway, up the Gorge and heading for Grand Junction.

We lay back that night on our cardboard mattresses, listening to the rain pelt the car. I can't report on the thoughts of Freddie and Bo, but for me, I was laying there, thinking and thinking, "Now, I can't be sure, and there's no way I can ever prove it, but. . . . about the power of the stick . . . is it just barely possible that it just might be . . . true?"

Hobo Hotel

I awoke early, got up and looked out the boxcar door. It was still dark and we were stopped, apparently at some siding. I was happy to see some neon lights over near a highway that seemed to parallel our track, but the best thing was that these lights were advertising an all-night convenience store. Yippee! What it meant to me was a cup of hot coffee and a sweet roll for breakfast – something you don't always get on a long-distance train, unless you carry your own stuff – like fuzees (railroad flares) or stove, plus the necessary cans or utensils for heating the water and coffee crystals, cup, spoon – the whole outfit – which no one had along that trip.

I was still traveling with Santa Fe Bo and Uncle Freddie. Not wanting to waken them I slipped quietly down and jogged the quarter-mile over to the store, hoping our train would not start up in the meantime and leave me stranded. Hell, it was worth the chance. I surprised the clerk, as he hadn't heard any car stop outside and I judged he didn't get too many customers from off the trains. I poured a large cup of hot black coffee, grabbed a Danish and while the man was putting it in a sack I asked him what was the nearest town, as I had no idea of where we were. He said "Cañon City." I ran for the train, thinking "I can't believe we've gone just to Cañon City – why, that's only a few miles out of Pueblo." We'd left about midnight in that driving rainstorm and here we were only a few miles up the Gorge. Well, that was okay, too, as now we'd get to see the Royal Gorge and all the mountains clear across Colorado in daylight hours.

That train couldn't have been very high priority as we didn't get under way for another hour, giving my buddies plenty of time to cross over for their breakfast snack, too. We trundled along up the canyon enjoying the scenery, spotting a mountain goat, some deer and other animals and got into Salida mid-morning, where the rails set out some cars and picked up, too. The old D&RGW depot was still standing, deserted and forlorn, a nostalgic reminder of what a busy railroad center this town had been in years gone by. My own mother had told me many times of her first trip West, when she'd left her family home in Denver to travel to Washington State for a school-teaching job at age 19. She'd gone this very way over what was highly touted and advertised then as the Royal Gorge Route. Ninety years later, here I was retracing her steps by freight train.

Colorado was breathtakingly lovely that day as we climbed the Rockies, shouting out greetings to the many rafters we'd see up close, floating down the Arkansas River. Santa Fe and Freddie would holler "Ya Ta Hey!" I asked Bo what "Ya Ta Hey" meant? He had acted in Hollywood movies and told me it was just a greeting that John Wayne used in his Indian pictures. He'd ride up to an Indian party, stop, hold up his right hand and say "Ya Ta Hey!"   Bo said he thought it meant something like "Hello there, how ya doin?"

Late that afternoon, we reached the summit of Tennessee Pass and started down the steep grade into Minturn, the division point where we'd be stopping for a new crew. We had no plans, just winging it, but decided to rest up and spend the night there if we could. Too much train riding can wear you down and you find you require some down time to get rested up. After that you can tackle another division or two and feel really enthusiastic about it.

We split up in Minturn, each to see the town at his own pace. I walked a couple of miles up the main road through town without finding any sign of a grocery store and was on my way back to the yards, when I recognized Uncle Freddie standing in the doorway of what appeared to be an ice-cream parlor. Knowing Freddie, that was not the kind of place you'd expect to see him, but I walked in, discovering it was a combination ice-cream parlor and beer bar. How's that for a combo? Bo was there too, with a crowd around him, as usual, telling a bunch of guys about our adventure back in Pueblo. He introduced me to what turned out to be the very crew which had brought our train in, an hour ago. One (the older man) was the conductor, and his son was the engineer. We had drinks all around, and by this time a few bikers had straggled in and joined us in the session. They were returning back south from the famous Harley Meet at Sturgis, South Dakota, one of the largest gatherings in the nation.

Harley riders are free-spirited adventurers same as hobos and railroad men, so we had a great old time in the beer bar – ice-cream parlor in Minturn. We learned that the locals pronounced the name of their town as Min-urn and that Pueblo was pronounced Pyoo-eblo. The conductor, after hearing us mention the super steep grade from Tennessee Pass Summit, told us that just a short time ago they'd had a break-in-two on that very stretch of track. Seems a really heavy drag using six units on the headend plus three helpers in the middle was laboring up the hill when a coupling broke just forward of the helper engines. The front section made it to the top, hoping to drop off the load and back the six engines downgrade to help rescue the last one-third of the train that had the three helper units. They couldn't get back in time, as the rear end, unable to hold the load, lost their brakes and slowly started sliding down track, picking up speed and leaving the rails at the first turn. Three locomotives plus several cars ended up in the canyon lost without hope of salvage. The helper crew had stepped off when they realized they had no way to hold it.

The conductor asked us "Where you boys gonna stay tonight?" Santa Fe told him we hadn't decided. "Why don't you stay with us at our hotel?" We exchanged glances, wondering just what he meant. "Yeah, won't be no problem, there's quite a few crews on the road at this time of year, so we've got plenty rooms to spare." We eyed him, saying nothing, wanting to hear more. "Yeah, come on over with me and I'll show you the ropes."

Hey, how good can things get? We all tagged along down to the Turn-Table Café, an all-night eating spot, which led directly into the two-story crew-only hotel. He led us into a room that had a board on the wall with numbers at key hooks – looked to be about 40 or 50 keys. The presence of a key indicated a made-up room available. Where there was no key, this meant the room was already occupied. "Now, there you are, boys, whenever you're ready to turn in, just come in here, pick a number, take the designated room, and have yourself a good night's rest. I'll see you later." With that he left us alone.

Santa Fe said "Whitey, you go first" I said okay, took key number 102 and, grabbing my gear, strode off down the hall to locate my private suite! Opening up 102 I was pleased to find a small but complete little motel room, similar to that of a Motel 6, with showers and all. What a deal! Would wonders never cease? The friendly freight conductor had acted like it was no big deal; the least he could do for three upstanding drinking buddies who'd also made the trip with him from Pueblo, was to see that they were taken care of with a crash pad. Hey! All in the day's work. Why not?

Freddie and Bo selected rooms upstairs and the next morning we all met at the counter of the Turn-Table, where we had Cream of Wheat and coffee and discussed our astounding good fortune. We'd slept eight solid hours, showered, rested up, had breakfast, and now had a couple of hours to wait around for the next Westbound, which the dispatcher had told us was due in about 10:00 am.

What if someone had gotten wise, and apprehended us coming or going from our rooms? What if some person of authority had asked us to show railroad employee ID? Would we have been charged with defrauding an inn-keeper? Would it have led to jail time?

It didn't even cross our minds. It doesn't pay to argue with fate!

Bad Order Boxcar

It looked no different than any other – just another empty box-car. It was the last car on the train. Santa Fe Bo, with eyesight like an eagle, spotted it earlier on while we were dodging raindrops in a center divider lumber car. It looked like more rain coming, so when we pulled into Helper, Utah, we walked the length of the drag to pile into this car.

We all three sat in the open door surveying the town of Helper. This was obviously named for being the place where "helper" engines were hooked on the D&RGW freights to get them over Soldier's Summit, the first real steep grade coming west to Salt Lake.

We sat there eating peanuts for an hour or so, until a two-unit helper nudged our car, whereupon our train groaned forward, and up the mountain we started. The boxcar was fairly clean so we congratulated ourselves at getting out of the rain, spread out our beds, preparing for a fast, smooth ride into Roper yard in Salt Lake.

At the summit, the helpers backed off and headed for home. As darkness fell we discussed our fantastic good fortune at how well the trip had gone so far. As the train gathered speed on the downward grade we began to suspect that our Lady Luck had done gone.

The car began to bounce and sway. I snuggled deeper into my sleeping bag, hoping to drift off and not have to concentrate on the rough ride, but it was not to be. The faster we went, the worse the move-ment. Something was wrong. This motion was definitely not normal. I was bouncing off the floor at one moment and getting slammed against the side wall the next. I crawled out and looked to see how Uncle Freddie and Bo were doing. They were on hands and knees trying to keep their balance. They both looked worried, too.

This was turning into a serious crisis. None of us tried to speak. We were too intent on trying to maintain a sense of balance in a careen-ing boxcar gone completely berserk. It appeared that this car might leave the rails at any minute – either that, or the car itself might roll off its truck-carriage and be sent sprawling down the side of the mountain.

No doubt about it, we had inadvertently climbed aboard a bad-order piece of equipment. We'd not seen any tags posted on the side indicating "Home shop for repairs," or the usual "Bad Order" sticker. But at this rate, the way this car was slamming and jerking and swaying and tipping – it couldn't stay on the rails much longer. Santa Fe was doing pushups in an attempt to stay calm. Uncle Freddie was lying prone while I was down on hands and knees wondering how we could possibly survive the 100 miles yet to go. It was imperative to stay clear of the walls as the sudden jerks could easily have knocked you out and moving about inside the car was impossible as you risked being tossed clear out the door.

I can't speak for my two buddies, but for me I know I started praying; something along the line of, "Please, Dear God, I didn't mean to do anything wrong, and if you'll just let me live through this night, if you'll only save me this one time, I swear and promise faithfully I'll stay home, get a job, go to church, never leave my wife again and never, never, never steal another ride on a train," or words to that effect. At the time I was serious – deadly serious. I'd never experienced a bone-crushing ride the likes of what we were getting that night.

How we held on, how long we suffered that brutal tossing, how we kept our balance (to lose it might have proved fatal) and how we maintained our resolve I shall never know. It was an endless, Hellish two hours or more before a slight slackening in speed reduced the arc of the boxcar's roll and things began to settle down somewhat. Were we to survive, after all?

By the time we'd reach Provo the train had slowed, our deathtrap of a car started to behave nicely, just as though nothing had ever been wrong. We knew better. This was one of those cars we would NEVER climb into again.

As we crawled into Roper Yard, we shook hands all around – once more bonded for life by an unforgettably scary experience. All three of us had grown much older, much wiser – yet somehow we'd come out of it alive. We split up there in Salt Lake City, Bo and Freddie heading for L.A. while I was looking to catch the "Modoc," an SP train that went all the way to Oregon.

I loafed along in the darkness of the yards till I spied a carman readying up a long string of cars. His lantern was bobbing around as he checked air-hoses and couplings. My sudden appearance sort of surprised him. I called out, "Is this train leaving out westbound tonight?" He sounded kind of irritated and out of sorts as he replied, "I can't tell you nothing about any of these trains." I thanked him and walked on. I guessed he'd been raked over the coals lately for giving out information.

It was about 2:00 am. I was dog-tired, plus the reaction had set in from the anxiety of our wild ride down the mountain. I needed to crash, so found a clean grain car, unrolled my bag and stretched out – falling asleep almost instantly.

I woke up slowly. As if from a long distance, a voice kept repeating, "Hey, wake up, there." I was so tired it was like I was drugged, but I managed to wake up enough to see that I was the center of attention. When I'd crawled in, the car was in the dark, but now there were lights all around me and one extra bright one shining in my face. Then I really woke up and came alive as I saw three or four men standing there watching. The lights were coming from a huge diesel locomotive – just ten feet away.

It dawned on me what the situation was; the power had arrived for this train and my car, the grainer, was to be first in line. They were waiting to make the coupling, but had seen me sleeping there, and had not wanted to bump the string in case I panicked or got rolled off. So they had radioed for the Special Agent, and here he was, flashlight in my eyes, asking me to wake up. The other guys were the engine crew and the conductor. I was holding up the departure of one of their trains.

Seeing I had come-to, the Bull spoke quietly, "Do you suppose . . . I could get you to . . . climb down off this train, and . . . leave the yard?" He was so polite, and he was using the same tone of voice that he would likely use if he was inviting me home to dinner. I was speech-less. I asked him, "Do I have time to roll up?" He looked pained and spoke again as if he was talking to a small child, "No, just get your stuff and leave the yard; there's a gate right over there," he pointed, "You've held up this train long enough."

I meekly gathered up my gear in my arms, left the car, and head-ed for the gate, noting that four units of power had coupled on to my car, and that if I'd felt up to it, I could easily have circled right around and boarded the last one. But weariness had set in and I didn't feel like any more bravado. Besides, I didn't even know where that train was going.

Two hours of walking the dark and lonesome streets of Salt Lake put me up towards the center of town. I spotted a Denny's – the tramp's haven of rest as they are open all night and are found every-where. I layed down in a little grassy plot, sort of out of sight (I thought) for a rest till daylight broke, when I would go inside for a Grand Slam breakfast.

I hadn't even gotten off to sleep when I was aware of some lady standing over me, watching. I sat back up, said, "Good morning" and waited. "What are you doing out here?" I told her I had just that minute laid down for a rest and that I'd soon be entering the restaurant for breakfast. She didn't look too happy about me being there and said, "I'm the manager, and if you're not gone the next time I check, I'm going to call the police." I told her I was leaving. Which I did.

A couple of blocks away was a McDonald's, just opening up; I stashed my gear outside and went in, ordering a cup of coffee – so I could sort out my thoughts and try to figure out my next move. I took my coffee outside and was sitting on my bedroll, not bothering anyone, when here comes a spick and span little man dressed in a white shirt and tie. He began sweeping up the ciggie butts, all the time eyeballing me sort of suspicious like. I was beginning to feel like I had the leprosy or something. Rejection has always been hard for me to take. It had been a tough 24 hours with no sleep and no rest and now, here were all the people in Salt Lake acting unfriendly. I felt bad. Two solid days of rid-ing trains had made me so dirty – my appearance was scaring the public.

I hoisted up my pack and took off back in the direction of the old D&RGW passenger depot. I remembered a park near there where I could possibly lay down and rest up without some uptight citizen calling the law on me. On the way I discovered a little side-arm working man's café on a dead-end street down by the tracks. It was like home sweet home. My kind of people. I enjoyed a great breakfast, rubbing shoulders with guys just as dirty and messed up as me.

While lingering over my coffee, I wondered if I should return to the yards and try to hop another freight, or hold true to my promise to lay off them, and instead, hit the freeway on-ramp to thumb a ride. I debated this awhile. Just last night, in my terror and in my extremity, I had prayed that if the Good Lord would just allow me to escape my imminent predicament – well, that I would be a good boy and never ever hop another train. Had I said that? Yes, I sure had. Well, then, did I mean it? Was I sincere? I wasn't sure.

After thinking hard I gradually realized that . . . I had probably lied. It was only my terror – my uncontrollable fear that had caused me to try to plea-bargain with God. Now that I was safe, the ordeal passed, and I was once more out of the woods, my old smugness returned. I'd really had <u>no</u> intention of ever keeping that promise. No, I was just another selfish kid who would do anything – say anything, to save his own skin. Not a thought to make me feel proud of myself, but at least I was leveling with God. That was something. There's something about the <u>Trust</u> that is comforting, even though it shows you up in a sorry light.

At that moment I accepted myself for what I was, accepted my weaknesses passing it all off as – "Well, that's just the way I <u>am</u>."

Free at last, I walked, refreshed, happy and relieved back down to the SP yards, on the lookout for a certain train known as the "Modoc."

What a Disappointment

I figured I still had time for some hotcakes and coffee, though I could see the power was hooked on and the caboose had smoke coming from the chimney. My Westbound was ready to go, but knowing how the Southern Pacific operated, it could be an hour or more before it actually left. Sanderson was only a tiny little stop way out here in the West Texas sagebrush, so I hurried though my breakfast at Jerry's Café as I didn't want to miss my train and end up stuck in this burg. I paid the bill of $1.50 and left the blonde the remaining 50 cents and started legging it for the tracks.

I got fooled and missed my train. I heard the two short toots and slowed down and watched her move slowly out of Sanderson without me. No way could I have hurried up and nailed her.

Checking at the combination freight and passenger station, I learned there would be nothing coming through westbound until after midnight. It was now only 7:30 in the morning. I took a dismal view of the whole scene. Eighteen hours to wait.

"Unless you want to take the Sunset Limited." It was the agent offering a possible out. He regarded me questioningly. It's due through here at 9:30 this morning – only a couple of hours from now."

So that's what I did. I bought a coach ticket to El Paso where I knew I could find me a ride. Besides, I wanted to keep moving. No fun to lay around a town this size for a day and a half. Sanderson was only about a thousand people.

As the Sunset Limited grinds to a stop I am the only person on the platform. I see lots of faces staring down at me from the high-level cars, wondering who is this dude in the dusty clothes and the Mexican straw hat and what's he doing way out here in the middle of nowhere?

The train porter shows me to a seat upstairs. The car is packed. A middle-aged couple directly across the aisle introduces themselves as George and Brenda from upper New York state and that they are on their way to San Diego to visit some relatives. They seem interested in me and eager to talk. As the train gathers speed they start firing questions. It seems they saw me standing all alone by the station as the train pulled in, and made me the center of attention – wanting to know all about me; where I'd been and where was I going?

The lady, Brenda asks, "Do you live here?"

I tell her no, I am just traveling.

"HOW FAR ARE YOU GOING?" This time it's George. He seems just as curious. I tell him I am going only to El Paso.

The couple confer a moment, then turn toward me with, "That was such a tiny little town, we were wondering just how you got there?"

In their eyes there seemed to be an aura of mystery surrounding this strange passenger (me) who, with no luggage, got on a train way out in the boonies. They appear consumed with curiosity and can't wait till they can ferret out my story.

Now, I have a bad habit of usually telling the plain, un-varnished truth and just letting it hang out there – take it or leave it. I know that people sometimes don't want to hear the truth. It's too prosaic. They'd rather hear a story. The child in each of us longs for a gilded fairy-tale – to sort of take us out of ourselves and give our lives some sparkle. It crossed my mind that this couple, coming perhaps from a humdrum existence, and seeking a touch of excitement, saw in me a fascinating vagabond – a mysterious wanderer of the wastelands and wanted to rub shoulders with and get to know him a little. So, instead of giving them a short and straight answer – a truthful and plain answer – I paused and mentally fantasized on what I <u>Might</u> have said,

"You people seem to be intelligent and keenly observant. You sense that perhaps I might be something other than I seem – that I just might possess a secret – right?"

They nodded enthusiastically. They'd taken the bait. I looked around cautiously as if to see if anyone was eves-dropping. "You wanted to know what I was doing way out here on the desert, and how I'd gotten there. Well, I'd like to confide in you totally . . . ." I lowered my voice as they automatically leaned closer, "But, due to the nature of my work, I can only hint at the reason I am here."

Brenda whispered, "What <u>is</u> the nature of your work?"

Riveting them with my gaze I murmured, "I insist on strict secrecy. You must never divulge a word of what I say. Understood?" They stared at me, their faces showing almost hypnotic glaze.

"Yes, yes, – of course. Please do go on."

Reassured, I continued, "These old clothes I'm wearing – they're just a disguise to throw people off the track so they won't suspect my mission. I'm really doing covert surveillance for the . . . ."

I stopped, again turning to check on our fellow passengers. I spoke confidentially. "Let's go down to the lounge car where we can talk more intimately – I'm afraid someone here may overhear us."

George and Brenda couldn't wait to follow me to the lounge.

"Can I buy you a drink, Mr . . . er . . . ."

"Oh, no thanks, I'm not allowed to drink while on duty, but I would like a coke."

They ordered beers and a coke for me. We sat, the three of us at the tiny table watching the scenery slide by.

Then George says, "You were saying?"

We huddled, faces close around the table. I kept my voice low, "As you probably suspect, I work for the government in a secret . . . ."

Brenda hissed "Are you a . . . a <u>spy?</u>

"I can't tell you in just so many words, but the agency for which I work would sound very familiar to you both." The two of them were hanging on my every word as I continued, "When our train arrives in El

Paso, I will be met by two men. There will be a plain, unmarked sedan waiting to whisk us away. Please, if you see them, give absolutely no indication that you know me or that I have ever spoken to you. Will you promise me that?" They solemnly agreed, nodding emphatically.

"I must apologize to you both for refusing to give you the details, but our whole dragnet operation depends on secrecy and surprise. I'd like nothing better than to include you both in on it as accomplices, as I can readily tell that you are trustworthy people – but I <u>dare</u> not implicate you further. It might prove dangerous and I wouldn't want anything to happen to either of you. I hope you understand?"

They just stared at me, seemingly mesmerized. George recovered first. "My wife and I – we're not in any danger, are we? You haven't told us <u>more</u> than we should know?" His face was troubled.

"Oh, no, you're in no danger – not yet – but I should warn you the three of us should not be seen together." The train was approaching Alpine; I knew it would be a five-minute stop. "I've got to make a phone call at this stop, after that I'll sit somewhere else till we arrive in El Paso. Please ignore me the remainder of the journey . . . ."

I got up, then placed a hand on both their shoulders. "Thank you for keeping this whole thing to yourselves. It's been a real pleasure to meet such bright and understanding people." I left.

So went the scenario of my fantasy. George and Brenda were so gullible and so yearned for some spice in their lives, that I could have enlarged on this fabrication for hours. They'd have gone for it hook, line and sinker. They'd have bought the whole package.

So, did I tell them a story? I did not. When they asked, "How did you get here?" I replied, "I came in on a freight train last night."

"A freight train?" they echoed simultaneously.

I nodded "Yes, a freight train."

George says, "Then . . . are you a . . . hobo?"

"Yes, I am. Sometimes."

"Oh. I see . . . ."

They turned away, staring out the window. No more interest. End of conversation. It seemed to me that I could detect a definite look of mild revulsion on their faces. Not out-and-out disgust, but rather a sense of disappointment – a lingering bad taste in the mouth.

I sit silently gazing out at the West Texas plains thinking of that good old Buck Owens song, "Streets of Bakersfield"

> "You don't know me – but you don't like me,
> You say you care less how I feel.
> How many of you that sit and judge me,
> Ever walked the streets of Bakersfield."

One Night In Jail

Everybody should spend one night in jail. Just for the experience. You cannot grasp the feeling any other way. It must be lived
through. In my own case, because, by nature, I am a harmless, inoffensive sort, the kind who tries to deal in good faith in most all situations, I
have been spared nearly all of the injustices of the justice system. In the
late 30's I had asked for and been allowed to sleep in a few jails, but it
was because of a cold, rainy night. The police regularly permitted people to do this. But as to getting locked up, it's only happened once.
Looking back I realized it was a good thing. I'm a better and more
tolerant person because of it.

NY Ron and I had caught ourselves a round-bellied hopper car
out of Staples, Minn. one frigid October morning hoping to reach
Minot, ND.

Why not Minot?
Freezin's the reason.

We are riding on the back porch out in plain sight. We pass
through Detroit Lakes and the train slows down through a section of
track where they had a derailment a few days before. There was quite a
crew of track workers busy making repairs, plus a number of "White
Hats" doing the supervising. They looked us over sharply as our train
crawled by.

We thought nothing of this until later that afternoon when we
entered the Dilworth yards. This was a regular crew change but we
weren't getting off. That's what we thought!

I peeked around on my side as the train came to a stop and saw
three cars, and three guys walking towards our car.

"Hey, Ron, there's something going on. Take a look!" He
took one peek.

"That's Mutt and Jeff, surer than shit! And they've got a town
clown with them!" Mutt and Jeff, as they were aptly named by the
tramps were two well known BN Special Agents assigned to this area.
One was tall and skinny (Mutt), while the other (Jeff) was a shorty. Ron
knew them by sight. He started to toss his gear off on the far side. Too
late, the Bulls came up on us fast – like they knew exactly where we
were on the train and had arranged a welcoming committee.

"Okay, you two, get off the train!" I reached for my pack.
"Leave your gear right where it is. Both of you climb down and stay
right here!"

What was going on? This wasn't the usual procedure. Why
would they order us around like this? Evidently this was not just a

routine I.D. check. Oh, no, this was serious. They meant business. We did as we were told.

"Now, turn around, put your hands behind you" I did. They handcuffed me. First time in my life I've ever felt the cold steel. I didn't like it. "Now you." Ron got the same treatment. They led us towards the marked patrol car. The uniformed cop opened the back door, we got in, and sat down. We'd been arrested.

Ron asked, "Aren't you going to get our packs? They're still on the train!"

The well-fed officer says, "Don't worry about it, we'll take care of your stuff." The Bulls retrieved our packs, put them in the trunk of the police car, then conferred with the cop. Jeff, the shorter one addressed us, "You two were reported to us as seen riding illegally on that train. We're on the lookout for an escaped murderer out of the North Dakota Pen. There were three men escaped, two were caught, but the third got away. He's known to be a rider of freight trains. You're charged with STEALING SERVICES. We're taking you to the county facility in Moorhead."

The handcuffs were so tight they were cutting off my circulation. I asked the driver as we sped off, "These things are cutting into my wrists. Could you loosen them a little?" He answered, "We're almost there, now. We'll have them off in just a few minutes." I looked at Ron. He said, "Somebody dropped a dime on us!" I'd never heard that expression before, but I knew what he meant. "One of those supervisors back at the derailment phoned ahead to alert the bulls to our presence?"

"You got it, Whitey."

Ron had asked both the Special Agents, back there in the yard, "Can I have one of your business cards? I collect them." They shook their heads, "We're not in the mood to play games." I know that Ron had a wallet full of bulls' cards, he'd shown them to me.

NY Ron was a BONAFIDE HOBO. A true HARD-CORE. He'd logged untold thousands of miles on freight trains since 1966 when he got started as a teenage kid. Small, dark-complected, thin and wiry, he had an amazing strength for a man built so slight, together with an untiring stamina and a cheerful never-say-die mental attitude. He spoke in a rapid-fire New York accent that hardly anyone could understand, at first. His sentences came like machine-gun bursts, and he was street-smart beyond his years. Raised in upper New York state, he welcomed cold weather. The only man I ever knew who preferred his train riding in sub-zero temp. He was one of the very few hobos who kept "out there" the year around, though he was know to take the occasional vacation and drop out of sight for months on end. His every move was QUICK. His judgment immediate and SURE. Never had to deliberate before taking action. His overall appearance suggested a wild animal – like a ferret. He hated a phony and could spot one instantly. Smoked some twenty cigars daily and was perhaps the most KNOWLEDGE-ABLE in the ways of the hobo of any man I'd ever ridden with.

Watching him board a train on the fly, NY Ron displayed the grace and agility of a ballet dancer. His grasp of railroad procedures and train movements was uncanny. Traveling with him was like attending an advanced course in hobo-ing.

Arriving at the county jail in Moorhead, we were stripped, given the orange jump suits, finger-printed and all our clothes and gear locked up. It was a dull and dismal day for me. I felt I had been violated. Sure, I knew I wasn't supposed to be on that train, but I considered it as only trying to uphold a long and time-honored tradition. I'd always made it a strict policy to never damage equipment, never steal the railroad's stuff, and never harm a person. All I ever took was a RIDE. Now here they go and lock me up like I was a Dillinger. I was hurt – my feelings, I mean. For them to put ME in jail for simply being caught on a train, was just a craven case of OVER-Kill. I paced the compound like a caged tiger, my whole mind and outlook in a furious turmoil. Jesus Christ! How could they do this to me?!

NY Ron, cool and unperturbed, lay back in his bunk reading magazines, sort of unfazed. Didn't seem to mind it at all. They'd told us at the desk that this was a smoke-free facility. Poor Ron, a guy who puffed on twenty cigars a day, unable to get even a whiff!

"Take it easy, Whitey," he looked up from his reading. "We'll be outta here by noon tomorrow." How could he be sure of that? I was not so optimistic.

"What if we get 30 days for illegal riding, like on the UP?"

"No way, you mark my words, Whitey, we'll be on our way west tomorrow."

There was room and bunks in this complex for twenty or so, but only about six men were present. Others, I learned, were out on work release and would be back for supper. Seems like most of them were young guys here on drug-related charges. They seemed incredulous to learn that we were in for as innocuous a thing as hopping a train!

At around 5:00 pm, the working prisoners came back, then the dinner trays were slipped in. Not bad. Institutional but okay. One worker admitted to smoking a whole pack of cigs on his eight-hour shift doing roof repair.

I passed a miserable night, cold under one blanket and worried. Not like me to worry. Not like me to be in jail, either!

Next morning about 9:00 am, fifteen of us prisoners were hand-cuffed together in line and marched out in the twenty degree cold (wearing nothing but those silly jump suits and canvas sandals) to the court-house a block away. We had a single public defender lawyer-man get up and break for each one. The judge was a matronly type middle-aged lady. When my turn came she asked me where I lived, would I be returning home and would I promise to stay off the freight trains. I said, "yes, your Honor." I knew from watching movies about courtrooms that you were supposed to end every sentence with "Your Honor."

She must have been favorably impressed for she sentenced me and Ron with thirty days for "theft" (stealing services) with twenty-nine suspended, credit for one day served, and that we must leave town, and never go near the Burlington Northern trains. That is all.

We got our clothes back on, valuables returned from the envelopes, packs unlocked and strapped on, didn't even wait for lunch, and OUTTA THERE! Like two scalded dogs. A man told us there was a HARDEE'S nearby, so we made for it.

As we clumped down the streets of beautiful downtown Moorhead, Minnesota, we could easily tell a storm was coming in as the day was growing bitter cold. "See, Whitey," Ron was all cheerful and smiling, "I told you we'd be out by noon! Let's get a couple of hamburgers then head for the yards. There'll be a local from Wilmar going west this evening about 5 o'clock."

"Yes, Ron, but we don't want to be pinched again here in this same town. Shouldn't we cross the state line over to Fargo and try for something over there? We sure don't want to run the risk of that judge slapping us with the other twenty-nine days, so we?"

Ron grinned, "You worry too much, Whitey, we can do it easy. I'm determined." I was twenty-five years his senior, but I felt like an inexperienced kid. He was the master strategist and I was only going along for the ride. I said okay.

Living On the Edge

NY Ron and I never did find that train from Wilmar. Instead, Ron insisted we retrace our steps and go back to the same yard where we were arrested – Dilworth, MN. I didn't really want to do that, as all I could think about was what if we got caught – again! Here we had just received twenty-nine days suspended with a warning to stay off the BN trains. It seemed like we would be pushing our luck to go straight back there and try again, but Ron was adamant. "We'll slip into the yard about midnight when no one's around, find our train and be gone by morning. They'll never even know we been here."

I wasn't all that sure, but went along for lack of a better plan. "Maybe we should take the lowline this time, Ron. We could hitch-hike to the first division. What town is that?"

"Jamestown."

"Okay, we could hitch-hike to Jamestown, and catch out there. How about it?"

"No, I don't ever hitch-hike, Whitey. Not unless I'm near death!"

So I gave up and together we plodded the road to Dilworth through the fast-falling snow, arriving at the yards about 10:00 pm. Silently we hurried past the offices including the office of Special Agents. No one around. There was a sign saying to call 911 after dark hours. We hustled over several sets of tracks, but found no trains. What to do? Where to hide? Snowing like mad, but the wind had died. Our tracks in the snow were covered almost immediately. A railroad yard in the middle of the night during a snowstorm is a dreary sight. It didn't look good! Then we spotted our SALVATION! A yard caboose sitting alone. I whispered "Let's check it out – see if it's unlocked!"

"It don't matter if it is – we'll still get in." Ron grinned at me. Then I remembered – He carried caboose door keys with him. Where he got them I never knew, but good old NY Ron prided himself on being equal to any and all situations.

He said, "Whitey, you try the 'B' end – see if it's open, and I'll try the 'A' end, okay?" He loved using technical terms known to most "rails" but unnecessary for most tramps.

I stepped up on the "front porch," tried the handle. It opened to my touch. All dark inside, but Glory be to Heaven above! The stove was going full blast and the caboose was toasty warm! Thank Heavens! We were out of sight, safe for the moment and warm at last. How good it felt.

I'd heard all kinds of stories about NY Ron, his travels were already legendary in hobo circles even though he was only about 45 or so. He was so alive, so intense, that he sailed through life with a reckless abandon, seeming to never get enough thrills. I found out, by riding and living with him that he was a paradox – a contradiction. You thought you knew him – then you found out you didn't know him at all!

In the words of Kris Kristofferson,

> "He's a walking contradiction – partly truth and partly fiction, taking every wrong direction on his lonely way back home!"

For example, one night we'd found ourselves a ride in a clean boxcar, and were just waiting for her to pull out. He'd say,

"Listen, Whitey, I'm gonna go check out some of these other cars. Be right back." He'd jump down, disappearing into the night. I'd call after him, "Ron, if you get left, what do you want me to do with your gear? Shall I kick it off – or leave it on, and wait for you at the next division?"

He'd always say, "Drop it off."

This very thing occurred in Pasco; He'd taken off to hunt for a couple of aluminum cans (we used these to heat coffee water in) and sure enough, without warning, the train started. I hollered his name, and whistled, but couldn't see him anywhere. The train began to pick up speed. Then in the gloom, I saw him running like crazy, angling over to our car. I was standing in the doorway with his enormous Camp Trails pack – ready to jettison it if he failed to catch back on – then I realized just what an acrobatic master he was as he tore alongside, caught hold of the hasp and swung lightly aboard! Just like nothing happened.

All he said was, "No freight train can get away from me!"

I was starting to believe him. He'd repeat this sticky maneuver daily – especially when he'd run out of cigars. The train would stop in some little crossroads village for a set out or a red light – for a minute or two at the most. "I seen a 7-11 back there, Whitey. I'm gonna trot over and pick up some cigars! Do you want anything?" And off he'd go on a dead run. Sometimes he'd get fooled and be unable to return in time to the same car. In this case he'd cut directly to some other catchable car towards the rear of the train, swing on at the last possible second and ride it out – rejoining me at the next stop. I'd have to sort of hover over his moves to be able to tell if he'd made the train! Couldn't mistakenly dump his gear off!

At first I thought he was a hot-dog! Then I sort of got the idea he was foolhardy – taking too many stupid risks! As I got to know him better, I realized that – no – he was not show-boating in order to impress me, it was simply that HE LOVED LIVING ON THE EDGE! That fine line he drew between safety and IMMINENT DEATH gave him the spice he required to live an EXCITING LIFE.

Ron seldom spoke about his past. I'd heard from others that he had survived a gunshot wound to the head, and now wore a metal plate in his skull. He was popping pills constantly, so perhaps he was operating in continual pain, but you'd never suspect it as he was about the most positive and cheerful rail buddy I'd ever known. Fastidiously clean – he carried a small whiskbroom that he'd use to sweep out his corner of the car before depositing his gear. He'd take out a plastic trash bag, insert it over his pack so the blowing dust wouldn't soil it. Carried one of these state-of-the-art Camp Trails packs, with zippers and compartments and pockets all over it. Ron was so organized that he could find, immediately and in the dark, most anything he needed – from a band-aid, a safety pin or switchblade – never had to dump out the contents (as I did) to retrieve an item. It occurred to me that this all-consuming penchant for dare-devil risk-taking he loved so dearly might possibly be an unconscious DEATH WISH, sort of a near-suicidal defiance of fate – like giving God the "Finger!"

A great partner to travel with – ready for anything. HE TYPI-FIED,

> "I want to love life, live hard and die young and leave a beautiful memory."

Ron lived on canned beans, coffee and peanut butter and jelly sandwiches. But if he couldn't get the food it didn't bother him as long as he had a goodly supply of cigars and plenty of coffee. He'd make instant coffee five or six times a day, using fuzees he'd "found" in the locomotives or cabooses.

He'd lay one blazing fuzee pointing at two aluminum coke cans filled with water. Inside of five minutes the water would be boiling in both cans. He'd holler, "Coffee, Whitey!" He'd pick up his can with his gloved hand, pour the scalding water into his plastic cup, coffee crystals already in, pop on the lid and VOILA! Piping hot coffee fit for the Gods! I'd do the same.

NY Ron took care of me like I was his Father. That miserable, snowy night in Dilworth, he let me lay down on the leather settee in the caboose and sleep most of the night, while he sat up in the cupola keeping a look-out for incoming trains or inquisitive Bulls.

Just before dawn, a mixed Westbound freight pulled in. He woke me, we gathered our stuff and made a run for it before daylight broke; found an empty, complete with about twenty clean airbags! We curled up in the corners, air bags under us and air bags piled on top of us and lay there contentedly watching the state of Minnesota drop away and lovely North Dakota pop into view. A heart-warming sight! Free at last from the long arm of the Moorhead County Jail!

Crow's Nest Pass

Riding freight trains in Canada is a real satisfying experience. It seems there are very few riders doing this up there and so you have it pretty much to yourself. So far I have been the only rider on every single one of the trains I've ridden. The local citizenry reacts in astonishment when you chance to ask them, "Say, where do the trains stop in this town?" They have a hard time understanding why anyone would want to hop a ride. One man I asked acted kind of irritated, replying bluntly, "Up here we don't steal a ride on a train – we buy a ticket and ride the BUS." So there.

I caught the Medicine Hat local at Taber, Alberta, and rode it into Canada's highest elevation city – Lethbridge. At least that's what the sign said at the entrance to town along the highway (visible from the train, too) where it was all spelled out in a gorgeous flower and shrub garden – one of the prettiest displays I've ever seen. I'd guess the elevation was right close to five thousand feet. I was reminded again that most of Canada is lowland, exceptions being Alberta, British Columbia and Yukon, which partially explains why nearly half of all the fresh water in the world is in Canada. Another reason for why I love to travel up North is that this huge, sprawling giant, our Northern neighbor, has more land even than the contiguous United States, but surprisingly has fewer people than the State of California. So if you're the kind who, like me, appreciates wide open spaces and not too many people, you'll love bumming around up there.

When we pulled in to Lethbridge my train was history, so I hunted around till I saw a young, good-looking guy in dashboard overalls hooking up the hoses on a little short train – about six cars. One of them was an empty box. I accosted him in a friendly manner. "Is this train getting ready to leave out?" He nodded. "Where is it going?" He told me it was first going to Fort McCleod for a "meet" with another train coming from Calgary, and that later on it would proceed clear on up to Crow's Nest Pass. I asked him if he minded if I crawled in the empty and rode along with him. He smiled and said, "That's okay with me, but if anybody asks you, don't tell 'em I said so. All right?" I grinned and told him not to worry.

Before long this short stubby of a train got underway and we hadn't gone but just a few miles till we came to a high trestle crossing a deep canyon over a shining river way down below. I stood by the open doorway, hanging on tight, gazing down hundreds of feet at this unexpected sight. I love to see new scenery anyway, which is the main reason I'm constantly looking of new and different railroads to ride. This magnificent bridge was worth coming up to see just for itself. I wondered what the name of the river was. Less than an hour put us into Fort McCleod, which has quite a railroad action for a small place. Historically this was one of the original Royal Canadian Mounted Police outposts and is still a Mounty center, even though they use very few horses anymore.

I stowed my bag in the weeds and saw an old house surrounded by gardens and vines, with an old man sitting in the sun on a wooden bench. He had on a floppy straw hat, had a deeply lined face and a large drooping mustache. I was reminded of the old-country Italians I'd seen in Southern Italy around the towns of Bari and Brindisi during the war. He was eyeing me inquisitively as I came slowly up the path greeting him softly. "Good day. Can you tell me if there is a store – a grocery store, nearby, please?"

He pointed, "Yah, you go uppa da road, two – tree block. You see it there." Not only did he look like an old country Italian, he spoke like one, too. I had another question, "Would you know the name of the river the train crosses on that big high bridge?"

"Yah, dat's da Old-a Man-a River." I didn't get it. It sounded like he was saying "Oldahmanah River." He repeated it slowly and this time I got it. Of course it was THE OLD MAN RIVER.

I moseyed up to the little village store, bought a small sack of plums and three apples, then returned to the yard to eat my lunch, all the while watching the trainmen building a Westbound that would be leaving this evening. It was a great summer day. I spied my friendly brakeman and offered him some of my fruit. He declined, saying, "Thanks, but I've got my dinner in the engine. By the way, that empty boxcar you rode in on . . . well, it's going to Vancouver if you're interested."

It's so gratifying to learn that these casual acquaintances you meet out along the rails not only tolerate your presence on their trains – but often, they seem to take an interest in seeing that you make your train and go out of their way to help. The hands-on working railroad employees are a breed apart and are universally respected by the rail-riders. The reason must be that, down deep, a good many of the train crews have a lot of HOBO in them, too.

In late afternoon the CP local from Calgary (our meet) pulled in with a good long string of cars. This was my signal that my afternoon nap was over and I'd best find that same boxcar, which by now had been shuffled back to near the rear of the train. With good luck I thought maybe I could hold her down all the way to the Coast. Seemed strange to be the only tramp in this yard, but no one paid me any attention as I climbed aboard, saying goodbye to Ft. McCleod heading farther west.

The countryside grew more wooded as we left the Alberta prairie and headed into the magnificent Canadian Rockies. At dusk we roared by a large campground full of family groups standing around their fires, holding coffee mugs and waving like crazy. I guessed this must be Waterton-Glacier Park (Just North of our Glacier Park). I noticed most of the campers had on down jackets, anticipating a cold night ahead.

This bothered me a little as I didn't have any warm clothes, nor had I even brought along a sleeping bag. I was traveling streamlined on purpose to test myself. At the time I wanted to find out how much I could stand, how little I could eat and how much gear I could do without. I was on a Spartan-like program of self-inflicted misery. I don't do that anymore as I've since discovered that I'm really not very tough, nor can I survive out of doors sans coat and bedroll.

It was dark and growing ever colder as we toiled up a long grade, arriving at Crow's Nest Pass (the summit) around 10:00 pm. Now, if the train had merely changed crews and gone on, I'd have stayed with it no matter how chilly the night – but I learned this train was to remain here until morning, when a fresh crew would take it on into Cranbrook. I did want to see the pass by daylight, as it was reported to be in a beautiful part of the Rockies, but I knew I could never get to sleep in that boxcar without anything to keep me warm. No 1,000-mile paper, no air cargo bags – nothing. Neither did I dare build a fire along the tracks – that would bring the Law quicker than anything.

I was shivering, my teeth were chattering, there was only one thing to do. I deserted the train, started walking at a fast trot on a downhill angle to try to intersect a highway I'd seen coming up. About a mile downhill I came to Highway #3 – one of Canada's main transcontinental throughfares, where I got lucky, getting picked up in just a few minutes. This ride took me into the little town of Fernie, a really pretty place, where I found a workingman's bar and hotel combination. So relieved to come in out of the cold, I drank a couple of beers, ate two hot-dogs and got me a room for five bucks. I was asleep by midnight.

I never did get to see Crow's Nest Pass by daylight, as I've never been back to that Canadian Pacific line since, but if I ever do get another chance, I'm gonna make sure I bring my down army mummy bag.

A Close Call

I've jumped off trains that were going too fast and got rolled in the cinders; I've torn my hands up occasionally on the jagged metal of door hasps, and have been thrown around inside boxcars, but never have I been seriously hurt. I came close once. It was not a train, no, it was kids.

NY Ron and I were walking up the track between two trailer courts in the city of Moorhead, Minn. This was where the BN branch-line from Wilmar, Minn. joined the East-West Main. Ron was trying to remember just where the Wilmar local stopped to change crews.

It was late October and cold. Only the night before, a freak weather pattern had crept in changing Indian Summer to serious winter. The T & T signs we'd passed coming through town showed a rapid drop in temp of about one degree every five minutes. My feet were freezing. I told Ron, "Let's go in behind those trees, over by that wooden fence and rest; I've got to put on some more clothes." I had a pair of wool socks and a pair of red long-john bottoms. It was time to put them on.

We'd seen some teenagers a few minutes before, over by the opposite trailer park, but paid them no mind. We were pretty well hid by the trees and I didn't figure anyone could see us, so I proceeded to unlace my boots sitting bent over against the wood fence. If I had been sitting upright, or standing, I would never have know what hit me, but, sitting peacefully in the quiet, with the snow falling, I was totally unprepared for what happened.

A rock, nearly the size of a baseball came hurtling over from across the tracks, striking the VERY BOARD against which I was leaning, with such force that it left a gouge in the wood – just 16 inches above my head! Whoever it was who threw it exercised perfect aim – his elevation was a little off – and that error saved my life. Had the rock struck me anywhere on the head, it would have been instant curtains. No doubt. As it was, I was so startled and shocked that I froze, petrified on the spot. Would there be another projectile on its way? I couldn't even run. Both boots off, I was helpless to move if these kids had wanted to finish me off. Ron dropped his pack and dashed up on top of the roadbed, but could see no one. They'd taken to cover. Trembling and feeling violated, I put on the extra clothes and we lit out on a trot.

If a boy decides to pelt another boy or a stray dog, or another local person, he knows he may be called to answer for it. But a tramp? There's practically no risk at all, as they have no clout and the kids sense this – no, it's more like "just having fun." It's a national pastime and if I don't want to risk the hazard, I'd best stay home.

That was my closest call. I never want a closer one.

Riding an Amtrak train one winter morning, leaving Washington, DC for New York, I was startled to see a group of six or seven teenage kids appear suddenly on a bank not fifty feet from our train and start a rock barrage. One big kid saw me, I think, sitting by the window and aimed a giant-sized rock at my head. I watched the trajectory, it seemed it would strike my window. I involuntarily ducked down, but he underestimated the train's speed and the rock banged like a clanging bell on the aluminum metal just inches from my double-pained window.

The conductor walked by just then; I called him over. "Did you see that?" I pointed out to where these kids were still throwing. "One of those rocks nearly hit my window; you could hear it land all over the car." I guess I expected him to jump right on his hand-held and radio the authorities. He seemed unperturbed, explaining patiently, "Oh yes, its nothing new, we get it every day."

I was furious, "How come it's tolerated?"

With a look of resignation he went on, "Well, until someone gets seriously injured the police just look the other way. They figure if they stop these hoodlums from rocking the trains, they'll just go uptown and start mugging the tourists."

Our nation's capital has never been one of my favorite places.

I Always Sit On This Side

I was just finishing breakfast in Ann's Cafe in Britt, Iowa one Sunday morning when in walked Leroy McClary, known the whole country over as the legendary hobo, "Cardboard." He sits down across from me,

"Are you headin' back to the Coast today, Whitey?"

I nodded, "Yeah, thinkin' about it."

"So am I; How about you and me ridin' back to California together?"

"Okay with me. When do you want to get started?"

"I already got me a ride up to Minnie. You find yourself a ride with somebody and we'll meet right there in that parking lot, it's a bar, I think, across the street from the entrance to Northtown Yards. Okay?"

It was agreed upon. I caught a ride up with Rod and Frisco Jack and that same afternoon, I got let out in the agreed upon parking lot. No Cardboard. At first I didn't see him, but on closer looking, there he was pretty well hidden, jungled up in the weeds, looking smug and well-satisfied. He greeted me with a big grin. "See ya made it all-right, Whitey, sit down and I'll pour you a cup of coffee."

Cardboard was a well set-up man of 70, looked for all the world like the quintessential Irish hod carrier. Always wore the same outfit – black Frisco Jeans, large suspenders, checked shirt, eight-inch boots and a black cap. He and I had a lot in common as respects our background; We'd both served in the Merchant Marine, had done Navy time, had started out on the road as kids, and had traveled and worked at various menial jobs all over the nation. I was almost exactly one year older than him. He carried a staggering amount of gear, for a tramp who traveled as much as he did. Some of it was just a bunch of stuff he would never use, but that he couldn't bear to part with.

The one thing he ALWAYS had was several rolls of cardboard tied up with drapery cord. He was just NEVER without it. It was the reason for his having been give the road name of "Cardboard." He was pegged in tramp circles as being a "Hard Case," not too easy to get along with. No doubt about it, he surely was feisty, argumentative, contentious and quarrelsome, but had always been okay with me. I gave little thought to his reputation and looked forward to our proposed trip together.

I was traveling pretty streamlined then, so when he offered me a cup of coffee I didn't even have a cup with me.

"What the Hell, Whitey, don't you even carry a cup? Well, never mind – you can use my extra one."

I was prepared to overlook his petty outbursts as I prided myself on being able to get along with just about everybody, and didn't insist on being RIGHT every time.

We moved our camp over into the Northtown Yards, kept out of sight, swatting at the mosquitoes all afternoon. Along towards evening we spotted some power backing down onto a string of grain cars and got ready to make our move. I was carrying a small shoulder pack and a lightweight summer bag. Cardboard carried a large, metal-frame pack so heavy he could hardly stand up with it, plus two five-gallon gunboats loaded down with stove, fuel, food and assorted junk that I would have deep-sixed long ago, and of course, three rolls of cardboard. Plus we each carrier a plastic one-gallon water jug.

"Here, let me pack some of that load" I offered, but he wouldn't hear of it.

"I don't need no help, I been doin' it this way for years."

I was beginning to wonder; he'd told me about his fall – said he'd fallen down an elevator shaft as a boy of 14 in an abandoned building, several stories, and had miraculously survived. He said he recovered completely, but it did occur to me that he might still be suffering, mentally, from the trauma.

We watched from the weeds till we saw the Bull, in his Chrysler sedan, drive way on down the yards, then we headed for a BN grainer pointed the right way, with the back platform empty, no air equipment. Carrying a lighter load and being a bit faster, I made it into the car first, putting my gear down on the right-hand side (facing backwards) and sitting on my bedroll. I helped him on with his donkey load of stuff, setting each piece on over to the other side of the car, then got back over to "my" side and sat back down.

Now, the back porch of the standard grain hopper car has two distinct corners: the right hand side (which I was on) is flat and clear, with room to sit and with room to lie down; the left side (again, facing backwards) is cluttered up with a brake-pivot lever, which is not only in the way, but that moves each time brakes are applied or slacked. It's a damn nuisance but you learn to live with it.

Something was eating Cardboard; he kept looking over at me, and just couldn't seem to settle.

"Whitey, I always sit on that side." He stood up, looking expectantly.

"Cardboard, get down, quick, here comes the Bull again."

The Bull drove on by, not noticing us, and pretty soon, with a series of hisses, groaning, bumps, jerks and squeals, we lurched ahead and started our way out of Minneapolis, heading for Staples and points West. Hurray!

"Whitey, I always sit on that side." It was him, again, not giving up. Would he never keep quiet?

"Yes, I know, Cardboard, but I'm just like you, whenever I'm on a grainer, I always sit on this side, too." Seeing his hurt look, I added "Besides I got here first, so I get to sit here."

"Whitey, I always sit on that side." I looked at him, hard; What's going on here I thought, does he have an obsession about where he rides?

"Now Cardboard, I'm older than you, so as the senior tramp, I should get first pick anyway, so just sit down and enjoy the ride."

"Whitey, I always sit on that side."

Now I'm an easy-going guy, usually agreeable and wanting a friendly, amicable relationship, but this was getting to me. He was being unreasonable and acting like a little child, and I didn't want to let him think I could be pushed around.

"Now listen here, I got here first, I took this side, I'm the Senior man and I'm gonna stay right here till we get to Staples." Then I relented a bit, "Our next car out of Staples, I'll see to it that YOU get to sit on this side, and from now on, clear across the country, we'll take turns."

"Whitey, I always sit on that side." He was pleading with me now.

All of a sudden, everything changed. I realized in a flash – I wasn't dealing with a rational adult. No, I was in a strange position with a person who was suffering and who had a fixation in his mind that he couldn't change. I saw that it would be impossible to reason with the man or to convince him to do things my way. He only knew one way and couldn't budge.

To defer to him from a standpoint of backing down would be disastrous. The only thing I could do was to stand pat till we arrived in Staples, then part company, with a huge sigh of relief. Good riddance! Jeepers!

For the last fifty miles, I thought it over good and hard, then decided to turn it around; Why insist on stroking my ego? Why should I DEMAND my rights? I didn't really give a damn about which side I rode on. Why not turn the other cheek, and try to HELP the poor guy? If it was just some idiosyncrasy, I could live with it. After all I had said I'd ride with him all the way back to California. How much could I stand? I decided to try it.

I stood up, "Okay, Cardboard, you can sit on this side."

We traded places and re-shuffled our gear. Did he say, "thanks Whitey?" No, nothing like that. He sat down with a look of injured innocence, then broke out his propane stove, put the water pan on, put coffee crystals in both cups, then looked over at me with a cherubic smile and said, "I'm makin' us both a cup of coffee, Whitey, do you take sugar?"

Travels With Cardboard

I woke up before 5:00 am, my usual time. Cardboard was still sawing them off, so I left him there, peaceful as a baby and walked over to the Lark, the 24 hour café for breakfast. I was the only customer. Those eggs and potatoes and toast together with three cups of black coffee set me right for the day. I took my time and by the time I got back to our little "Nest" behind the big propane tank, he was up and stirring.

"What the hell, Whitey." He started the day off grouchy, like he'd made up his mind not to be nice to anyone. "You shouldn't have left your gear out in the open like that – anybody could've come along and swiped it."

I was feeling too good to be anything but amused at his very first outburst. "That would have been okay, Cardboard, if they wanted my old stuff that bad, they'd be welcome to it!"

I've always had this idea about jackrollers and other assorted thieves, that they are seldom seen real early in the morning, so to walk away from your gear at 5 o'clock in the morning presents no real risk. Most crooks are night owls anyway, preferring to operate under cover of darkness. They don't function too well early in the morning, as they are mostly heavy boozers or users, too, who generally drink or whatever up into the wee hours, and then take the oblivion express, waking up around noon. That's just the way I see it. There are exceptions.

I stood my turn as camp watchdog while my partner visited the café, then had to run his clothes through the laundromat. That took two hours. He'd washed all his stuff at Britt – just two days before, but that's the way he was, couldn't stand to have to carry any dirty clothes. While waiting for him to finish, I layed around swatting those enormous Minnesota mosquitoes, and counted two viable westbound trains come and go. I checked the depot for a call sheet and was handed the very latest. Those employees in the Staples Freight station are truly helpful. The sheet indicated several stack jobs due through that day and one mixed freight late in the afternoon. I forget the train number, but it could have been #1071 – an odd number – indicating westbound. The BN used a number system that was hard for me to remember. I preferred the four-letter system employed by UP and SP where the first two letters abbreviated were the point of origin and the last two showed the point of destination. That would be, for example, OGRO – Ogden to Roseville, or WCWS – West Colton to Warm Springs. Simpler to figure out and keep track of.

We did find ourselves a decent ride in a boxcar late that day, holding her down all the way to Minot, North Dakota. The yard there is six or seven miles east of town, so we didn't try to walk it, even though Cardboard said we needed grub. I didn't think so but kept quiet.

He was on the prod something fierce that day. We'd left our boxcar and taken refuge in the tall weeds to wait out an afternoon train, when along came a couple more riders off the same train who passed by and made their own camp nearby. I acknowledged their "Howdy" and that infuriated Cardboard. "How come you spoke to those bastards, Whitey? I never talk to nobody out here." I let that go also. Let him fume. Now these guys were all right. I could tell by the way they packed their gear, a couple of seasoned veterans, but to my partner, everyone was suspect.

We found our train, boarded a clean grainer porch, (yes, you guessed it, Cardboard sat on the "Good" side) enjoying a lovely summer-night's tour of highline prairie country, de-boarding at Glasgow, Montana at around four in the morning. We jungled behind a huge grain elevator, out of the wind. My buddy was having a hard time to keep his stove lit, as the breeze kept blowing it out. We drank coffee and ate sweet rolls. I found out that he hated to be left alone. He'd stew and fret like a little kid waiting for its mother, so I made it a point to let HIM do most of the foraging. He loved to go out poking around the track side businesses looking for cardboard. He had a mania for always having rolls of it with him, and seemed to know exactly where to find it. This was a good thing, as we always had some of it for sleeping on, or for padding a steel deck; but at the same time it was a drag as it reduced our mobility and made it a lot tougher to catch a train when we had to move fast. He had me trained to carry just as much as he did, so there we were like a pair of pack mules struggling along life's railway.

We hung around Glasgow all day even though two stack trains and one piggyback came through. Cardboard wouldn't even hear about trying to catch one. "I never ride them damn hotshots, Whitey. Ya can't get out of the wind and the Bulls watch 'em too close." I'm not sure but I suspect the real reason was that, with all his mountain of gear, he was unable to move fast enough to board one. These high-priority, fast-stepping trains change crews and are gone in just a couple of min- utes. Too quick for Cardboard. I didn't complain, but I knew then why it had take him 31 days to ride from his cabin in West Sac to Britt, Iowa. If he wanted to go slow, why, fine! I'd go slow too!

Then he got on me about the food. I'd returned from the little market with a couple of apples, two oranges, a grapefruit, some dried dates and a small sack of "Gorp" (trail mix). He snorted, "That all you bought? Jesus Christ, Whitey, don't you ever buy any real groceries?" Defending myself, I assured him that this type of food, mainly fresh fruit, was all I ever ate while traveling, and saved it for munching on the trains. When I arrived at a division, I'd usually chow down in a restau- rant and eat a real good meal. I told him it was easier to pack a little money, than to load up on all the canned goods they would pass out at the food banks or Sally's.

He blew his stack at that and stomped off to the store, returning with pork and beans, white bread (sliced), white crackers, canned spaghetti, baloney and a hunk of cheese.

I had given up long ago, using standard fare that had to be heated or cooked, and had quit even building fires except maybe for warmth, and then I'd make the fire in a five-gallon gunboat, using a track spike to punch a few holes in the bottom to insure a draft. But munching carrots, celery, oranges and apples – anything that would stand up to travel, was what suited me. I could go with that by the week on end. But I'd never try to proselytize anyone else – I knew by experience that few persons would settle for my fare.

Cardboard didn't like that. He wanted me to eat just the same as he was eating, and he thought I should buy the same old canned goods and then we could "share." He sure didn't go for this every man for himself stuff. His disapproval showed. I was a big disappointment to him. Like I'd let him down. This old-time tramp had never known the niceties of life; the wife, family, children, a home, and as a consequence he'd never had his rough edges rounded off. All he'd ever known was a man's world of trains, ships, skid row hotels, engine-rooms, flophouses, hobo jungles, jails, and had been all over the world as a wiper on merchant ships, but admitted, "All I ever seen, Whitey, was through the bottom of a whiskey bottle." A fairly well built man, he was in good shape and strong, too. But people baffled him; he didn't know how to cope. His only reaction to any problem was always the same – he'd blow his stack. His cantankerous ways were legendary among hobos.

I made up my mind to make a project out of getting along with him. I'd determined to overlook his feisty tongue and ride out each storm; hadn't I said I'd ride with him all the way? Maybe the poor guy was in constant pain from all the times he'd been clubbed and beaten. I'd stick it out.

We'd been here in Glasgow nearly 24 hours, and still no junk train had shown. Late afternoon I strolled down to the yard office to get the skinny on train movement but had no luck. I poked around town a while and was gone about an hour. When I got back Cardboard exploded. "Where the Hell ya been? You said you'd be back in a couple of minutes, and here you been gone more than an hour. Christ, Whitey, I had to protect our gear all by myself." What was this thing he had about being left alone? I said nothing, just rolled up my gear, sat down and waited.

It was nearly midnight. Cardboard jumped to his feet. "We got a light." I followed his gaze, sure enough, a headlight was visible way down the track towards the East. This was our man. It was a good many minutes before three big green lokies rolled by. Oh, oh, something wrong here. What gives? Here's the power, but no train. Where did he leave the rest of it?

Pretty soon Cardboard points. "Take a look Whitey, don't that look like a string of white grain cars way down there?" I couldn't see a thing, no matter how hard I strained. He was certain he could make out something, so we started down the main to check it out. As we got close I began to see the cars too. "Cardboard, you sure have got better eyesight than me." I had to hand it to him. That wise old boy was able to spot a train in the dark nearly a mile away.

We hurried down the track, stumbling and huffing, hoping we could get there before the power beat us back. They'd backed their train down onto a siding, then ran the three engines by themselves to the crew-change point; this way they wouldn't be blocking a whole bunch of traffic crossings, and as it was we needn't have hurried. We found us a nice back porch, unrolled and still waited a half-hour. Gone at last.

I woke up to a lovely, warm Montana morning. Sun just beginning to rise coloring up the big country all around. It had been a good night. We'd both slept well. These grain hopper cars ride so much better than boxcars. I lashed up my bedroll just as we pulled into Havre.

This was where all the engines were fueled up, so I knew there was no hurry. I nudged Cardboard, "We're pulling into the Havre yards, time to get up." He raised up, took a squint around, saw me sitting on my gear and immediately started cussing, "What the Hell, why didn't you wake me earlier, here you are all ready to go and I'm only just now coming to? You're a no good partner to be with, God Damnit Whitey. You should have known to wake me up way back there." And on and on he went heaping his verbal abuse all over me. He ran out of the usual four-letter vocabulary and then started calling me a "Freeloader." I took it for a while, then, in sad disgust, I realized there were no more excuses I could make for him, and that I was at the end of my patience. I could take no more. Sorrowfully, I waited till he had run clear down then stuck my face right up to his, and speaking softly but in deadly earnest said, "I can take no more of your filthy mouth, so I'm going my own way, right now. You're on your own."

I climbed down and without looking back hoofed it out of the yard. He screamed at me till I was out of sight – I can still hear that hated word – "Freeloader."

I walked up to the Park Hotel, stashed my gear then went into the Iron Horse Cafe. Ordered French toast, bacon and coffee and sat there nursing my bruised ego. To myself I thought, "Yes, I've made lot of blunders, let a few people down and probably been a disappointment to many, but, never, by any stretch of the imagination, could anyone ever have accused me of being a Freeloader." It wrankled. It hurt. It wasn't fair.

Breakfast over, I felt real good. I felt free at last. Putting up with Cardboard and suffering his abuse and his moodiness had weighed me down like an anvil around my neck. Now that I'd gotten him off my back, I began to brighten right up – like my usual cheery self. I'd take a meander around town, get a shower down at the Sally, have lunch and then head for the yards. No argument, no discussion, no explaining, Thank Heaven, no packing a five gallon gunboat full of canned food, and no more carrying three rolls of pasteboard. Hot Dog, it sure felt good to be out from under all that junk and rolling along by myself. I felt so good, so loose, like being a kid again. I began to whistle a railroad tune, wishing I'd brought my trusty guitar along.

I turned the corner and stopped. There was Cardboard standing in front of the laundromat waiting for them to open. I knew what I had to do.

I fished a $20 bill out my jeans, walked up to him like I meant business, stuffed the bill into his hand, saying, with intensity, "Here, this is for you to buy your own damn groceries; take it; and don't you <u>ever</u> – don't <u>never</u> call me a freeloader. Ya hear?"

He looked at me like he was going to cry; he threw the bill on the ground, "I don't want your fuckin' money, Whitey. You shouldn't pay no attention to all those crazy things I said. I don't ever mean any of that; something just comes over me and I guess I go out of my head. You always been square with me. I don't even care what you eat."

We stood looking at each other maybe a full minute. His face showed apology, contriteness, his eyes were PLEADING with me. He looked for all the world like a whipped dog that is trying to lick your hand.

Then he totally floored my with, "Listen Whitey, let's you and me be good buddies again . . . ."

Could I believe my ears? What was this he was saying? All my self-righteous resolve was melting away; he was charming me like I was putty. My heart went out to him. He was doing the best he knew how to APOLOGIZE. "Whitey," he went on haltingly, lamely, "Do you suppose you and me could go back to riding some more together?"

Me and Cardboard

We caught out of Havre mid-afternoon. The power had already hooked on so we had no time to look for a good ride. We took the first grainer that had the porch facing the right way, and we were out of there inside of ten minutes. I'd made sure I got to the car a couple of steps ahead of Cardboard and flopped down on the "Good" side first. I waited for the moment of protest but it didn't come. He was on his good behavior and really making an effort to be cooperative. He even started telling me about his remarkable release from the clutches of alcohol.

"Was it easy to quit?"

He snorted. "Easy? Hell, Whitey, when you're as sick as I was, anything is easy. I was in and out of Detox so often, I finally got so I'd do anything to get well again."

"How old were you when you quit?"

"I was 49. The Doc asked me how old I was and I told him, 49. He said if I didn't quit booze and cigarettes – I'd never see 50. I believed him and I cut 'em both out the same day. I got lots more energy now. It's better."

I thought to myself, this is going to be a good trip, what with Cardboard turning over a new leaf and acting rational, as when he was smiling and happy you couldn't ask for a better partner. My hopes were premature. Our car was pretty far forward and we hadn't given any thought to changing to a better ride farther back, so we were caught by surprise in Shelby when we stopped and then backed up.

I spotted this "rail" standing by a switch. I yelled out, "Are you setting us out?" He answered back "That's right. You'll find the train three tracks over, sitting on the main."

Oh Christ, what a scramble. We had to get all our three tons of stuff gathered up and ready to run. Packs, water jugs, five-gallon cans, plus rolls of cardboard; pile off the grainer, then climb through two cuts of cars between us and the mainline. I'd climb over first, then stand by the coupling, taking each piece of gear as Cardboard handed them across. Then he'd climb over and we'd repeat this move through the second string of cars. It was hot, sweaty, and Cardboard was cussing.

Now it doesn't take more than a few minutes normally to execute a set-out maneuver, but this time it took a little longer – otherwise we'd have missed the train. When we finally got through both trains we looked at our original train, hoping for a reliable car not too far away.

We were in luck. Not a hundred feet ahead was an empty boxcar. We made for it. Throwing all our stuff up into the car we had to help each other climb aboard – all this hoping the train didn't suddenly start moving. I wish I had a movie of me and Cardboard pushing and shoving each other into that boxcar.

I'm just a little guy, but my buddy is a good-sized man, so I'd swing my feet up as he pushed my back and shoulders till I was in; then he'd grab the door hasp, swing up, whereupon I'd brace my feet, then clutch ahold of his arm and together we'd manage to roll him in. Neither of us had the upper body strength enough to swing on unaided. There we were, exhausted with the lifting, climbing and hoisting, filthy dirty, wet with sweat – just content to lay there, panting for a few minutes till we could catch our breath.

Talk about the blind leading the blind. Now it's plain to see why we usually chose a grain car. They had a stirrup and grab irons allowing you to step right on up fairly easily.

Just in time, too, that train took off right now. The reason for all the panic moves leaving the set-out, and scurrying over to re-board the same original train is – that Shelby is not a regular stop on the BN, most EAST – WEST through freights roll right on by, so if you do happen to get left – you might have to wait many hours or even days before another one stops. The average hobo just HATES to get side-tracked!

From Shelby to Whitefish was a night run, arriving in early morning. I made my breakfast run first, then relieved Cardboard, who by now was back to being his usual miserable self. I paid him no mind, letting him vent his misery all he wanted. He was particularly up-set because when I left him alone to watch the gear while I went to eat, a guy and a gal came along and started talking to him. He hates that. They'd evidently come in on the same train as us. They had traveling gear too, and just wanted to be friendly, but Cardboard wouldn't talk, so they moved off.

First thing he said on my return, "Jesus Christ, Whitey, how come you have to run off like that? We could build a fire and fix our own breakfast. That way all these tramps wouldn't be bothering me!" All I could say was for him to relax a little. Didn't help.

About 1:00 pm we made a unit grain train all the way to Spokane – about six hours, which is pretty fast. On the way, it being another hot day, I was thirsty and grabbed the nearest water jug for a snort. We carried three one-gallon Clorox bottles, which is a clear case of overkill.

Cardboard saw me drinking and was immediately in a rage. "What are you doin' drinking out of that jug for? I told you that's the one we use for coffee water only! Why don't you use your own jug, that way I won't have to worry about having to drink your crumbs – out of your mouth!" Would you believe it?

I refused to talk or answer his remarks all the way to Spokane, which he didn't like at all. I was going to show him that I didn't need him, and could get along just fine without him and his hostilities.

We were stopped in Spok-a-loo about a half-hour for a crew change, as I'd found out this same train was continuing on to Pasco, so we stayed right with it. I was at the point where I was wishing this trip was over, so I could fulfill my commitment to seeing Cardboard all the way to Sacto – and then be done with him! So the better speed we could make just pleased me down to the ground.

Leaving Spokane we passed the Northern Pacific Depot (the only one still standing) and I was reminded of a newspaper article I'd read recently. Seems three high school boys from Seattle had hopped a freight out of Balmer Yard, for a joy-ride to Spokane. It was their first time out. MISTAKE. They'd no idea of how trains work, or where or when they stop, so when they passed this very NP Depot, the train didn't stop, but kept barreling on through at about 25 miles an hour. The boys panicked, thinking the train was not going to stop in Spokane (they evidently figured that freight trains stop at passenger depots – not realizing that the stopping place was in Yardley, just three miles further on). They foolishly piled off at that speed and got rolled badly, one boy breaking an ankle and the other two sustaining cuts and bruises. A real KID'S mistake! A stop at the hospital for a check up, then a plane ride home ended their hobo play-acting. I recalled my first time out and how, because of poor judgment, I too, came close to meeting a violent accident. It's so easy to get yours!

As usual, the train stopped way out on the North end of Pasco yard, where the trains are lined up from the hump. This afforded us the necessity of carrying all our stuff the two or three miles down to the only shade – the highway overpass, where everybody waits for their trains. Cardboard took off to find some water. He is good at finding things. Has an uncanny knack for poking around, discovering where the water faucet is or where he can find wood or cardboard, or where there is a convenience store. Sure enough, he returned with two jugs full.

"Ya gotta remember, Whitey." Yes, we were speaking again. "Never pour out what water ya got left, just because you run onto a spigot. Oh no, it might be dry or might not work, then, you're really screwed." I nodded, thankful for any tips.

Checking with a couple of car knockers on four wheelers, we learned to our dismay there was nothing down river to Wishram until 9:30 that night. We had twelve hours to kill. The heat was unbearable in the sun. The temperature was close to 90 even that early. We were sitting together discussing other trips and talking about the old ice-house that was such a busy place years ago when a gray sedan appeared, cruising the yard a few tracks over. As it passed, the driver looked our way and gave a friendly wave. We didn't acknowledge the gesture – just looked at him. He drove off.

"That just had to be the Bull, Cardboard. Don't you agree?"

"Sure looked like one. Wonder why he'd wave like that?"

Pretty soon here comes this same car back. This time it stopped and a small smiling-faced man gets out and walks up to us.

"Why didn't you fellas wave to me just now?" I spoke first.

"I guess you sort of surprised us." I grinned. "We're just not used to being waved at by the security." He laughed at that one, then

held out his hand, "My name is Mannie. I'm new here." We introduced ourselves, shaking hands all around. This was the first time in my
life I'd ever shaken hands with a Bull.

I said, "There used to be an older fellow here in Pasco. Are
you his replacement?"

"No, he's still here. Been here 44 years. While I'm at it, I
might just as well check your I.D.s."

We fished out our cards. This new Bull was so amiable, so
friendly, we couldn't get over it. I asked him if the old SP&S (Spokane,
Portland & Seattle) line along the Snake River had re-opened, but he
said he was not familiar with it. Old Cardboard, who'd been studying
him intently asked,

"Did you used to be a prize-fighter?" That got Mannie's attention right now.

"Yes, I used to fight out of Portland. I was a lightweight.
Why?"

"I could tell by your cauliflower ear." Indicating his right ear.

"Yes, I retired out of the Portland City Police. This is my first
job with a railroad." Then Cardboard took out of his wallet one of
those Tourist Union #63 cards, signed it and presented Mannie with it.
He seemed impressed.

"Now you're a hobo, same as Whitey and me!" Mannie grinned from ear to ear. A nicer, more congenial Special Agent I have never
seen.

There was a train called The California Man that made up here in
Pasco that went all the way to Sac and Stockton, but we couldn't find
out just when it left, so we decided to catch the first thing out for
Wishram and make our California connection there. The car knocker
had told the truth – the first thing out got started about 9:30 that night
with us on it. The yard had gradually filled up with riders all day; they
kept popping up in twos and threes and there was an older man with a
bicycle. I see more and more of that all the time. Pasco was a huge
classification and marshaling yard on the BN with trains being humped
and assembled all day and night for departures in at least five directions.
Out of Pasco you could catch out for Yakima, for Walla Walla (State
Pen called "The Wall"), you could go to Pendleton, up to Moses Lake,
North to Spokane and down river to Wishram, Vancouver and Portland.
So it was a big mystery to us why no trains were leaving for over twelve
hours that day.

Ours was a slow drag, taking the hole for everything else on the
rails, so it was four o'clock in the morning before we made Wishram.
Cardboard wanted to go find a train right then but I said, "Listen, old
Buddy, there won't be anything leavin' out southbound across the river
until after seven am. That's when the Amtrak comes through.
Everything else will wait till she leaves – so we've got two or three hours

at least. Let's sack out and get some sleep till daybreak anyway." With that, I unrolled next to the freight station and went right to sleep.

I woke up about 6:00 am, looked around. No Cardboard. I got rolled up and walked over to the crew shack. I was looking for a cup of coffee – my number one priority in the morning. It was daylight – looked like another nice day, sunny and warm coming up. I put a quarter in the coin-op machine and sat on the depot steps enjoying the steaming hot amber stuff. Delicious! Then I took a hike up the tracks, thinking Cardboard might have found himself a jungle under the trees and be expecting me to hunt him up. That was just like him. I wandered all over, saw nothing, but noticed that a few more trains had arrived. The yard was filling up.

Pretty soon I heard the two-tone chime of the Empire Builder (Portland Section) and here she comes, sailing into the station, stops momentarily and takes off again – right on time. I've got my gear all rolled up so I'm ready and waiting right by the crew shack to ask about the Bend train when the rails come out and start walking to their trains.

I get me another cup of coffee, and am sitting there, wondering where the Hell my buddy went, when out of the little yard comes the first train out. I see right away it's not the one I want as the consist is mostly woodchip cars, empty (the retaining nets were rolled up and tied down), with a few grainers near the back end. This train was obviously heading for some sawmill in the Portland area. I gave it no more thought. I sipped my coffee contentedly. As the grain cars came abreast of me I spotted something on one of the back porches. I looked! Could it be? Yes it was! I'll be damned!

It was Cardboard, sitting by himself, surrounded with his gear. The train was clipping right along by now. He saw me and hollered out, "Hey Whitey! You missed the train!"

Mixed emotions filled my head. Why had he boarded this particular train (which was obviously going nowhere)? Why hadn't he told me – even if he had to wake me up? Did he actually think that THIS was the California man? Why hadn't he waited till I had awakened, and then board a train together? Was he deserting me? Was this his way of terminating our relationship?

All these unanswered questions flitted through my mind. I will never know the answers. Less than an hour later I'd found me a ride on the Bend train and was crossing the mighty Columbia.

To this day I still wonder, "WHY?"

Is the Yard Hot?

I woke up first, got my stuff rolled up, looked out at the lightening sky, felt hungry and dying for the first cup of coffee. The Train Doc stirred, looked up,

"What time is it, Whitey?"

"About five. It's light already. You want to sleep awhile yet?"

"Yeah, it's too early for me."

"Okay, I need me some breakfast. I'll head on over to the all-night place and meet you at the other end of the yard. Take your time, sleep all you want. Our train doesn't run till this afternoon. Okay?"

"Okay, if that's what you want to do. I'll be along later."

I hit the ballast, hoisted my gear and took off on an easy stride, crossing about a dozen sets of empty tracks towards the western edge of the yard, right under the tower, walked past the building that said "Railroad Police – Southern Pacific Transportation Co." No hurry.

At this time of the morning the Eugene yards were deserted, the day switching crew hadn't come on and the Bull was not around. A fifteen minute walk put me in front of the long, low building. The sign read MILE POST INN. Next door was the crew hotel. I was their only customer. I ordered up hot cakes and eggs and cleaned up in the men's room. I loved these Mile Post Inns. Seemed like every SP division point had one. The food was real good with reasonable prices.

I took my time, after breakfast, slow but sure, enjoying a crisp June morning, keeping to the blacktop road till I was past the second tower. I cut back into the yard through the Berry Patch jungle. Abruptly I came across two guys resting on their packs.

"Good morning! Is the yard hot?" They appeared to be two bindle-stiffs about middle age.

The older one said, "No it ain't hot; not now."

I asked, "Has it been hot?"

They laughed, quietly. "Yeah, it was hot – yesterday."

"Why? What happened?"

Seems there was this newly hired Special Agent, a young guy, who found these two tramps going through some empties looking for cardboard. He I.D.'d them, told them they were under arrest for trespassing on Railroad property, ordered them into his Blazer and took them downtown to the main police station in Eugene.

They had just started the booking process when the head cop, I guess he was the Chief, walked in, looked the situation over, then asked the SP Harness Bull, "What are these guys charged with?"

"Trespassing, Sir. Trespassing on Railroad property."

"Trespassing?" The chief glowered, "Just trespassing? That's all? No breaking into cars or piggybacks or anything like that?"

"No sir, just trespassing."

The chief told the booking clerk to wait, then turned to the Bull. Meanwhile the two hobos were just standing, watching and listening.

"Now, let's get something straight." He was boiling mad, but tried not to show it. "We've got the GRATEFUL DEAD coming into the stadium tonight." (This stadium was the football field for the University of Oregon), and that means we'll have forty thousand hippies here to see them." He came closer to the Bull. "Do you have any idea what that's gonna mean? Can you imagine the number of parties and fights we're gonna have to break up? Can you picture the amount of controlled substances we've got to confiscate? Or the amount of hard liquor we'll have to pour down the drain?" He went on, a bit quieter now. "I look for our jail to be full tonight. These Grateful Dead audiences get pretty rowdy. Yes, we'll have a full house; so . . . ." He lowered his voice, "I sure don't want to see you filling up my jail with trespassers, is that clear?"

The Special Agent didn't have a word to say. The chief concluded with, "Now, get these guys our of here, and fast!"

The two Bo's told me they were ushered out the door, told to leave town, and here they were, the next day, back in the departure yard, looking for another train.

I hadn't seen Train Doc go by, so I parted with the guys and headed farther up the line to see where he'd got to. I'd asked him to meet me at the other end of the yard. Found out later he'd done just that, gone clear up to where the Northbound engines back down on their respective trains. I, on the other hand, camped within sight of the rear ends of these same trains. So, there we were, separated by a mile, with each of us wondering where the Hell the other was. This was easy to do, this miscommunication. I'd been trained to watch the back end where the caboose was; as soon as you saw the crew boarding the crummy or getting a fire going inside, you knew it was a matter of minutes till departure. Train Doc had done the bulk of his riding in more recent years, and much of it since the railroads has done away with most cabooses and had adopted the little gray boxes known as end-of-train-devices. So, as there was no caboose, therefore no one at the rear end to ask info from – you just naturally worked from the power end.

I still preferred to keep tabs from the back for this reason; in the departure yard in Eugene were ten or so tracks, usually with trains sitting on them awaiting their call time. These trains were of differing lengths; one might consist of a hundred cars, the one on the adjacent track might have only sixty while the second track over might contain a train of 125 cars – so the front ends would be staggered. The back ends of these same strings would be usually pretty flush – all lined up – clear across the ten tracks. Reason was – this was the end where the underground compressed airlines were buried. There were outlets by each track; the carmen would connect a flexible air hose from these outlets to the hose connection on the last car and pump air through the entire train. An enormous yard air compressor kept the pressure up and it expedited the air system considerably faster than road engines alone could possibly accomplish. The net result was that, when the power was called for a certain train, the engines could come out of the roundhouse, cruise clear up along the edge of the yard on the "runner" track, back down onto its particular string, and after just a few minutes of testing the "Air" be in all respects ready for the "Bell." It eliminated the slower process of the engine using its own compressors to get the whole train "Aired up."

So, by watching this rear end activity, looking to see which cars had the EOTD set-up, watching the runner track for the units to arrive, then watching close to see which track they backed down onto, and finally listening for the tell-tale hissing of the pressurized air – you could identify the next train out and still have time to select your "Pullman." Simple, eh?

So, Train Doc, assuming I'd been delayed, went ahead and caught the BN afternoon train up to Vancouver, WA. I kept looking for him all that day, and finally caught an evening train to Roseburg, where I knew I could eat a hot meal and get a decent flop at the Roseburg Rescue Mission.

So I left north again the next morning on the 9:00 am local back to Eugene and finally on up to Vancouver, where I ran onto Train Doc. I was waiting by the herder's shack up at the 39th Steet Yard, when out of a boxcar where he'd spent the night, crawled my long lost road buddy. All he said was, "Where Ya' been, Whitey?"

A Reason For Living

We were waiting at the crew-change point in Portland for the Eastbound Union Pacific.

"Whitey, we've got a green light. Let's head down the track!"

It was the Train Doc pointing to the signal mast, which had been dark up till now. I got my pack ready first and headed down the track toward where we knew a train would be approaching. Pretty soon a headlight showed, then three big yellow UP SD 60's roared by hauling (thankfully) a mixed freight. Then it stopped.

Train Doc and I had met only the week before and didn't really know each other's habits yet. But we were learning fast. I was an early riser; Doc liked to sleep in. I just <u>had</u> to have my morning coffee; Doc didn't drink coffee. I loved a good breakfast; he was indifferent about the morning meal. I enjoyed meeting and talking with strange Bo's; the Doc was a loner. He preferred traveling alone. I was to find out why.

He had been given the moniker of "Train Doc" by some of the L.A. train riders who were giving him a lift to the train yards one morning. They passed one of those "Roto-rooter" trucks that had a sign saying, "Drain Surgeon." Someone picked up on this, "That's what we should call you – the 'Train Surgeon'. Or, better yet, how about 'Train Doctor'?, and shorten it up to just 'Train Doc'?"

So that's how it got started and the name stuck. It suited him perfectly, as the Train Doc was a rare bird indeed! I had met no one quite like him. A well set-up fellow over six feet tall, vigorous, energetic, in his early 40's, smart – really whip-smart and an interesting talker. He had other qualities I hadn't as yet divined; one especially – he was dedicated! By that I mean he had found something that he liked so well that it gave him a new lease on life; riding freight trains. He simply loved them; couldn't get enough. He'd found his heart's desire!

The background is pretty sketchy, but as I know it, he was in his mid-twenties when he got out of the army after a stint in Vietnam. He hated the army, seeming to begrudge every minute he had to serve. Was so elated when finally was released that he recalls noting the year, the month, the day, hour, minute and exact second when his discharge was effective. Possessing no marketable skills to speak of, he was at a loss as to what he should turn his hand to in the way of work or job.

Fate intervened. He decided to hop a freight train. Why, I don't know. Maybe he knew someone who did this sort of thing or maybe he just saw someone else riding and thought it might be a gas.

On a certain day in July, 1976 (I think) he caught his very first ride on a freight train in some little New Hampshire town, and, in so doing became a hard-core devotee, hooked irretrievably for life. He'd found it! It was simply euphoria – instant euphoria. His life took an immediate turn. No longer was he groping, grasping and wondering at

what should he do? Instead, a clear-cut and instantly discernible path
was disclosed. He'd found not just a way of life; oh, no, the Train Doc
has discovered a mission!

He had no family ties to speak of, was uncommitted, had no
plans and little money, but he did have one thing: he saw an opportunity
to do something he wanted to do and do it his way. After those years in
the service this freedom loomed large. Why not? Just climb on a train,
travel the nation and see what might come of it. I doubt he sought any
advice from friends. He's a person of strong convictions, an intense
personality and afraid of nothing. He once said to me, "I've never tried
to avoid controversy."

He outfitted himself with some good gear (always carried the
best state-of-the-art camping equipment) and took off. He'd been on
the road 15 years when I met him. He'd devised an ingenious system
and had stuck with it. He worked at piddling little stop-gap jobs for six
months of the year (From Oct. 15th until April 15th) saving every penny
possible. He kept a modest apartment in Boston (year round), rode a
bicycle, had no expensive habits (other than drinking copious quantities
of chocolate milk), then when April 15th rolled around,

> "When springtime does come, oh won't we have fun,
> We'll throw up our jobs and we'll go on the bum."

He'd quit his super-market clerk job, or his night shift desk-
clerk thing in some skid-row hotel, ask his landlady to hold his apartment, that he'd be returning in the fall, and off he'd go, splendidly geared, well groceried up with a song in his heart to find and board the first
freight out of town. He'd been doing this six months on and six off
thing for fifteen years. For him it worked like a charm.

Not the sort to stay out year around, having to resort to various
welfare giveaways, foods tamps or homeless shelters, he enjoyed having
money and being able to pay his way. Nor did he like being out in cold
weather. This part-time lifestyle suited him perfectly. Of late however,
the finding and securing of an instant job when he came in after the
season was becoming a littler harder. He had to choose one that he
could walk away from come spring. He learned that employers don't
like this. They just assumed he intended to stay on for the rest of his
natural life and were more than a bit chagrined when he'd leave. Money,
retirement, security or any long-range goal meant nothing to him. He
preferred to ramble, and ramble he did – logging as much as 25,000
miles a year. Riding the rails became more than a hobby – it turned into
an obsession!

Then it was that he discovered something to do, besides just
travel. Being of a studious, detail-oriented, record-keeping disposition,
he turned to making notes of his train movements, his destinations and
arrivals, the daily mileage, names of the various railroads and, most espe-

cially, the exact places where freight trains stopped to change crews! This was of prime importance because it was only when the trains were stopped, that a hopeful rider could get on or off without suffering the possibility of hurting himself. It was the only safe way to do it. Therefore to be able to know in advance exactly where these crew-change points were was a key bit of information – knowledge one could use over and over and even pass on to other rail riders.

Thus it was that his idea took shape. He immediately put it to use and it became his driving interest, ever expanding to finally include (after several years) a rather complete and exact body of little-known information of such comprehensive scope that it covered the nation, plus parts of Canada! He put it all together in a neat typewritten (then photocopied) slim little volume, alphabetically indexed state by state, city by city, and even including a section on timely and helpful how-to hints. He called it A BASIC GUIDE TO RAILROAD CREW CHANGE POINTS and JUMPING FREIGHT TRAINS IN NORTH AMERICA. It was a concise and neatly done piece of work, which could be slipped into one's pack and referred to daily. I loved it!

Compiling this thing required years. The info it contained was a Godsend, a literal gold mine! But, to whom?

Beside myself I know personally of only about a hundred people who would ever have use for it, but my knowledge is extremely limited. I may be under-estimating its potential, as it is possible that there may be hundreds and even thousands of guys and gals who would spot it right now as a find! Who can say?

The Doc refuses to publish it for mass sales, feeling it should be kept as an underground thing, known and used only by the rail-riding brethren. He will make it available, however, to the select few who take this lifestyle seriously, for just what it costs him to reproduce and mail out, about $12. It would be cheap and a bargain at any price!

Getting back to the man himself; he has this penchant for being well-heeled, usually starting out in the spring with around $4,000 in traveler's checks. He spends it mostly on food and living expenses such as topographical maps, chocolate milk, ready-made sandwiches, admission to major-league ball parks (he's a baseball nut – favors the Cincinnati Reds), sweatshirts with railroad logos, stamps, postcards etc., but never on a room in a motel, preferring to sleep out in the weeds or in boxcars, and he boasts that he has never, ever bought a ticket on a passenger train.

On being stopped one time by a town clown somewhere in Minnesota, the cop asked him if he had funds. Train Doc nodded in the affirmative.

"How much have you got on you?"

"Close to four thousand dollars."   The cop was plainly skeptical.

"Let's see it."

Doc produced several books of traveler's checks. The officer slowly counted the lot, handing them back. He asked, with surprise in his voice, "Well, just where are you going?"

"Chicago."

"With that kind of money, how come you don't fly?"

"Officer, I just don't like to fly." The cop was incredulous.

"But you do like to ride these filthy old trains?"

"Yes, I do." (The Train Doc is a fastidious person concerning personal cleanliness, keeping himself and his gear in immaculate condition. More on this later.)

One evening he found himself in a small New England town looking for a place to crash. He came to a city park, spied a picnic table, spread out his $300 sleeping bag underneath, crawled in and was just dozing off when an old man with his little dog came by and sat down at the table. The old man didn't notice our hero in the darkness but his dog was immediately interested, proceeding to sniff all around while the Doc was eyeballing the situation. He was reluctant to say anything that might startle the old man and possibly cause him to become alarmed and even call the law.

So he kept quiet, didn't utter a peep, even when the little dog lifted his leg and proceeded to urinate contentedly on the lower part of Doc's sleeping bag.

Too late. He couldn't react now. The deed was done! Finally the old man led his dog away, unaware of the calamity while Doc had to suffer the ignominy and say <u>nothing</u>!

This fetish for cleanliness was getting him into more trouble! One night in Ashland, Oregon, passing a house that had a nice, grassy backyard, complete with garden hose all invitingly hooked up, it occurred to Doc that this would be a great chance to have a shower! A dog barked furiously from inside the house but no lights came on, so Doc assumed there was no one home.

Wrong! He stripped down, broke out his trusty bar of soap and had himself a hose-shower.

He was just getting dried off when a police patrol car pulled up in front. A man got out and shone a spotlight right on him.

"Don't move!" The cop came closer. "What are you doing here, anyway?"

The Doc patiently explained that he was only using the water to clean up with and meant no harm to anyone. The cop studied the situation for a minute. "We got a call from the lady who lives here saying that there was a naked man in her backyard and that she was terrified!"

"I'm terribly sorry, officer – I didn't realize anyone was home. If I'd have asked her she would probably say, 'It's okay, go ahead'."

The cop wrote out a citation for trespassing (odd how that word – that same word keeps cropping up!) and let the Train Doc go.

Getting back to that UP train we were trying to catch out of Portland; I was ahead of Train Doc and the first to reach an open-doored boxcar (quite a find on the UP, as they've been sealing up empties for years). The car already has a forlorn little old wisp of a man sitting by the doorway stroking a bright-eyed little puppy. I stopped and asked if my buddy and I could share his boxcar – that being the proper protocol. He said that would be fine.

I asked him what was his dog's name? He said, "I call him BOXCAR." He said he'd caught this train down in the UP main yard and was trying to get to Spokane. Said he'd been "cannin'" and had blown all his money on Silver Satin whiskey. The car was a nice clean one with a wooden floor, just the ticket for an all night ride to Hinkle.

About then the Train Doc caught up with me, and like I said before, I had a lot to learn about his habits. I hollered, "Throw your gear up here with mine. This guy said it's okay to ride with him."

He surprised me with, "No, Whitey, I'm gonna catch one of these grainers I can see further on down." He hesitated, like he was waiting for me.

I didn't get it. "Listen Doc, this is a great car, wood floor and all. I'd rather ride this than any cold old grainer."

"Oh, come on, Whitey," his voice sounded edgy – "this ride means a lot to me." He headed down the train. After a bit I followed him, feeling miffed. What was this thing he had about not wanting to ride with anyone? That poor old tramp and his dog "Boxcar" wouldn't hurt anyone. I was still grumbling when I caught up with Doc, swung into the grainer and noticed he'd left me Cardboard's Good side.

It occurred to me that perhaps Doc has spotted something about the old man I didn't know and was reluctant to speak in front of him.

"How come you didn't join me in that boxcar?" I was still hot!

"Well Whitey, you know, with all this money I carry, I'm sort of the J. Paul Getty of the hobos. I don't like to take chances."

"Chances? Come on, Doc. That old man was purely harmless."

"Yeah, he <u>looked</u> harmless, that's true."

"We had nothing to worry about from him – we were two against one."

"Yeah, Whitey, but what if he had a gun?"

I just kept shaking my head. It didn't make any sense. About then the train started nudging slowly ahead. We were finally on our way up the Columbia River Gorge.

Sensing my irritation, the Doc said, "He might not have been dangerous at all, Whitey . . ." his voice trailing off. He couldn't seem to justify his action and was searching around for an excuse.

Then he brightened up. "Ya know what might have happened? His little dog would have probably pissed on your sleeping bag!"

Hiding Out In Hinkle

The Train Doc and I made that night run from Portland to Hinkle on the UP enjoying a pleasant, smooth ride. The Union Pacific seems to maintain their roadbeds better than most. Now Hinkle is nothing but a huge classification yard stuck out in the Eastern Oregon desert about five miles from a town – Hermiston, not on a main highway, with apparently no convenience store anywhere around. You are really stuck out there; no trees, no shade, nothing green or pretty, so the SPORTSMAN has to lay low or skulk around out of sight of the tower, watching out for the Bull's white sedan – the one with the radio antennae and spotlight as he zips tirelessly up and down the yard. The word had been out for years UP takes an uncompromising attitude towards illegal train riders, doling out a much-discussed "automatic 30 days" if apprehended. I have yet to experience their wrath, but that's the story you hear dozens of times.

So when the Doc and I discovered this little gray building housing a restroom, ice-water dispenser and even a chair to sit down on, we claimed instant squatter's rights, proceeding to make that our Jungle until train time. It was a yard worker's rest stop. They kept popping in all day, driving up in their pickups, paying no attention to us at all. Security in this yard was so tight we didn't dare wander around checking out the cuts of cars to hopefully zero in on our SPOKANE man. The Doc sat down to scribble out some postcards (has an enormous bunch of acquaintances he writes to regularly), so I confronted an overall-clad, amiable looking carman to ask a favor. I requested he inquire from someone as to just when the Spokane train would be called – and on which track would she leave from. "Sure, I'll see what I can do." About a half-hour later here comes this guy with a piece of paper in his hand. "I picked this up," handing me the sheet, "it was laying on the dispatcher's desk. It doesn't make any sense to me but it might tell you something. See all these mixed-up letters, I don't know what they mean, but it's yours if you want it." This obliging mechanic had secured for us the precise bit of "dope" which told us everything – it was the "CALL SHEET" indicating every train's departure time and destination! We couldn't have done any better with an employee's timetable!

He stood reading it over my shoulder. It was plain and simple, I said. "See this one, it reads 0800 HKPD?" "That means that at 8:00 this morning, a train originating in HK, that's Hinkle," I stopped and looked at him, he nodded. "Now," I went on, "the PD part, that's the destination, and it's pretty obvious that PD means Portland. Got it?"

He smiled. It was beginning to make sense. "I've got to get back to work, hope this will help you find your train." And he was gone. Wonderful people, I meet them everywhere.

We checked the whole sheet. We found a HKPO (Hinkel to Pocatello), a couple of PD's to SLC (Portland to Salt Lake) and a few more to various places (Hinkel was a busy place) – then we spotted ours – 1430 HKCP on #9. "What's that CP, Whitey, Camas Prairie?"

"No. I'm pretty sure that CP means CANADIAN PACIFIC."

"Is that going to be our train? Will it go to Spokane?"

"It's got to be our man, and I think we can see it from here!"

I pointed "See that string straight across from us, the cars that say BCR, CP and CN – those grainers and tank cars?" He nodded. "Well Doc, that's just got to be OUR train!" He agreed.

It was past noon by then, so with a 2:30 call time we figured we'd better low-line over and pick a ride. Filling up water jugs and sharing an orange, we planned our assault and bided our time. The very minute we stuck our noses out of the water shack we would be in plain view of the tower, so we had to make our move AFTER the Bull had gone by. This took some alert surveillance. Finally our chance came.

"Whitey, the white sedan just left the tower office!" He was watching him through the window. "Here he comes now!" We watched approvingly as the Bull sped by raising a lot of dust, then tracked him as he hurried way down to the far end of the yard, out of sight.

"Go for it" yelled the Doc. And go for it we did.

On a dead run, we tore out of our hiding place, crossed eight sets of tracks and headed for #9. This was like running in plain sight across a battlefield – No-man's-land, exposed to anyone in the tower. Reaching the cut of CP oil tankers we slipped behind the string and hurried up the train to where the CP grainers were – quite a number of them. To our surprise we came upon the wispy tramp and his dog, "Boxcar" – already up on a grain platform and grinning down on us. "See ya' both made it" was all he said.

We hurried on up, selecting two hopper cars right together. We needed one apiece as we planned to hide in the "Hole" of our hopper until after clearing the yard. These Canadian Pacific compartments just forward of the back-porch platform were much larger and more comfortable than the usual U.S. version. So up we went, each in his own rabbit hole and sat panting, prepared to wait.

After sitting cramped and hot, with a temp of around 95, we endured about an hour's worth of clanking, groaning, hissing and creaking of the brake linkage until we slowly got under way, laying low till we were out along the Columbia River where she stopped at a place called Wallula Junction. Then we got down, stretched, laid our gear out on the cleanest of the two porches, and relaxed, looking forward to a pretty ride to Spokane.

We'd done it again. Sure enough, we'd survived Hinkle, one of the hottest yards in the state. We looked at each other in mute congratulations. Was there ever a better way to travel?

Down Time

Labor Day, Sept. 5, 1983. Livingston, Montana. Woke up after a peaceful night at the Fix Hotel, $10 a night, bath across the hall. Real clean and quiet. Could have had a room for $35 a week or $90 a month. Come to think about it, that's fairly reasonable!

Climbed off a westbound BN mixed freight at noon yesterday. I'd ridden in from Laurel enjoying one of the most pleasurable trips of my life in an open boxcar, cruising along the Yellowstone River all the way. What a gorgeous fall day, sunny and bright as I gazed off at the Crazy Mountains to the north and the snow-capped Absorkas to the south. Big sky country never looked prettier.

At the eastern edge of town I dropped off at the Trail Ride Restaurant for breakfast. This place is adjacent to the highway and the BN yards — really handy. The waitress was God-awful slow, so I missed my train by about three minutes.

Waited around all afternoon for another one but there was nothing going west except a piggyback. Too cold and windy for me, plus these trains are watched too close. Weather turned cold as the day wore on, wind came up, felt like right off some snowy mountain pass, so I decided to stay over at the Fix Hotel one more night.

The previous day I'd met an old railroad boomer who had the room next to mine. I was fascinated by his belt buckle, which was a beaut; Great Northern logo showing the Billy Goat standing on a mountain peak. He told me that anything pertaining to the old GN was really scarce since the merger (GN, NP, SP&S and CB&Q) into Burlington Northern. He told me he had worked thirty-five years as a freight brakeman on fourteen different roads.

Talked to an Indian from Pine Ridge, South Dakota who had just bailed off an Eastbound piggyback from Helena. Asked him why he got off in Livingston. He said it was just too cold riding outside. He'd left her up in front of the old NP depot and while walking down toward the yard he'd found a crumpled up dollar bill. Said it was his lucky day — now he could eat. He'd slept under a viaduct in Helena the night before and shivered all night. He was carrying a broken suitcase, a sleeping bag under his arm and a plastic bleach bottle for water.

"I don't know what I'm doing on the road; I got a wife back home; she couldn't find me in Cheyenne. We were at the Frontier Days and I got throwed in. She didn't know where I was so she must have gone back home. She can't run around with me no more cause she's preg-a-nant — yeah, four months gone aw-ready. Good luck to ya, pardner," and off down the tracks he went.

Had a dinner salad as usual for my supper; only this time they threw in a basket of French bread and butter. Plus I had a glass of Rose' wine. Cost a total of $3.00. Delicious.

Then I slipped the piano player a buck. She was a young, horsy-looking gal who played all the old songs from a stack of sheet music (you don't see that much anymore!). Not really a sharp entertainer but tried her best. This was at the Livingston Bar & Grill where these ranch folks came in and ordered monstrous steaks. They charged by the ounce; $1.29 per ounce for top sirloin and $1.49 for filet mignon. The place was jammed. People seemed happy and the drinks were generous. Saw a cowboy in there wearing a magnificent pair of silver-mounted spurs. The business-ends were big wheels with sharp-pointed tips that made a neat jingling sound as he walked. You could tell he loved them.

Next morning I waited around the BN crew shack till 10:00 am, looking to catch west for Helena but nothing came by. I was in no hurry, I liked the town and felt really good about the idea of bumming around with money in my jeans, and being able to afford a flop in a cheap hotel and eating in restaurants. Only the month before I had received my very first Social Security check, realizing I had unconsciously beaten the system; I had outlived my usefulness (job-wise) but figured I still had some good years left (for travel) and now had a check coming in every month for the rest of my life (everlasting money as it's called in the Navy).

How come I'm always so lucky? Did I really deserve it?

About then I spotted three units of Green BN power backing down onto a string of boxcars in the lower yard. I shouldered my gear and lit out for it. Two days of downtime had made me ready! I was itching for a ride. I wanted to ramble! I figured she wouldn't stay long so I hustled but was carrying such a heavy pack I couldn't move quick.

As it turned out I paid for packing too much gear, as before I could reach the only rideable car — one, lone empty box, all the way down just ahead of the crummy, the train got underway. All I could do was stand alongside and watch it pull out. With my oversized pack I wouldn't think of trying to nail her on the fly like I would have — years before.

Missed another one! Stuck in Livingston, facing yet another Rocky Mountain High freezing cold night. So here I am sitting on an old farm wagon next to the tracks. As I scribble these words the sun is bright, but the wind brisk. It seems to me this town could be a very cold, uncomfortable place to live ten months out of the year.

Coming in from the mid-west, I'd flagged a ride on a big freight truck from Rapid City to Belle Fouche, then a long ride on another semi all the way to Laurel over Highway 212. Had an interesting day of it talking to Jim Hensbruck, the driver, learning his philosophy on life and why he considered truck driving a poor way to go. He got me a room at the Husky truck stop in Laurel for $6.00, which was a bare-bones crash-pad! Just a bed and a chair in a monk-like cell with bath across the hall.

Here is the exact wording of a sign posted in the yards near where I was sitting:

BN RAILROAD   NO TRESPASSING

Walking, loitering, hunting or using firearms along tracks or
on right-of-way, and hopping on or stealing rides on trains is
Prohibited. Persons so doing will be subject to arrest under the
law.

It would sort of make you want to go ahead and do it — right?
You see this sign posted everywhere along the BN. The train riders,
hobos, tramps, homeless, bums, hippies and other assorted vagabonds
pay them no mind.

The word "loitering" is an interesting word. Years ago as a kid,
I recall seeing "No loitering" signs posted in public restrooms and in
railroad depots. I think today's phrase "Hangin' out" means much the
same.

So, here I am, putting in some Down Time, but it has been a
restful break. No one bothering me. Haven't laid eyes on a Bull. This
vagabonding life suits me. I love to travel incognito, cloaked in the man-
tle of un-accountability, answering to no one for my actions, drifting
serenely through life. Not in a hurry, having no appointments to keep,
no deadlines to meet — no one to please but myself! Sounds kinda
smug and selfish — but then — I've paid my dues — or I hope I have.
Here I am at retirement age still hobo-ing around the USA. Maybe I
should quit all this nonsense — this irresponsibility and go get a job!
I'll think about it . . . .

The Big "G" and Luther the Jet

Train Doc Norton had told me about this guy he'd met at Britt, Iowa, who, it seemed, rode, not only the prosaic freights like the rest of us mortals, but who also had the temerity to steal rides on the Amtrak passenger trains. No small feat, considering it could turn into a Federal offense, if apprehended.

"Just exactly where does he ride?" I queried. Train Doc thought he must ride in the engine, somewhere, but wasn't sure.

"If you go to Britt this summer, Whitey, you'll meet him; he's always there." Sounded like someone I ought to know, so that's how it happened. That meeting, with Luther the Jet, turned out better than I could ever have hoped for.

I knew it was him; he fit the description perfectly; a tall, skinny, black-bearded string-bean of a man; soft-spoken, undemanding; self-effacing, gentle person, friendly, attentive, dressed in camo-clothing and black boots; so much at ease and seemingly acquainted with everyone there at the hobo camp. We hit it off right away, discovering our mutual interest in song-writing. But first off I wanted to learn his modus operandi for hopping Amtrak.

He seemed to take no small delight at his audacity. He told me he would enter Union Station, Chicago, head for the commuter train gates (where you didn't require a ticket), then cross over a dozen or so sets of tracks to the well-guarded Amtrak section, timing his arrival to coincide with the departure of the Broadway Limited. "I saw this employee checking something on the engine, so I asked him, 'Would it be okay if I ride the second unit?' The man seemed unconcerned. 'I don't give a fuck where you ride.'"

Luther climbed aboard (on the off side), disappearing into the cab and laying low. Said he rode her clear on over into Ohio. Said he'd only done it a few times and that he'd found everything quite easy. I couldn't get over it, as I'd heard of lots of Bo's riding between the coal tender and baggage car (outside, known as riding "blind baggage") on passenger trains back in the steam days, but never ever even considered doing it myself.

The longer I knew him, the more impressed I got. I could tell by his speech and manner he was a refined and educated person — with a degree in French Literature! This guy was a paradox; I could tell he spent a lot of time in libraries, and had gathered old-time American railroad history till he was full of it — but, though obviously book smart, he was also quite a traveler on freights, had slept out in the weeds, and rammed around the whole U.S. over a period of twenty years. He was just the opposite of so many macho-typed swaggering railroad tramps you see out there. He seemed to float, unharmed around the scary yards and jungles like a mild, genteel gentleman hobo — leading a charmed life.

He'd composed a dozen or more long-winded story songs of happenings on the trains and rails of old-time, long-forgotten companies. He sang these songs himself, unaccompanied, never missing a word — stanza after stanza, carrying on thirty or forty verses and lasting ten minutes or more. In the commercial music industry, it is conceded that a song should not last more than three minutes — audience attention span is the reason. With Luther, not being aware of this limitation, he kept right on, verse after verse, blissfully unaware, and the crowd loved it. They bought every word.

So one day he and I headed north out of Dunsmuir, California, on the SP, hoping to make K Falls the first night. We discussed the history of the Great Northern Railroad, and it was like tapping an oil well. It seemed he knew more about this road than I did, even though I'd been raised around it. Did I learn?

The Great Northern had the neatest logo — an enormous " G " (first letter of "Great") with a picture of a mountain goat standing on a mountain peak, and their slogan, also painted on the sides of the cars was "See America First."

I was raised in Seattle, the Western Terminus of the "Big G," so was familiar with it from an early age. This was Jim Hill's road, the man responsible for creating a standing order, "Always see to it that there is at least one empty boxcar on every GN train. The hobos helped build this road, and I want to see that they always get to ride it." This was implemented and continued right up to the day of the merger with NP, CB&Q and SP&S. The GN people were ambitious, wanting to expand, always shooting out branch lines and hoping to capture new markets. The Northern Pacific, the first transcontinental to arrive in Washington State, was, on the other hand, a smug, self-assured group of men who sat on their assets, ran with the status-quo, and weren't interested in expansion, knowing full well they were No. 1.

The Great Northern wanted desperately to crack the coveted California market — then held and controlled by Southern Pacific. No way would they (the SP) allow any upstart to horn in on their ever-growing trade from down South.

Sometime in the 1920's, the GN conceived a plan whereby they would create a new railroad (ostensibly a NEW line), run it from Spokane, down to the Snake River, then follow the North Bank of the Columbia all the way down river to Vancouver and Portland. It was to be named the Spokane, Portland and Seattle Railroad (SP&S). Now comes the hanky-panky part.

Ninety miles upriver from Portland, a mighty bridge was built across the huge Columbia at a place called Wishram — to an old spur-line on the Oregon side near Biggs Junction on the Union Pacific. Many years before, the Oregon-Washington Railroad & Navigation Co. (OWR&N), or better known as the Oregon Short Line, had branched off from UP and built a road south up the east bank of the Deschutes

River up to Madras, Redmond and Bend — three tiny little villages in the vast sheep and cattle ranching country of Central Oregon. This line was, by now, long defunct and abandoned.

So the ever-restless and ambitious GN went ahead and constructed a new trackage along the west bank of the Deschutes, through lava beds, with tunnels, over rivers and mountains, all the way through Madras, Redmond, Bend — and on — clear down to a tiny settlement known as Chemult, which was (by no coincidence) where the SP mainline going south had recently been built. Well, what have we here?

Somehow GN persuaded SP to allow them to use their trackage from Chemult to Klamath Falls. This is hard to believe — much less to understand, but that's what happened. Now then, GN built their own freight yard in K Falls, just two miles south of the big SP yard. From there, it was only ninety or so miles down to Nu-Bieber, Ca, where they made connection with Western Pacific, a friendly road. This wasn't all done at once; it took years to complete this maneuver but when finished, the result was remarkable!

The Great Northern Railroad could now run trains all the way from Seattle or Spokane, down river to Wishram, across the Columbia, up the canyon to Bend, on down to Chemult, use SP tracks into K Falls, then finally conclude the run down to Nu-Bieber where they could turn the traffic over to WP, which ran it the rest of the way down into Oroville, Sacramento, and finally Oakland and San Francisco! They'd crashed the market! It was a done deal. It's being used to this very day!

Luther and I were discussing this adroit piece of connivance while hiking through the K Falls yard looking for a train north — any train. We'd arrived the night before and had opted to stay at the Rescue Mission as the night was windy and cold — even though, here it was June! We sang Amazing Grace, had a decent dinner, took a shower and passed a restless, miserable night of it, unable to get much sleep for listening to the grunts, groans, hacks and coughs of fifty or so shot-down drifters.

Trudging along, we heard a car coming up behind us; I took a quick look, "We've bought it," I muttered. "It's him!"

"Who?" asks Luther. I broke out singing softly a bit of old English Rhyming,

> "Who's that a-coming? . . . Oh My God!
> It's Rodger the Dodger, the lodger, the sod!"

The nemesis of the premises, Rodger, got out of his white Cherokee, greeted us with the usual, "You guys know you're trespassing, don't you?!" He checked Luther's I.D. "How old are you?"

Luther answered, "Fifty five." Then he checked mine, "And how old are you?" This question was redundant as he was holding my driver's license, but I went along with the gag. "I'm 72."

Rodger stared at me hard. "What's a man of your age doing out here on these trains?" I gave him the reply I often use, "Well, I get the fever so bad, sometimes, that I just can't help myself!"

The words of Merle Haggard singing "White Line Fever" came to me.

> I wonder just what makes a man keep pushing on,
> Why do I always sing this same old freight-train song?
> I've been from Coast to Coast a hundred times or more,
> Ain't seen one single place where I ain't been before!

A man with 35 years steady as a railroad cop could hardly be expected to share the wistful dreams and mysterious urgings of a foot-loose wanderer. We told him we were walking down to the BN yard (where we would no longer be a threat), whereupon he softened his talk, then becoming almost paternal, warned us of the "weird" characters lurking in that yard, concluding with his timely tip,

"I hope you two have got food and water. There's no stores or markets or anything within walking distance down there. Good luck, and don't let me catch you trying to get out on an SP train!"

The day was warming up as we met a small gang of teenage boys who said "Hi," seeming friendly enough. Then, after they'd gotten a hundred feet past us, turned and let go a volley of rocks plus a mouthful of words that sounded like, "Dirty Bum" and "No-good, worthless tramps!" and stuff like that.

We kept on a-plodding. Luther took it all good-naturedly, totally unaffected by these annoyances, so disarming and determined to enjoy himself, no matter what. In addition to spouting gems of history, he'd mention gardening, raising roses — how long and lush the Calif. growing season was compared to where he lived, in Madison, Wisconsin.

All quiet in the BN yard this time of day. We set up in a shady spot and began the long wait. For how long, neither of us knew. I checked out the area, noting a large factory-looking building, surrounded by cars in a huge lot, about a quarter of a mile down the road. It had a sign, too, but I couldn't read what it said. Later that afternoon, I took a stroll down the blacktop road and as I got closer to the building I saw it was a large store of some kind — then, of all things I recognized the name "WALMART"!

What do you know? How lucky can a guy get? I'd seen these stores all over the South, but couldn't get over seeing one here in pokey little K Falls! Inside you could buy anything from building supplies, to gardening shrubs, to clothes, auto parts, just anything a person could ask for — and best of all, a whole department of snacks, groceries, and even a small restaurant.

I thought, "Now why did Rodger make a big point of warning us that there was nothing around within walking distance — when, all the time, here was this giant Walmart complex in plain sight of the yard?" Could it be that he really wasn't aware? Doubtful, as he also patrolled THIS yard, for the BN. He couldn't help but notice the size of the place — plus the fact that it was brand new, and everyone in town would have heard about it! What sort of a bill of goods was he trying to sell us? And why?

I loaded up on some fruits, peanuts and trail mix, and headed back to where Luther the Jet was waiting. Spotting a green BN pickup pulling up in front of the office, I hustled on over, bracing the driver with "Howdy!" my friendliest smile and most courteous manner. "Maybe you could tell me about what time the Northbound will be leaving out of here tonight?" He didn't return my greeting; just looked somberly at me for a long ten seconds. He acted like he was sore at me.

Then, slamming the door, "I wouldn't know!" he disappeared into the office. Interview over.

I retreated, licking my wounds. I don't take rejection very well. Guess you can't expect to win 'em all. Maybe he'd had a bad day, you can never tell.

It was Luther's turn to make the Walmart run and here he came, loaded down with goodies. What a find! Too bad ALL train yards didn't have a store like this.

We laid around the weeds all afternoon, making up more rail history talk. No action yet in the yards, so I took a walk down to the overpass about a half a mile, to the other end. Like always, there was a jungle under the bridge, the concrete all blackened by years of hobo fires. I came upon two guys sitting on five-gallon gunboats, one of them was reading out loud — looked to be a letter of some sort.

I gave them ample warning of my approach, "Howdy! How you guys doin'?" The conversation stopped, they looked up. "Okay, how are you?" I said I was fine, and asked if they knew when the North-bound was supposed to leave.

The answer came immediately and authoritatively, "Midnight . . . but could be later. All depends on when the Man from Beiber gets in."

I thanked them and left. I thought, "So these were probably some of those 'Weird' characters Rodger had warned us about!" It was always the same; if you wanted a straight story, ask a hobo, and never — but never, ask any supervisory personnel, white hat, or anyone wearing a tie!

There was a string of empty boxcars waiting to be picked up when the Beiber train would arrive, so, weary and happy, Luther and I found the cleanest one and piled in, drifting off to sleep in short order.

Must have been midnight when we were jolted awake by some loud talk. We could see a couple of figures standing, peering into our car. I could tell right away, the loud-voiced guy was a Southerner.

"Hello in there. Is this the train to Pasco?"
I did the talking, "Yes."

"How many of you-all are in this here car?"

"Just the two of us."

"Are you guys F.T.R.A.?" (Freight Train Riders of America – a youth- oriented, violence-prone rail-riding group).

"No."

"Are you-all going to Pasco?"

"No, Wishram."

"How many hours it take to get there?"

"Twelve to eighteen hours."

"Would you mind if we rode up in the same car with you-all?"

"No, climb on in."   If this loud-mouth would only shut up, anything for a quiet night.

They sort of discussed it together, then drifted away, evidently choosing not to join us. That was fine too. I can't handle much talk in the night. We discovered the next day that the reason for all the precautionary questions was because he wanted to make damn sure just <u>who</u> he would be sharing a boxcar with. His "partner" was a GAL!   Sure enough. Can't be too careful!

Must have been after 2:00 am when the Beiber train picked up our cut of empties and rumbled on out of K Falls, past the Klamath Lake country and on up through the high, timbered plateau towards Bend. We slept a little, then rolled up, thinking we'd slip off for a quick cup of coffee when she stopped in Bend for a crew change.   I'd remembered that normally we would stop on the mainline anywhere from ten minutes up to an hour or more, which would give us plenty of time – but for some reason, this time the change took less than a minute and wham, we were gone again.   Damn! I could have used a quart of that stuff, too! Neither of us was into carrying all the gear required to heat water and make our own, as it was nearly always possible to jump off at a 7-11 and still get back aboard.   This time we had to eat an orange, instead, and . . . wish!

When we stopped at Madras, that gave us a chance to change over to another empty car with the door open on the <u>right</u> side — so we would be gazing out at the Deschutes River going down the canyon, instead of the rocky bank!   We walked right by another open-doored boxcar and spotted two people, still sleeping — both in the SAME sleeping bag!   One was a dark-haired girl, and the guy just had to be the loud-talking Southern boy of last night's episode!

All the way down the canyon, Luther pointed out various items of interest as the talk resumed of the rail history of this part of Oregon. He could have taught a college level class with all these neat, little-known facts. He'd point out across the river and on the far bank showing me just exactly where the old UP roadbed had been.   The rest of the time was taken up with waving to boatloads of rafters floating the Deschutes.

Luther told me the Great Northern had even made plans to run another section of their crack passenger train, "The Empire Builder," from Spokane, clear on down the route I've already mentioned, terminating in Oakland/San Francisco – but never did inaugurate it. They'd even started constructing the depots in towns along the way — including a big one at K Falls. If you'd ever studied the maps of this route, it would be plain to see that this overly-ambitious plan would have to fail. Not enough ridership potential. None of the little towns along this run were of any size, and could not be expected to develop in time to create a demand for rail passenger traffic. It was doomed. On that score, the GN sort of missed the boat. But the freight part of it did work, and is still working, as we could testify that very day.

Made it to Wishram, now just a few tracks, no longer the busy, bustling Division Point it had been, with roundhouse, beanery and crew hotel all gone. It was still a crew change, but on its last legs. Luther and I talked a while with a couple of tramps we knew, "Smilin' Sam" and "Tall Man," had a great supper at the Bar/Grill combination, the only business still operating, bedded down in the weeds, then caught a grain car down river to Vancouver the next morning. Luther the Jet headed back to Wisconsin, I left south for California.

So ended another journey, a lesson in history and an adventure with one of today's premier rail-riders. See ya down the line, Luther the Jet.

The Scanner

Choo Choo Johnson was explaining the merits of his scanner. It was a black, plastic gadget with all sorts of buttons, dials and colored lights, reminding me of a transistor radio, which it was, I guess, except that it could pick up voices but would not allow the operator to talk back.

We were having a late breakfast at the Turntable restaurant in Minturn, Colorado, following a restful night's sleep (free) at the adjoining crew hotel. We had come in the night before and were now waiting to continue on east to Pueblo. There was a train expected around noon. We were packed up and ready; just marking time till then.

I suggested, "Maybe we'd better walk back down the track and wait, in case she comes in early." I always liked to give myself plenty of time to "roll" the train as she pulled in, picking my ride in advance, so that when she finally stopped, I would know just where to head for.

"Relax, Whitey, there'll be plenty of time. We'll get advance notice of the train's approach by listening to my trusty scanner. Either the engineer will have something to ask the dispatcher, or — more likely — the dispatcher will have instructions for the engineer. Besides, there will have to be some chatter as they cut in the mid-train helpers."

I was still a little dubious of these electronic gadgets but reasoned out loud, "Yeah, I guess you're right, Choo Choo, this is all part of the wave of the future, and I'd best just learn to accept it."

"Whitey, you are right," he says, "You'd better get acquainted with these things and start carrying one yourself. Don't be so old-fashioned and close your mind to the new innovations in the industry, like so many of the old hobos do. Get with it and you'll find how useful they are. By listening to my scanner I can get a good idea of just what's happening up and down the line for several miles."

I was puzzled. "How can you tell what road is talking when you're in a yard like — say Pueblo — where there's the Rio Grande, the Santa Fe and the Burlington — all in there together?"

"Oh, that's easy." Holding the scanner closer to me, "See these six little lights? Well, each one indicates a different band or channel; the first three are this road we're on — the D&RGW. The second is Santa Fe, the third is Union Pacific and the last one is Burlington Northern. All you have to do is learn the frequencies, set them according to the lights, then, when you hear a voice, you glance down to see which light is on, and you know right away who's on the air. Simple!"

It didn't seem all that simple to me, as the only gadget I'd ever carried on the road was a knife and a P-38 for opening cans. My grasp of the workings of complicated machinery was stymied by anything beyond a pair of pliers.

My skepticism showed. "I still think we ought to finish our coffee and get out of here. It's almost noon already; we sure don't want to miss our train."

"Take it easy, Whitey, we won't miss it. We'll just stay right here where it's nice and warm, have another cup of coffee, and I'll explain some more about this marvelous instrument. When you finally see how handy they are, you'll start carrying one yourself. I'd never be without mine!"

We had heard not one peep out of this machine yet, but we kept listening. He went on.

"Suppose you hear a voice saying, 'Set 'em up when ready.' Well, that's the tower telling an engine driver to release his brakes and prepare to depart. Then he might say, 'Get ready to take the little yellow-brick road,' again, meaning for him to prepare for the highball. Then, the final transmission might be — still from the tower — 'Ten thirteen, you've got the bell!' That means Highball and away he goes."

"What if they just want to bullshit back and forth between themselves?"

"There's almost no BS between crew members, as it's strictly forbidden and voices are easily recognizable when people have worked together for years. There is what's called "chatter," which is talk between any two parties, but is not important to you at the time.

"Now, Whitey, don't get the notion that a scanner is practically fool-proof — oh no — it is an aid, nothing more, but it does give you the human dimension to railroading as you hear real people doing their daily jobs (to provide us hobos with transportation), and, I will admit a scanner is more useful to trackside rail photographers than to hobos. But there are times when it has made the difference in catching the first train out — or waiting for hours for another. I repeat — I'd never be without mine!"

Did he love his scanner, or WHAT? I mentioned that I still felt unconvinced; it was just one more weighty thing to pack around. I agreed with Peace Pilgrim's saying, "EVERY OUNCE COUNTS." Besides, they cost several hundred dollars and required fresh batteries at every turn. I shook my head.

"Choo Choo, I'm not sure I'm ready for a scanner. Seems the older I get, the more I want to lighten up — not pack heavier."

Disappointment showed on my partner's face; he was the kind of guy who loved new things, new gadgets, and was always trying out stuff on the road such as heat blankets, alarm wrist watches, and gadgets to sit on while riding the cars. He always carried a camera — a real good one; a tripod (small, collapsible type); assorted maps, bulletins and mags such as "CTC Board." Oh, Choo Choo was well organized all right; I'd never met a better photographer or map-reader. He was also deep into planning and organizing and had our trips all worked out in advance like a travel agent: Day one! Day two! And so on — just where we should be and what we would do!

I was more of a winger, a seat-of-the-pants traveler, taking each day and each situation as it came. Together we made a good team. We resembled Mutt and Jeff — me short and slight — Choo Choo tall and thin! Yeah, Mutt and Jeff!

Choo Choo bored in on me even harder. "Whitey, just trust me on this scanner thing, and I guarantee you that before this trip is over, you'll be a believer . . . and you'll be taking one along yourself and just loving it . . . ."

He stopped in mid-word; we both froze; we stared at each other in disbelief! No doubt — we'd heard a train whistle — loud — up close! How could it be? How could a train slip up on us without our hearing a word – nothing – from the infallible telltale scanner?

We tore madly out of the restaurant, hoisting our packs as we went, ran around the corner of the building (it adjoined the trackside) and stopped in wide-eyed dismay! The Eastbound (our train) was already leaving the yard, heading uphill, picking up speed for the grade ahead and — worse luck — it was all tri-frame auto racks — closed up so tight a mouse couldn't slip in.

I experienced that sinking feeling I knew so well! After waiting long and patiently, to have to stand there and watch her slide on by — letting her go! Missing our train! What a shame, out here in the mountains, you only get, at the most, two chances a day — so you hate to miss out! I looked at my buddy, he looked at me; shrugging his shoulders, like saying, "I don't know what could have gone wrong; too bad, we just weren't ready, and now we've gone and missed out!" The last cars were passing. It looked like no chance.

Then the scanner-man hollered, "Whitey, that third car — see it? The one with the open top? — yeah, it's open on the third deck. Shall we try to make it — or is it going too fast?"

"Let's nail it," I shouted, already starting to run. We ran alongside, pacing ourselves up to train speed, grabbed the rungs as our car drew alongside, then, getting a foot in the stirrup and swinging on, we scampered up to the top — over the side, and dropped down to the deck — exhausted but triumphant!

We sat there breathing hard. We'd done it! We'd taken a chance nailing her at that speed and pulled it off! Another Brownie point! Another gold star on the hobo report card! We shook hands, not saying a word, then got up and watched the town of Minturn fade away. We were off on one more rail journey.

My thoughts were interrupted by a strange sound. I recognized, instantly, it was the SCANNER — still turned on in Choo Choo's vest pocket! Voices . . . and it sounded like they were talking about us!

The helper units were apparently informing the lead unit.

"We've got a couple of riders!"

Hobo vs. Train Buff

Choo Choo Johnson told me this incident that happened in Salt Lake City a couple of years back. He was checking out the UP yards, trying to figure out how to tell the destinations of their double-stack trains without asking the rails. He was looking to catch a fast ride back to L.A. in a well. The well is that portion of the low-boy type container car (the latest innovation designed to carry two large containers, one stacked on top of the other) that is not being fully utilized. For example, if the car can accommodate a 48-foot container, but is loaded with only a 40-footer, then the four-foot unused portion at each end is extra for the hobo to ride (our assumption, not the railroad's). It's like being in a metallic swimming pool, eight-feet wide by four-feet long and four-feet high, completely out of sight of any surveillance (except from directly overhead). You can lie down, sit up or even stand to watch the scenery flash by, and flash it does, as these "stack trains" are all hotshot (high priority) jobs that simply scream down the rails at passenger train speed or better. The new wheel-truck designs give them a soft, smooth ride. They're known as the Cadillacs of the rails.

All westbound traffic on the UP leaves out on the same single track, but a few miles out, at a place called Garfield, it branches off – one heading for Oakland, the other swinging south to L.A.. As the trains are standing in Salt Lake to change crews, it's sometimes a puzzle to determine their destinations.

Choo Choo is hiking down the yard when he comes upon two hobos sitting under the freeway bridge at the south end of the yard, each taking hits off a quart of beer apiece. He asks them this very question, "How do you know which goes where?"

"Oh, that's easy," one of them says. "If she's got five units, she's bound for Oakland. If there's only four engines, she's headin' for L.A."

Still unconvinced, Choo Choo asks, "Why would they put an extra unit on the Oakland train?"

"Well, I guess they need the extra power to get 'em over Silver Zone Pass, that long grade out there, you know, about seventy miles this side of Wells."

"Oh, I see . . . . By the way, are you two heading west today?"

They nodded, sipping on their beers.

"You're not going to L.A.?"

More sips on the beers. "No, we're gonna catch the Oakland man."

"Okay, well, thanks a lot. See you later."

Choo Choo headed back to the crew-change point. A train was just pulling in — a westbound, to boot. He counted the power; five big yellow and red units. "Damn." This wasn't his train.

Then he thought of the two guys he'd just left. Hadn't they said they were waiting for the Oakland train? Thinking to do them a favor, he jogged back to where they were still relaxing in the shade, still nursing their beers.

He knew these stack trains didn't stay long — maybe five or ten minutes if that.

"Thought you guys might like to know," he said, nearly out of breath from running, "there's a hotshot pulled by five units just came in and won't be here long, so I guess it's what you've been waiting for."

They didn't seem to be very concerned.

"Thanks," one said.

"If you hurried right on up there, you could probably still catch it."

Neither of them budged. They exchanged glances, then they both raised their quart bottles showing about half full.

"We haven't finished our beer yet."

The Engineer On the A&C

Driving into Parker, Arizona, I was surprised and pleased to see a good-sized mixed freight standing on the mainline. I parked my car (yes, I was rubber-tramping it that trip) and strolled over to see what was happening. The three engines looked freshly painted with the white, green and yellow of the Arizona & California Railroad — a newly formed company that had bought part of the Santa Fe's desert trackage. This train had been known as the "Parker Local." It connected at Matthie, Arizona (near Wickenburg) with the Santa Fe's "Peavine," and at the other end at Cadiz, Calif., the Santa Fe mainline on the desert. It also served a spur, south from Rice down to Blythe and Ripley.

This was the very line Choo Choo Johnson and I had tried to ride a couple of years earlier. We'd caught out of Barstow intending to sleep out in Needles where it was warm (this was in April) and continue on to Winslow the next day. At Needles, they surprised us with one of those one-minute crew changes; I was relieving myself over the side of our grain car before getting off, but hadn't even finished when the train got under way again. Choo Choo was as surprised as I was; he didn't have his gear ready either; so, too late, we had no choice but to go back to bed, watching Needles fade into the night.

Once past Kingman the weather was cold, so we waited it out, finally arriving in Winslow the next afternoon. We chowed down at that fast-food Mexican joint right across the street from the Santa Fe depot, then my fearless companion donned his "disguise" and went over to squeeze the information out of the dispatcher as to when the "Peavine" train left.

His disguise was a Rock Island cap (this company had been out of business for years), a fanny pack, a high-quality camera around his neck and a pair of steel-rimmed glasses. Tall and lean, Choo Choo looked for all the world like a train buff who was out on a photo crusade. He always felt he should pretend he was a rail buff in order to get info from the guys in the office. That wouldn't have occurred to me, as I usually got all the facts I needed just by marching straight to the window with, "What's on the board for Phoenix?" — like I belonged there. But his way worked for him. He came out of the office with the scoop, "Nothing till tomorrow morning — early — like 6:00 am."

As it worked out, we DID get into a boxcar at 6:00, and then laid there, in the yard until <u>noon</u> before it left out. He'd found out something else, too. That very day, a deal had been consummated, whereby the Parker section was to be taken over by a new operator (later to be named the Arizona & California Railroad), but no trains would be running for a few days. That meant our proposed journey from Matthie to Parker to Cadiz was out. Too bad – we'd have to take a rain check on that run. What a strange coincidence! that this should happen on the very day we showed up for the ride!

That evening just before dark, we passed a whole herd of elk just south of Ash Fork. Choo Choo, usually alert with his trusty camera, was busy shooting something else and missed it. We got into Phoenix, at a place called Mobest Yard, around midnight. For some reason we felt we didn't want to stay, so within the hour we'd crawled into another open boxcar and were on our way north. Short stay, but typical of hobos, who would rather be constantly on the move.

We had a scare on that trip. In the back of your mind, there is always lurking the fear of getting trapped inside, should a boxcar door slide shut. From the inside these doors are close to impossible to re-open, as the doors themselves, and especially the tracks, are usually bent.

We must have been extra weary that night, 'cause neither Choo Choo nor myself thought to wedge the door open — something you invariably do. In fact it's the first thing you do on entering — put a spike in the track, or a wooden wedge between the door and the wall.

I had gone to sleep as we left Glendale, thinking to myself what a lovely clear sky with stars so bright, as they usually are in the desert. A couple of hours later I woke up, glanced over to again enjoy the stars, but couldn't see a thing where the open door had been.

Then I sat up — alarmed, something was wrong! Then I knew, in a flash, what had happened; the jerking and slamming of the train's slack action had slid the door shut on us! Oh, my God!

I scrambled out of the sleeping bag, nudged Choo Choo, hollering, "Wake up, wake up, the door's closing on us!" I scampered over to see how bad the situation was and was relieved to find a small gap, maybe six inches — still left. Another good forward-motion jolt would have sealed the door completely shut. What might have happened had I failed to wake up? We gathered some short two-by-fours that we found in a corner, started prying and soon, with my partner's expertise in physics, we managed to slide the heavy door back and wedge it good.

A close call! How many stories we'd heard about tramps, imprisoned by this very happening, sometimes trapped for days before rescue by some car-knocker who happened by and heard the muffled cries and banging. It was our own fault. You just can't be too careful. We should have known better, and for sure, there's no fool like an old fool — meaning us.

So, two years later, here I am in Parker, strolling up to the units to meet the approaching engineer and "give him a line of talk." He was carrying one of these large-size plastic coolers, and was having no small amount of difficulty climbing up the stairs to the cab.

"Howdy," I said, in my cheeriest voice. "Are you getting ready to leave for Cadiz?"

He stopped, halfway up, turned to answer me . . . it was a gal! A heavy-set lady of about middle age, baseball cap, sweatshirt, jeans and white tennis shoes, smiled and said, "Yes, we'll be leaving soon."

Normally glib and articulate, this time I was tongue-tied, couldn't think of anything to say. I blurted out, "Are you the hog- . . ." I corrected myself in time and came out with, "Are you the engineer?" If I had used the term HOGGER, she might (due to her ample build) have taken exception. "Sure am." By this time she had struggled up into the cab. My attention was drawn to another – yet another — could it be?

Yes it was — a second lady appeared on the scene and was also getting on board. "What is this?" I thought. "Ladies' Day? Where have I been? Is this now, the NORM?"

The pair of women paid me no attention and went about their job of readying the locomotive, like they'd been doing it all their lives. I'd noticed the second girl was a younger version, could have been her daughter, almost a carbon copy of the Engineer-gal, so I supposed she had to be the Conductor-Brake-person, if this was a two-person crew.

I stood there like a dummy till they pulled out of town. I got back into my vehicle, sitting there a long time, reflecting on what I'd just seen. I felt disappointed, somehow; depressed, but not knowing why.

I felt let-down . . . betrayed — seething with resentment. But why? This was totally unexpected, and not like me at all. Did I object to seeing two females in charge of a long freight train, and handling it with skill? What was the matter? Was it my age, preventing me from accepting the new wave of rail personnel? Was I being threatened? Had my attitudes crystallized to the point of unthinking, stubborn resistance to change?

I realized, ruefully, that my concept of engineer and fireman was woefully over-romanticized by a lifetime of story and song (songs were my very life!) of "The Brave Engineer — with his Sweetheart so Dear," Casey Jones, Wreck of the Old 97, Wreck of the Old Number 9, etc., as it invariably went in the lexicon of railroad songs. I was about two generations behind the times! I'd read about the railroads' hiring of females in recent years, but had seldom seen any.

Then it dawned on me; two on one train! How could that be? The answer was pretty obvious; whoever it was who had bought out this marginally profitable branch line from the Santa Fe, had set his wife and daughter up with a job running his engines. Or maybe a couple of sisters. No matter, he had a perfect right to hire whomever he chose. These girls were obviously competent — so why the big deal? Didn't women drive cars and trucks like champs? It had to be a combination of envy and jealousy on my part. Hadn't I always secretly dreamed of working on the trains, myself? Yeah . . . that was it. The workplace was different now, might as well grin and accept it; after all, these gals were to be commended for having the guts to tackle their jobs. God Bless 'Em.

I brightened up, started my truck, and headed down the desert, remembering what an old brakeman on the Great Northern had told me one time when I mentioned my wanting to be a brakeman, too. "Look, Mister, you might think that; but you're way better off hobo-ing like you're doing now — you get to travel around, all over, see new sights and try out all the roads — always something new ahead. Now us — we got to run up and down the same old hundred miles of track, and believe me, buddy, it sure gets old!"

How right he was, I thought; as I cruised along, it came to me just how lucky I'd been, not to have gotten hired at those railroad jobs I'd tried to get, years before.

"Besides," I said, right out loud, "Who'd want to be an engineer, anyway?"

All In the Name of Adventure

All the articles in the papers for months about the Milwaukee Road going bankrupt and wanting to abandon all tracks west of Miles City, Montana, stirred me into action. Wasn't this the very railroad on which I'd taken my very first train ride?

At age 12 a friend and I boarded the Olympian, the Milwaukee's crack passenger train, at the old Union station in Seattle one summer evening, and rode her clear across the state to Spokane, returning the next night. It was an eye-opening thrill for me and I was hooked on trains forevermore. My buddy's father was a signal inspector for the Milwaukee, thereby rating a permanent pass for family travel. He sneaked the pass, made the kid's perennial excuse to his parents of staying the weekend at my house, while I used the same ploy, claiming to stay at HIS house. It worked. We got away with it on the train with me posing as his little brother. I recall the conductor eyeing us both rather dubiously but saying nothing. We snuggled down for the night in the luxury coach, giggling delightedly and congratulating ourselves on our audacity.

That was the start of a life-long love affair with trains. Since that time I have ridden most of the major lines in the USA, Canada, Alaska and a few in Mexico, plus many obscure, little known roads, mostly long-gone and out of business. My enthusiasm for trains did not stop at traveling the conventional style of buying a ticket on a passenger train; oh, no, I discovered at age 13 that freight trains were even MORE fun. You could move around in the boxcars, see better the magnificent scenery of the Northwest, get on and off as you pleased, pick up helpful hints and sage advice from friendly hobos and road-kids so numerous at that time (this was in the depths of the Depression of the 30's) — and, best of all, it was free.

The Milwaukee was a most innovative company, being the first in the nation to pioneer long distance electric trains. They advertised 656 miles of electrification through mountainous Washington, Idaho and Montana — from Tacoma, Wa to Harlowton, Mt — a project of unheard-of ambition for those days, constructed around 1916 during World War I.

It was also one of the first Western railroads to inaugurate automatic switching yards, utilizing the ingenious HUMP system, where freight cars were pushed up an incline, then released on the downhill side — gravity-propelled onto any number of diverging sidetracks where the trains for various destinations were made up — and all controlled by one man in a tower.

But, for some reason the Milwaukee was never a money-maker. The Great Northern and Northern Pacific both were years ahead securing the best routes and more lucrative markets, leaving the good old

Milwaukee with whatever was left. Her passenger train, the Olympian, was the first transcontinental luxury train to be dropped — discontinued about 1969 for lack of riders.

Poor management was said to be the cause of the road's sorry showing. Instead of maintaining the roadbed and rolling stock, it was mostly left to fall apart, until, in recent years the track on the mainline through the mountains was in such dismal shape that de-railings became everyday occurrences. Even hobos considered it too dangerous to ride, and in Western jungles the word was out, "Stay off the Milwaukee." Even now, as you drive on highways paralleling their route you can still see a few mangled freight cars totaled beyond salvage lying along the right-of-way and in the bottoms of gullies, testifying as rusting evidence to train derailments.

So much for background; having always been a hopeless romantic where trains were concerned, I realized, somewhat guiltily, that I'd never beaten my way on Milwaukee freight trains, and that I'd better get to it — and DO it before they folded forever. They were still running two trains a day, just barely, in a hopeless last-ditch effort with no attempt at maintaining such a thing as a schedule.

I decided to do it. Living in Spokane at the time, I had my choice of catching out at either Othello, Wa or Avery, Idaho — the two nearest Division Points. I chose Avery.

On August 24, 1979, starting early, I hitch-hiked down through the Palouse country through Mica, Freeman, over to Plummer, Idaho, on to St. Maries and then up the St. Joe River road. Getting a series of short rides but no real phenomenal success, I pulled into Avery about 4:00 pm and all of a sudden got lucky.

There under the highway bridge and right in the station, was a familiar looking string of red-rusty boxcars hooked on behind three orange-colored Milwaukee diesel-electric units. (The original all-electric locomotives had been discarded years earlier.) She was standing still — like waiting for me to hop aboard.

I thanked the lady forest ranger who'd been kind enough to give me a lift, hoisted my pack and hustled for the yards. The dispatcher's door was open so I stuck my head in, asking, "What time is the Eastbound called for?" He smiled. "She was called two hours ago. They've tried twice already to leave but don't have enough power to start this long string on the up-grade. They're getting ready to reduce the train and try it again."

I thanked him and headed down the length of the long line of cars. I wanted to get as far back towards the caboose as I could before she took off, as trains are usually made up so they can set off the cars closest to the engines, and your chances of staying with the train and not getting side-tracked are much better at the back end. I had no time for this maneuver, as I hadn't got much more than started when, with no whistle and no warning, she began to move.

Slowly, very slowly, then gradually picking up speed, with no time to pick a ride I decided, "Hey, Whitey, if you're going, you better get on." There was one open-doored boxcar towards which I made a fast move; throwing my pack in first, then grabbing the metal door hasp with both hands. I ran along the train, keeping up with its speed, then with a jump, kicking upwards with both feet and simultaneously heaving all my weight forward, I swung up and onto the door platform, rolling myself inside the car, heaving a thankful sigh. This boarding on the fly is always a ticklish and often dangerous maneuver. I was pleased to see the inside of the car was fairly clean and noted with approval a pile of sheets of pasteboard at one end, which had been used to pack merchandise, which, for the hobo, made real fine bedding to spread out a sleeping bag on. I'd heard many times of riders, caught on non-stop fast freights going over the mountains in winter, rolling themselves up in this cardboard to keep from freezing.

I stood by the edge of the doorway, keeping pretty well out of sight as we rolled out of Avery and on up to St. Joe. The weather had changed from a bright sunny day to a cold, bone-chilling drizzle as the long drag toiled slowly through the Bitter-Root Mountains at about fifteen miles per hour towards St. Paul Pass. At the first horseshoe curve I looked back, noticing three helper engines about seventy-five cars back. Never could see the caboose — we were too long.

I'd noticed back in Avery that the Old Beanery Restaurant, right there by the station, was gone — burned down. The hotel was gone, too. It was easy seen that the once-bustling little division town was tottering on its last legs, the rip-tracks all pulled up, the round-house torn down. If the threatened closure came about the town would crumble, too. No question — with the Milwaukee gone there would be nothing left but the US Forest Service camp and a few gypo loggers. It would mean the end of an era.

As the train labored creaking and groaning over the dilapidated roadbed I stared out the open boxcar, unmindful of the rain, lost in thought, with memory evoking visions of other, similar peaceful jaunts by train and of how I loved it so. The sense of security, of being all alone and glad of it; the sense of prideful accomplishment that comes with the feeling of having done it — you'd beaten the system; you were carrying on an ancient and longstanding tradition fabled in story and song, of riding the rails, bumming a railroad train, "ridin' free on the Milwaukee!" as the songs go. Once more it hit me so strong of just what a marvelous way this was to travel – especially through the mountains with forest on either side, untouched, pristine, unsullied by billboards, road signs or the usual clutter found along any highway, and, oh, so peaceful! It's like going through a tunnel of trees, so primitive and clean. Oh yes, they had to clear the right-of-way when they first built the road, sure; but since then no activity except the passing of the trains, allowing the woods to close in again.

I noticed an occasional deer watching us out of sight, not panicking, just watching, seemingly unafraid. Yes, no doubt, this is the way to see America — unspoiled, the way it looked one hundred years ago; so superior to traveling by auto, bus or air where you see nothing.

I was glad I came. The tensions dropped away. I felt relaxed. From Avery, Idaho to Haugen, Montana, where you drop down out of the mountains, the scenery is breathtaking. Not a sign of human habitation, not a farm, not a town, not even a road do you cross all the way through the Bitter-Roots. This has got to be one of the least known and yet the prettiest train trips in the country.

The rain stopped as night came on. I settled down in the doorway, sitting on my pack, munching apples and plums, quietly content. At Haugen the helper engines were taken off, and after a fifteen minute pause the train continued on, this time picking up speed. We were now on the flats following the Clark Fork River. As we got up to 30 miles an hour or so, this car I was in began to sway rhythmically from side to side, gradually increasing the arc of roll until it seemed she would surely leave the rails. I was alarmed, thinking back on what everyone had said about derailments. I pondered the idea of jumping off but quickly decided against it — as plunging off into the darkness at this speed would be at least as foolhardy and possibly suicidal.

I gradually calmed down, laid out my sleeping bag, took off my boots and crawled in, hoping to relax. Thinking back on innumerable train rides, I could recall nothing as dangerous as this. It occurred to me that I might not survive the night. I silently vowed to leave her at the very first stop.

The motion of the train and the constant noise of the wheels however lulled me to sleep, as it always has (like a baby rocked in a cradle). I sleep calmly and peacefully as long as the train is rolling, but usually wake up instantly when she stops. This time I didn't.

Sometime in the middle of the night I was awakened by voices, men's voices, talking loud, arguing and cursing. Instantly awake and alert, I listened intently. I detected footsteps on the ballast along the tracks; sure enough, the voices were getting louder; they were headed my way! In a flash I realized my predicament; I'd been side-tracked, the train had gone off and left me (I had sure enough picked a car too far forward) and here I was, all alone, unarmed, in a car with only one door open (another mistake).

I was caught like a rat in a trap — all too conscious of my vulnerability. Weighing only 145 pounds, with good quality traveling gear and money in my pocket, stuck way out in some remote siding, beyond earshot of any help — in the middle of a pitch-black night. What could I do?

Desperately, quickly, almost automatically I groped frantically about in the dark, feeling for the sheets of pasteboard, pulling them over me, covering up my pack, my sleeping bag, all my gear — then huddling trembling, scared — and, oh, so sorry I came, just hoping and praying.

The footsteps stopped. Between the sheets of cardboard I saw the rays of a flashlight probing the darkness. There was silence except for my heart beating like mad; I even tried to stop breathing. Then low-pitched voices; whispered, hurried conversation; the moment of truth had arrived! Would they climb in and have a look around? If so, I was done for. It seemed like hours and was probably only a few seconds as I lay there, my thoughts flashing back to visions of my own snug house, with a wife waiting and all the safety and security connected with the word "home." Were these men a couple of switchmen or brakemen or car knockers out there just doing their job? Or were they, as was much more likely, a couple of streamlined jack-rollers looking for a pigeon to beat up and rob? This . . . I will never know.

To my intense relief the voices and the footsteps trailed off in the distance, leaving me weak and trembling and still afraid of making a sound. I must have laid there five full minutes before I dared to move. I crawled out of the jumble of pasteboard blankets and laced on my boots — realizing yet another mistake! In my stocking feet I would have been unable to make a run for it over the sharp ballast.

What a fool I had been! So many kids' blunders — and me, supposed to be an old-timer and experienced in the ways of the road. I shivered at my close call and offered up a silent prayer to whatever guiding force there is that protects little children and fools like me!

I rolled up my gear, slipped silently to the ground, half walking, half running up the track, headed for some lights glowing faintly in the distance. It was just beginning to get light.

Getting closer I began to recognize my surroundings; I was in Missoula, in the Milwaukee Yards along the Clark Fork River. A half-hour's walk put me into the 4B's all night restaurant where I gulped black coffee. Never had it tasted better. My hand I noticed was trembling as I raised my cup; my mind dwelling humbly, thankfully, almost unbelievably on my escape. I felt DELIVERANCE!

All this in the space of a single day. I had survived intact in body and in pocketbook. I shuddered at the things I do . . . all in the name of adventure.

If You're a Company Spy . . .

The original office of the McCloud River Railroad in McCloud, Calif., had burned down since I'd been there, so I had to ask where the new one was. I walked upstairs and asked to see the "man in charge."

A youngish, smiling-faced man came out of the inner office. "How can I help you?"

"Good morning! I'm with a group of rail buffs visiting the Dunsmuir Railroad Days celebration and we heard about your railroad. We wondered if you were still in business, and if you still ran trains."

"Oh sure, this road's been around quite a long time, and yes, we sure do run trains." He spoke enthusiastically — even proudly.

"Where exactly do your trains go?" (Like I didn't know.)

"We have service from here to Mt. Shasta, where we hook up with the SP, and in the other direction, we run east as far as Lookout, where we connect with the Burlington Northern. Oh yes, there's also a spur off that line that runs down south to a town called Burney. We haul ore and minerals from there."

"Well, that's interesting. How often do you go to Lookout?" (Where I wanted to go.)

"Just a sec, I'll find out." He dialed a number, spoke a few words, set the phone down. "We've got a train leaving for Lookout at noon today." He smiled. "You're welcome to take pictures!" He seemed pleased to be of service.

"That's great, you've been very helpful." I thanked him and left. I had about two hours to make my train.

McCloud was originally a company town with company stores, company-houses (all alike, so many peas in a pod), company bank, schools and all, sitting in the middle of a vast wilderness of trees.

Lumber was the thing. McCloud River Lumber Co. was a giant in its day, but now long since defunct. The town was still there and apparently doin' okay. Pretty place, nestling at the southern edge of the base of majestic fourteen thousand foot Mount Shasta, snow-capped the entire year. It was a land of pine and fir timber, clean air, sparkling streams, lots of wildlife and a fisherman's paradise. The McCloud River Railroad's logo, painted on the sides of all its cars, was the figure of a big old bear holding a fish in its mouth. I always liked to see it and thought of what a neat logo they'd chosen.

A half-hour's walk put me at the tiny little yard. I poked around, spotting a couple of small diesel units marked "Alaska Railroad." So I guess they buy equipment, used, wherever they can. There was a cut of loaded lumber cars on a siding, but no caboose and no power.

I found me a shady jungle, stretched out and prepared to wait. I figured this was to be my train.

Presently I heard the sound of a diesel cranking up. Checking my watch, I found it was exactly 12:00 noon, straight up. Great, the crew is on duty. Time to go.

I'd already picked the best car to ride, a bulkhead flat with a level load of wrapped boards. I crawled up, took a position well to the back and laid back down.

Someone had seen me. The two units of power came out of the roundhouse, backed down on the twenty car string; then along came a rail, stopped at my car and hollered up, "You gonna be all right up there?" a note of concern in his voice.

"Yes, I'll be just fine."

"Where are you going?"

"Lookout."

"Well, okay, but be careful, and hang on."

We moved ahead a ways, then backed down and picked up the caboose, then started our eighty mile trek, perfectly level all the way, through a clean, green, picture-perfect forest land, with Mount Shasta towering above us on our way to Lookout at about twenty miles an hour.

What a beautiful ride, me sitting way up high with a 360 degree vista of this breath-taking panorama — the sort of thing tourists on an excursion train would pay big bucks to see. I could hardly get over my good luck, the timing was perfect, the scenery spectacular; I felt happy and excited, like a little kid. That's what I was, a kid again! Could there be anything in this world so satisfying, so thrilling, so much fun — than a ride on a freight train through the woods on a warm summer day? Like the TEXAS MADMAN says, "If this is a disease, I sure don't want to get better!"

I broke out my oranges for lunch, sipped some water and feasted my eyes on the view. We passed a little ghost-town, the faded sign read "Hamburg." We crossed one blacktop road, saw no towns, no people and finally, about 4:00 in the afternoon chugged into Lookout. Nothing there but one house, a few rusty switching tracks, and the mainline of the BN. It was going to be a meet with a BN train, I found out afterwards. We had gotten there first.

I climbed down, found a shady place to rest and waited around while the crew began shuffling cars. Pretty soon the southbound BN arrived. The McCloud River and BN were going to exchange trains.

I decided to return to McCloud and asked a brakie would they mind? He said he didn't care. When the switching was finished the same man who'd asked me if I'd be all right climbed down from the engine, came over to where I was sitting, looked me over real close. He didn't beat around the bush.

"If you're a company spy . . . you'll tell us, won't you?"

I looked at him in disbelief. "A company spy? Where would he get that notion?"

"I guess you don't see many riders, huh?"

"None."

"No, I'm not a company spy. I'm just a guy who likes to ride trains. Your line is possibly the only one left in California that I'd never been on — so I figured I'd better ride it while it's still going."

"You think our road is liable to go belly-up?"

"I hope not. I did wait too long on the Oregon, California and Eastern. Now it's out of business and I hear even the tracks are gone."

"Is that what you do — just travel around so you can ride on trains?"

"Now that I'm retired and out of circulation, yes, I do quite a bit of it in the summer months. You could say it's sort of a hobby with me."

He relaxed, seemingly satisfied that I wasn't there to make trouble. He started back for the engine, then turned. "I hear you want to ride back with us. That'll be okay, but we'll be pulling pretty much of a junk train, and it could be a rough ride. If you want, you can take the second unit, won't be anybody in there. We should make it just before mid-night." I said that would be fine.

They were about ready for the trip back, so I got into the cab, thinking of what a great fraternity they were — these railroad guys. Once more I'd been invited to ride inside.

The return trip, in the dark, was mostly uneventful. Just before pulling into the McCloud yards, a brakeman appeared and stuck his head in the door.

"We're coming in now," he shouted. "Thought you might like a wake-up call!"

Pretty friendly treatment of a "company spy!"

It's Not For Everyone

At the 1st annual West Coast Hobo Gathering in Dusmuir, CA, there were a goodly number of venturesome guys and gals looking to return to their homes in Sacramento, San Francisco and L.A. Most were making the trip by freight.

Two couples had suggested to Helen that she come along. She had never been on a freight train and wasn't too sure if she should, but the others convinced her to do it, that it would be "fun" and that everyone (even gals) should ride at least one division. This trip would be from Dunsmuir to Roseville. So it was arranged, Helen to accompany the rail riders and her boyfriend to drive the van and meet her in Roseville.

I'm guessing she passed a worried and sleepless night, but having committed herself, she'd go through with it. These alive youngsters prided themselves on taking daring rides like this, with each new trip amounting to a sort of "certificate" to prove their hobo-ing ability. They were "making points."

Helen was <u>not</u> a Tom-boy, a dare-devil or even athletic-minded. Rather, she was more of a quiet, soft-spoken, sweet-natured girl, more at home in a library than a train yard. She decided to be a good sport and do it just this once. She wanted to feel that she belonged.

Now, contrary to what many people think, riding freight trains is no picnic. If you're the bold, adventurous, rugged type, with a "What the Hell" attitude and a disregard of imminent danger; if you don't care a fig what the railroad authorities think; if you're ready at all times to risk losing a limb, and insist on being a devil-may-care rail-riding hero – well, then you might probably enjoy it.

Beside being illegal, train riding gets you unbelievably dirty, plus the ride is often slam-bang and violently bone-crushing. Bathroom facilities are non-existent – especially for females. A spread out newspaper or a #10 gunboat (large tin can) in the corner of a boxcar is about all you can expect.

A girl finds herself continually at a disadvantage while hobo-ing. Most everything encountered on the road is more difficult for a woman. The reason they endure it, I think, is to please the boyfriend and not for any personal sense of accomplishment. What it comes down to is that freight hopping is a grimy, gritty, hard and dangerous way to travel and most gals do it only once. That's enough. It's not for them and they know it. I personally know of one or two staunch advocates who have ridden quite extensively – but I have yet to meet a girl who'll admit she really likes it.

At five o'clock Sunday morning our two couples plus Helen are congregated along the mainline on the banks of the Sacramento, awaiting the arrival of the daily PDROM (Portland to Roseville Mixed). The head end will stop at the Dunsmuir Yard Office for a crew change. This will require only a couple minutes, so our would-be riders will have to hump it to locate and board a rideable car. You must spot your "ride" in advance as the cars round the turn, then make a mad dash to reach it and board – before the train takes off again. This can be ticklish.

For a genteel, city-bred charmer like Helen, this becomes a terrifying prospect. Just then it all gets worse. The kids are alerted to the approaching juggernaut by the whining, screaming sound of steel wheel-flanges rubbing the rail as the train rounds a long curve on a slight downgrade.

Helen is losing her nerve. The monster-like engines roar past our little group huddled by the track, the air-brakes begin to apply, the knuckles, couplings and drawbars start to slam and bang – while all the while the flanges keep up this ear-shattering screaming sound. It's like something out of a nightmare to Helen as the one hundred twenty five car train grinds down to a stop.

The four experienced riders have spotted two grain car porches back to back. They grab their packs and head for it fast, calling to Helen to follow. It's all too much. She can't handle it. The noise, the smell of the train itself, the over-all confusion plus her initial fear – have taken their toll – leaving the poor girl a crying, sobbing, near-hysterical basket case. Unable to go through with it, totally humiliated, she sinks to the ground, ashen-faced, trembling uncontrollably.

It was a hurried crew change. The train is gone. One couple stayed aboard. The other guy and gal stayed behind to take care of Helen. They each take an arm and walk slowly up the hill back to camp, consoling her with kinds words.

The guy says, "Sorry it didn't work out, but don't feel bad. You gave it your best shot. There's always a next time. Now you know – this riding freight trains – it's not for everyone!"

Ride a Coal Train? You've Got to Be Kidding!

I'd hitch-hiked in from Prince George, B.C., with this man and his son from Ft. St. James, and had to wait down by the river while a long CP freight train trundled by. They were going to cross the bridge into North Kamloops so I thanked them and got off, thinking maybe I could still catch my Vancouver train – the one we waited for. No go, as she was going too fast, so I just stood by the tracks watching the caboose disappear. Can't always have everything go your way, besides I was almost at the freight station already, so maybe another one would be through soon.

I'd had some difficulty arriving in Kamloops anyway. Starting out in Prince Rupert two days before on a grain train, I'd overslept in Prince George, where I'd planned to get off, and instead had to hold her down all the way into Jasper, Alberta. I watched my chances there but could see nothing going west. Kicked around town all day checking out the prices of rooms in the private houses, as it had turned cold, even for the month of May, and I needed somewhere warm to crash. The cheapest price for a room in a private house was $39. The tourist season hadn't even started yet and here they were already gouging the tourists! A park ranger had told me about a youth hostel for $6.00, but it was located about eight miles out of town on a gravel road.

Here I was, cold and lonesome, night was soon falling, nowhere to bed down. I walked over to Elmer's Pancake House run by a friendly family of Greek people, had a delicious order of hotcakes and coffee, and, feeling better, headed back to the yards, thinking I'd tough it out in an empty and try again the next morning. My interest picked up right away as I saw the headlight of a big CN Westbound leaving town. She would pass right by. My hopes faded as she picked up speed. Too bad, I mused, for there was an empty boxcar towards the rear end. Going too fast; no way to get aboard at that speed. Then, as has happened to me so many times before, a minor miracle occurred.

The train stopped. It was like a guardian angel manipulated the situation in my favor, stopping with the empty quite close. Could I run and make it before she started up again? I tore down the embankment running my fastest, threw my pack in the open door, grabbed the hasp and swung myself in just as she lurched forward. I made myself invisible in the forward end until after passing the RCMP office by the depot, then got ready to turn in. It would be a cold night, but riding, it never seems as cold. I was hoping this ride would put me into Kamloops, or at least Blue River, so I stayed up, watching, until we came to Red Pass Junction where the CN forks off – the left turn towards Kamloops and Vancouver; the right turn going to Prince George and the Coast.

This time it held to the right. What? Back to Prince George once more? Nothing I could do about it, so I sacked out and shivered most of the way – arriving in PG about daybreak.

I walked thru town, had breakfast at the Greyhound Bus Station, the only place open, and headed for the highway south, flexing my trusty thumb for the journey ahead. It was here that the pickup truck carrying the man and his son from Ft. St. James picked me up.

Now I was in Canadian Pacific Country. Their yard office was just in back of a large shopping center and fronted by the Thompson River. I needed to replenish my water so I waited outside the crew-shack door till I saw my man. A young guy, wearing a big, bushy mustache came out, stopped and lit a smoke, eyeing me casually. He had a soft carry-all bag with him, with a brakeman's lantern showing, so I knew I could talk to him.

"Howdy," I showed him my jug. "Be okay if I get some water inside?"

"Sure, there's a cooler at the end of the hall – help yourself."

"Thanks." I got directly to the point. "Maybe you could tell me if there's something goin' out Westbound. I just missed one awhile back."

He looked me over, "Why, do you want to hop her?"

I smiled, "Yeah, I was thinkin' about it."

He walked back inside the office for a minute, then came out, checked me out once more. "There won't be anything through goin' West till after midnight." It was now about 2:00 pm.

"Okay, thanks, guess I'll just have to wait it out."

He hesitated, then said, "Unless you're willing to ride a coal train."

"A coal train?" Didn't sound too attractive . . . but at least it would be a ride. "How long before it comes through?"

"Less than an hour."

I was still skeptical. "Do you think I could ride it?"

He stamped out his cigarette. "Piece o' cake. Here's what you do.

"Walk about three blocks down this here street till you come to Dauphin Street, turn right, cross the tracks, then you'll see a couple of sheds. Wait right there until she comes in and stops. You'll be real close to where the Slaves stop."

"The Slaves?"

"Slave units. Radio controlled. Nobody in 'em. There'll be two; take your pick."

Not being used to their terminology, it had thrown me for a minute. We called the extra power "helpers" or "pushers." In Canada they're called Slaves! I gave him a great big handshake, filled my Clorox bottle and took off down the road.

Great timing, I thought. This time of year when it stays light a long time, I'd get a great look at the scenery along the Fraser Canyon. Just as my brakeman buddy had described, here came a loaded coal train with about one hundred fifty cars, with two un-manned units about two-thirds of the way back. It would be a fast crew-change so I hustled.

The first one was filthy with coal soot; the second was clean. I moved in, kept down till we'd left town, then took my seat in the lavishly upholstered engineer's seat, stretching out and relaxing, prepared for a first-class ride all the way into Port Coquitlam (Poco), a suburb of Vancouver – the ride was everything I could have asked for – and more!

She was a fast one and made no stops. I played conductor, waving to the people in the cars and along the towns, really enjoying myself. We were on the South bank of the river, while the CN held the North side. We saw some of their trains across the gorge. I waved at them.

I found out later from a rail rider named Adman that the crew in the CN units across the river will sometimes radio across to CP to alert them to the presence of an unauthorized rider (like me), and arrange with the RCMP to rendezvous at the next town where they'll stop and let the cops make their collar. But I was blissfully unaware of this, so behaved like a small kid, having a field day. It was getting dark as we approached North Bend, so I unrolled, crawled in and fell immediately asleep.

I must have been extra tired as I slept like a man drugged, not waking up once until the train started to make some bothersome short starts – then stops – then starts up again, then stops, and just kept this up until I got real irritated. "What the Hell. What's going on? Where are we?" I slid out of the sleeping bag, got to my knees.

Looking out the cab window I was momentarily blinded by hundreds of orange-colored lights. It looked like we were in some kind of industrial plant. The engines revved again as we jerked ahead a short distance and stopped again. It gradually dawned on me as to just where we were! Could it possibly be? Had I slept through all the stops?

Yes, it was all sadly true! We were at the end of the line – a coal unloading dock, and these short stops and starts were so the cars, one by one, could be scooped clean. God knows how long we'd been here.

The sky was black with a drizzle of rain falling. I rolled up my stuff, climbed down and made for the far end of the rows of lights. Then, away off to the south, across a body of water, I recognized the ferry docks at Tswawsson. Walking along I realized we were way out on a spit of land surrounded by water, with huge freight ships tied up and taking on their cargo – coal.

Finally I came to the office of this enormous coal station. There was a light burning on the second floor. I walked up, saw two men sitting at desks. They were surprised, "Where did you come from?" I told them I'd rode in on the coal train, had not intended to, but had fallen asleep and never woke up till a few minutes ago. They relaxed a bit, realizing I was not a "dangerous" person.

"Where did you come in from?"

"Kamloops."

"Were you trying to get to some certain place?"

"No, just traveling around the country . . . looking for work." I had learned years before to always let on like I was looking for a job, as most people could sympathize with that predicament.

"Well, listen Mister, you're seventeen miles from Vancouver. This here is called Delta, it's Sunday morning, raining and you're miles from a bus line. Take the wooden viaduct just across the parking lot and head east towards town. It's getting daylight now, and someone might give you a ride!"

I thanked them, shouldered my gear and took off. I hadn't gone a quarter mile before a car pulled up, I opened the door and a voice said "get in." It was the younger of the two guys I'd just spoken to.

"I can take you about three miles. That's where our property line is – then you'll be on your own." They'd evidently taken pity on me and gone out of their way to do what they could. I meet the nicest people.

Two more hours of steady plodding through the farmland and swamps, in the drizzle, along this country road, brought me to a cross-roads; I had not the slightest notion of where I was.

Lo and behold, there was a taxi cab parked there. What's this? I wondered. Looking closer, I noticed the motor was running but apparently no one inside. I wiped the mist from the glass on the driver's side and saw there was somebody laying down in the front seat, sound asleep. I tapped on the window. After a while, a figure rose up.

"Yeah?"

It was a gal. I asked, "How much would it be to take me to the nearest bus-stop?"

"Oh, a couple of bucks, I guess. This time of the morning, anyway." I told her okay. She opened the passenger's door. It was snug and cozy inside.

"Didn't really expect to find a taxi way out here in the country. This must be my lucky day."

"By the way, what are YOU doing way out here?"

I told her I had inadvertently rode a coal train clear out to the docks.

"Rode a coal train? My god, what an experience! Was it tough?"

"Piece o' cake!"

Self Portrait

1. I love to be by myself, going along at my own pace.
2. I love to read and then contemplate on what I've read.
3. I prefer an orderly existence and a lot of quiet time.
4. My real inner nature appears to be that of an introvert.
5. I can force myself to be an extrovert for a limited time.
6. I love to play the guitar – but mainly for myself.
7. I prefer the company of a good dog to that of most humans.
8. I love to travel – land and sea – but not air.
9. I am thrifty, conservative, careful and love a bargain.
10. I am usually generous with others – a Spartan to myself.
11. I dislike having to plan or to commit my future.
12. I am impulsive, daring and sometimes fool-hardy.
13. I prefer the unconventional ways of doing things.
14. I am impressed with nature and by wildlife – not man-made wonders.
15. I prefer solitude and require a broad margin of leisure for each day.
16. I care little for money – except for the freedom it will buy.
17. I have no ambition other than to be left alone in peace.
18. I love my fellow-man – at a distance.
19. I avoid loud, boisterous, rowdy people.
20. I have no desire to be a leader, or to be the boss.
21. Business and money-grubbing have grown distasteful to me.
22. I have a happy, sunny disposition.
23. My preference is to travel incognito through life, enjoying my obscurity.
24. My nature dictates that I take a back seat and remain quiet.
25. I lack the courage of my convictions, yet I am resilient, tenacious and stubborn.
26. I have always had an ability towards writing, but, until recently, have lacked the discipline and drive to tackle it.

Seven Days With the Gentle Giant

I first met Monterey Linc at the Hobo Poetry & Music Festival held at the Union Plaza Hotel in Las Vegas, Nevada in April, 1991. A tall quiet man, I was immediately taken by his warm human-ness. He was a freelance film-maker who was considering doing a PBS Special about hobos. He'd heard about the gathering from Captain Cook, who invited him down for the party.

We were attracted to each other right away. Seemed Linc had been pretty much of a gypsy most of his life, spoke several languages, had lived with the Gypsies in Spain, and what was more important, he was interested in doing a film about hobos mainly to see if he could capture and condense the philosophy, the mind-set behind the move-ment. He was interested in the WHY behind the exterior. I found he was not particularly interested in producing a film that would make money, as he was into creating a story that would capture the theme of freedom, of release, of self-reliance and independence – in other words, the spiritual essence of vagabonding, of the alternate lifestyle that hobos seemed to represent.

Being a singer of songs I recalled a tongue-in-cheek ditty that seemed to say it all – called "Acres of Clams" – very popular around Seattle. Here are the first and last verses,

> I've traveled all over this country,
> prospecting and digging for gold,
> I've tunneled, hydrauliced and cradled,
> and I have been frequently sold.
>
> No longer the slave of ambition,
> I laugh at the world and its shams,
> and think of my happy condition,
> surrounded by acres of clams.

This talented and thoughtful man had already done several short films, each one on an off-beat theme. He'd lived with the Nevada Native Indians on a reservation in western Nevada and filmed their lives and living conditions exactly as found. Not one to cover up or to make excuses, his picture came out brutally frank. The one thing that his backers objected to was the ever-present scenes of drinking and the way that alcoholism was wrecking the Indians' lives. They wanted all this cut out of his footage but Linc wouldn't budge, insisting that he photo-graphed reality – not Hollywood make-believe. The boozy theme was left in. He was looking for one thing, first and foremost – TRUTH and INTEGRITY, and if the sponsors wanted something else – then they should get another film-maker. He was a man of principle.

Linc asked me if I would consider taking him out on a freight train trip during the coming summer and film whatever happened. I told him I would, then sort of forgot about it until two months later, when I ran into him again in Dunsmuir at the West Coast Hobo Gathering, held in conjunction with Dunsmuir Railroad Days. He'd made arrangements to travel with some other hobos, but after that run – why, he'd let me know and we'd go out by ourselves. And that is what happened.

In mid-July we got together in Seattle to interview one of the legendary old-timers of the hobo fraternity, one "Fry-pan Jack," who, at age 75, was living in a skid row hotel quietly winding down a lifetime of hobo adventures. Linc wanted me to be the LIAISON, or go-between, as I knew most of these men and could ask them questions, getting them to open up and talk about their lives while he handled all the camcorder work and deftly steered the conversation in the direction he wanted.

Such as, "How did you get started on the road?" "What sort of background did you some from?" or, "Have you ever had occasion to regret your life as a hobo?" The main thing was to get him to talk and let it roll. Instead of it being just a question and answer-type interview, Linc wanted the man's experiences said in his own words. Our first attempt was a disaster – Linc discovered that extraneous background noise (car tires) drowned out nearly all Fry-Pan's talk.

These old hobos are a pretty independent sort and really don't like to be button-holed and forced into giving an interview, so that was where my job came in. Our next subject: Oklahoma Slim, age 78.

We tracked him down at his homemade shack in the little town of Beverly, WA, along the banks of the Columbia River. Most cooperative, bright and articulate, this old tramp was a dream to work with. The three of us were together a couple of days, filming around Wenatchee WA.

By now Linc had got this thing down to something that worked every time – we filmed in out-of-the-way places like jungles (Wenatchee jungles were nationally known) and freight yards – keeping away from city and streets. One especially good scene was near the town of Quincy, WA, where Okla. Slim showed us his gravestone, already carved, worded and placed near the BN mainline so that his hobo friends could wave at his grave with a "Hi-ya Slim" as they rode by.

Slim's philosophy carved on his stone was priceless:
PLAY THE HAND THAT'S DEALT YOU. He lived by that.

Catching the trains was a problem for two reasons. Linc had promised his wife that he would not unnecessarily endanger his life by hopping a moving train (on the fly). This meant we had to always find one that was stopped. Cut down on our chances a bit, but not bad. The other thing was this huge camcorder he carried in a hand bag. He had to protect it against bumps as it was as delicate as a basket of fresh eggs.

Of course he had a large pack to carry, plus a sleeping bag; all this making an enormous load of gear, which he struggled with uncomplaining. In his late forties, Linc was an ex-athlete, a professional base-ball player and in real good shape, but he found out firsthand just how rugged this hobo life can be.

We caught out of Seattle's Balmer Yard one afternoon where he learned how difficult it was to have to balance yourself on a jerking, jolt-ing, swaying boxcar, while using both hands to manipulate the camcor-der. No mean feat. He did a great job, getting the passing scenery, plus my moves and my jabber. I'd never been around any kind of a movie before so wasn't much help at first – but I learned a lot.

We had one close call. Linc was poking the camera out the side door shooting the engines of another train approaching on the adjacent track – about six feet away. He wanted to get the action up close so he kept standing in the doorway, not hanging on to anything, just bracing his feet. Meanwhile the approaching engines came roaring by (meeting speed around ninety mph), and as the engine got abreast of our car, it produced a vacuum effect – literally sucking the air out of our car and right into the passing engine. Most all experienced rail riders are acutely aware of this and stay well clear of the doorways when this occurs. Only Linc's strong legs and natural sense of balance saved him from being drawn out – sucked right out of the car. He was white-faced and scared and realized with sickening horror just how close he'd come to ending it all right there. Around freight trains you seldom get more than one chance. Thank God, after a week out there together I was happy to be able to release him back to his family, body and pocketbook intact.

Probably the most interesting sequence of the whole filming ad-venture happened in Roseburg, OR, at the Roseburg Rescue Mission. He wanted this scene included in the film, as it constitutes a very real part of the hobo culture. We found it was not easy to get permission to shoot any of the mission activities – especially the Chapel Service. He'd been turned down a time or two by the Pastors in other towns, so here in Roseburg, where they gladly permitted him to come in and film, he found to his dismay that the Bo's themselves didn't feel comfortable (some of them, anyway) and told the Lady Pastor that they didn't want any TV cameras taking their picture. The objections were, "Well, I'm not too proud to be here, and I'd rather the folks back home didn't see me on TV." Quite understandable.

This was finally resolved by the Pastor telling them to turn their faces away from the camera, so Linc went blissfully ahead, catching the whole service. It turned out to be one of the best segments of the entire thirty-three hours of filming.

We wanted to rest up and get some sleep in an empty boxcar down in the Roseburg Yard, then travel north the next day. We learned from a brakeman who was hooking up some air hoses that this train would be the last for two days. We got our packs on and walked the train all the way, both sides. Nothing open. What to do? Maybe we could ride the engine? I spoke to the engineer. He was non-committal, but did volunteer that, "We're nearly out of time and might not be able to make it into Eugene." And further remarked, "If we die on the law, you guys might be stuck way out in the country." (Rail crews are not permitted to work more than twelve consecutive hours – by law.)

We smiled our willingness to take that chance. He didn't want to come right out and say that it would be okay for us to ride, but left the gate ajar. We could assume the rest.

When he climbed back up into the lead unit, Linc and I waited till his back was turned, then slipped quickly in the darkness up into the rear third engine and sat down on the floor. This way we would be protecting our man so that in the event we were discovered riding the locomotive, he could honestly say he had not seen us get on. It was the very least we could do for this decent human being. As it was we slept nearly three hours on the trip up north and <u>did</u> arrive in the Eugene Yards within the twelve hour time limit.

I was beginning to appreciate this six feet four giant of a man. Such consideration he showed me. I could see why his two children adored him. The care and concern in his heart showed on his craggy face. There was another quality that came through.

Suffering. He'd obviously had a hard life, coming from a broken home. He'd been a center-fielder for the Cincinnati Reds farm teams – AA ball and AAA affiliates, leading the league one season with twenty-nine home runs. I asked why he left baseball. "I had a bad attitude – didn't realize my own opportunity." He'd knocked around the world, lived in Germany and Spain, finally going back to school for his teaching credentials and was now teaching German, English, Humanities and Film-making at a Junior College in California. Generous to a fault, wouldn't let me spend a dime, he seemed to value my suggestions and heed my occasional advice, while introducing me to the intricacies of movie making. We became fast friends.

He was intrigued with a story I'd told him. Said he wanted to film it but that it would require "staging." Here's the story:

A salesman, driving his big car, left Dillon, Montana one summer morning, only to be stopped at a rail crossing just out of town. It was a long freight rumbling slowly by, so the man got out of his car to stretch, leaving the motor running. Then, as trains will, it stopped. An empty boxcar directly in front of his car had a rider – a hobo standing relaxed in the doorway – looking right at him. The salesman said, "Where's this train going?" The hobo replied, "I don't know, why? Does it matter?" Then they both grinned.

The salesman was fascinated by the hobo's nonchalant attitude, and kept asking him more questions – hoping the train would stay a little longer. He enjoyed the chance meeting, reveling in the bright sunshine, the cool morning air, the snow-capped mountains on all sides. It felt good to be alive. He felt something taking a hold of him, a new perspective, a new boldness. Years and years of frustration and a growing dissatisfaction with his lot in life – all bubbled to the surface in the few minutes he'd spent talking to this total stranger – this carefree vagabond – so obviously enjoying <u>his</u> life.

It all culminated in a swift moment of RESOLVE. The answer arrived. He knew suddenly what he must do. It wasn't too late, then, after all. Yes, by God, he'd do it. At that time the train gave a bump and a lurch, starting to crawl ahead. Decisively, his mind made up at last – he called up to the tramp, "Do you mind if I come along with you?" The hobo's only reply was to lean down, extending his hand and arm and give him a boost up and into the car. The story ends with the salesman leaning out the door, looking back at his car, still sitting there with door open and motor still running – the first auto in what was by now a long string of waiting-autos. The freight gathered up speed, disappearing towards the north.

This very scene was, indeed, photographed in precisely that manner on the McCloud River Railroad in Northern California. Monterey Linc, suspecting however that the story's conclusion would be so bizarre as to be unbelievable, changed the ending, so that the salesman fantasized his sudden decision and escape, so that instead of riding off into the sunset with the hobo, he returns sheepishly to his car and resumes his desultory rounds. Just a dreamer. Can't recall who the salesman was in the film, but the hobo up in the boxcar was none other than Roadhog USA, who, acting out his own personal life-story, did a creditable and believable job. The whole scene came out perfect.

So, there we were, hoofing the streets of Eugene at 4:00 am looking for an all-night café. An hour's walk brought us to one of my favorite haunts – The Mile-Post Inn – the twenty-four hour restaurants sponsored by Southern Pacific (but also open to the public), situated usually near the crew hotel. We gobbled up a great breakfast, then lit out for the departure yard.

Had a strange experience that morning. I'd been telling Linc that if you want to get the true information re train movements, your best source is nearly always a car-knocker, the dirtier and greasier the better. They are out there on their four-wheelers, checking, repairing and readying the cuts of cars that are being made up into departing trains.

So, as luck would have it, when we reached the north end, there was a carman working on what looked to be a Northbound train. I walked over and asked, "Good morning, I wonder if you could tell me which of these trains (there were several all hooked up) will be leaving out first going Northbound?"

The car-knocker straightened up and turned. It was a GAL. First female car-person I'd ever seen.

She pointed to a string farthest over – "That one's first."

I thanked her and left. We crossed over to this designated train, found an empty boxcar, crawled in, spread out our cardboard and prepared to wait. And wait. And wait. Then wait some more. After several hours, wanting to make sure, I walked to the rear to see if it had a FRED (flashing rear-end device, the caboose's replacement) blinking and ready, while Linc walked to the head end.

Sure enough. Fred was back there all right. Linc reported that there were six units (locomotives) hooked up to the head end, but no crew was around, and the engines were not idling.

Something was not quite right. It just didn't add up. Why were six units ready to pull a seventy-car train made up mostly of empties? And, if what the gal car-person had told us was correct (and car-knockers don't lie), how come no crew and no activity around this train?

It was a strange situation but we hung with it till late afternoon (we'd been in a go-nowhere boxcar for seven hours), then we had a visitor. With no warning, we hadn't heard a car drive by, a small, older man comes climbing through the couplings and greets us, "Hello. What you boys doing in there?"

No uniform, no suit, just a plain shirt and pants, but on his hip a holstered gun. Sure was. The MAN. The Bull. He kept up a slow-talking, quiet conversation as he recorded our ID's, then asked us why we'd chosen this particular train. The protocol is that you never rat on any railroad employee, so we just told him that this one looked good to us. He said, "Now, both of you get on over to that road over there. I go off shift at six, so don't let me see you in this yard again. That's all."

The Bull took off. Linc said, "Why did he tell us what time he quit work?" I told him, "That was his way of being nice. What he just told us was to keep out if his sight till he'd gone home – then, after that, if we wanted, we could return back into the yard and find a train."

We laid in the weeds a couple of hours, then walked up to the herder's shack to again try to ascertain the next Northbound departure. The herder (man responsible for switching cars in certain order), a tall, gangling, youngish man told us track 6 around midnight. When we told him we'd spent nearly 10 hours waiting on track 2 – he looked stunned. He wondered why anyone would have given us that information, "Hells bells, man, that's a bad order track, cars in need of repair – that bunch of empties with the six engines – that's been sitting on that track nearly a month, now. It's not going anywhere."

Now it was my turn to feel stunned. I told Linc "That's the first time I've ever been lied to by a car-knocker." I got to thinking maybe she didn't lie. Could be she was new on the job and told me the wrong story. In any case, we waited a whole day for nothing. Next time, the wise thing to do would be to get a second or third opinion.

We pulled into Portland next morning, had breakfast at E.C.'s Hide-away, did a little filming around the depot, then shook hands and split; Linc for the Portland Air Terminal – me to the Vancouver Yards. It had been a memorable seven days with the Gentle Giant.

El Paso Kid Mystery

It's been 1991 since the disappearance of the El Paso Kid. This well-known, well-respected and well-liked man was a professional, year-round hobo who'd been elected King of the Hobos for 1989 in Britt, Iowa, had lots of friends and was a staunch attendee at most all hobo gatherings. Then, following an altercation one night at Britt in August, 1991, he just walked out with no good-byes and was swallowed up in the anonymity of hobo-dom. No one has seen or heard from him since. You might think it would be easy to disappear, but it's not. The way the hobo family moves around the nation, keeping in fairly close touch with one another, and all the places they visit, someone, surely, would chance onto the Kid sooner or later.

My first meeting with him was in L.A. at the closing of the Hobo Club. As King, he was expected to say a few words, and say he did. He got up and spoke on a variety of issues with an assurance and conviction that was surprising. He sounded like a labor leader castigating his membership. His tone was scolding, delivery bombastic and his wit scathing. Yes, the El Paso Kid had plenty to say. I was glad he wasn't mad at me!

The following June he shows up at Roadhog's for Dunsmuir Railroad Days, carrying a small canvas pack and, of all things, wearing shorts! Now that's something unusual for a hobo! I got to liking him a lot. He was unquestionably the real thing, and, as with most of the old timers, a real handy guy around a camp; good with fires, cooking and making do with very little. I suspected he'd had a tough life and maybe a hard boyhood.

A few weeks later I found myself in the SP yards in Bakersfield early one morning. A piggyback train was in. I spotted the Bull's blazer. Sure enough he was carding a Mexican he'd probably just rousted off the train. I walked harmlessly by, looking neither right nor left, and continued up the track.

I could see someone standing, looked like a rider, as he was geared up, but, as I was squinting directly into the sun, I couldn't tell for sure who it might be. Then, getting closer, I noticed a strange thing; he was wearing shorts! Wow, I thought, that's the second time this summer I've seen a 'Bo with shorts on. What's happening, anyway, is this the way things are going?

It was a hot summer morning in August, to be sure, but still, this was unusual. I walked up on him just as he stepped toward me with his mitt stuck out.

"Hello, Whitey, how ya been?" Sure enough, it was the El Paso Kid, larger than life.

I said, "If you're going to make the piggyback, be advised I just saw the Bull!"

He grinned, "Yeah, I was considering it, but I don't like those outside rides in the heat. A man could fry out there . . . heading north?"

"Going to Roseville, then East to Britt." I answered.

"Why not come with me? I'm taking the highline (Great Northern, now BN) to Minnie, then south."

I explained it was too late for me to go that route, as I'd already gotten a late start, giving me only one week for the whole trip.

He said, "Well, Whitey, think about it." The sun was bearing down, so we went farther down the yards to an empty boxcar, crawled in to sit in the shade.

It was noon before our Northbound drag got under way. The Kid opened up a sack, pulled out what looked like buns, and bit into one. "Found this package of McMuffins in the McDonald's dumpster this morning. They're a little dried out, but not too bad." He crunched into one. It was hard, dry and brittle like a crumbling cookie. My God, I thought! I broke out a tin-foiled package of fried chicken my wife had provided, tore off a big leg, offering it to him. "Here, this is home-cooked; my wife made it." He shook his head, "Oh, no thanks, Whitey, that's yours. You eat it." I insisted, "Go ahead, take it, I got lots more." I showed him the whole package. "Throw those stale buns out and help me with this fried chicken." He weakened, "Okay, thanks a lot, sure smells good!" He tore into that leg like a starving man and between the two of us, we killed the whole package before the train reached Fresno. He seemed to open up to me more and more. Instead of answering questions with short, terse replies, he started delivering a monologue on boxcar etiquette till I felt like I was attending a clinic on hobo lore.

"Ever noticed, Whitey," he began, "how most guys will usually go to the far corner of the car to take a leak?" I'd nod, "Uh huh." He pointed to the edge of the door. "Here's where you should piss – right down the crack of the door – where it will dry up fast and won't leave no bad smell; in the corner it will just stay there and stink and mess up the whole car.

"Another thing, you see guys standing two feet from an opened door as the train's highballing at sixty-five." He shook his head. "These guys don't realize that they can, in a second, get pitched out the door – so fast they'd never know what happened. And as far as sitting down with your legs and feet hangout over the side . . . well, that's the stupidest thing of all – that's just asking for sudden death." I agreed.

He searched in his pack, bringing out a small, metal, four-pronged tool. "I always carry one of these gimmicks; you know what it's for, don't you?"

"Yes," I said, "it's for turning on water faucets when the handle has been removed."

"I never like to ask anyone for water; I prefer to just help myself, and these petcock wrenches come in real handy."

We stood silent as the San Joaquin Valley rolled by. "Yeah, I'm getting to be just like a wild animal out here on the road, avoiding people and not wanting to ask anybody for anything. Another thing, Whitey, I never write my name or anything on the sides of cars like so many of these publicity-hungry guys do – sort of showing off where they've been and all. My idea is to stay out of sight, and never let anyone know I'm around." He was warming to his subject now – there was no shutting him up.

"A real hobo never leaves the railroad; even if he gets stuck in a town for a week, maybe – he'll wait it out, and eventually make his train. It'd never occur to him to get out on the highway and hitch-hike; no, he prefers to stay with the trains. That way, he don't have to talk to anybody or answer their silly-assed questions." I was non-committal on this one, as I'd been an incorrigible thumb-bum since age 10.

We slowed down coming into a junction. "Ya' gotta watch close here, Whitey, this is called Lathrop. The left turn takes you towards the Bay Area; we want to stay on the straight." He peered ahead. "We're all-right, she hung with the Roseville Track."

He had a tremendous knowledge and grasp of this area, pointing out things I'd never known, like, "You can always pick up large sheets of cardboard back of that shed," or, "there's a clean little creek right over there," he'd point, "I usually take a bath in it when I stop." I'd been through this way a few times myself, but I was a babe in the woods compared to this traveler.

I realized I was in the hands of an expert – a true Knight of the Road, yet the Kid was not old, I guessed him at under 50. How could a man amass this kind of varied experience and encyclopedic knowledge? The answer had to be that he'd done it! He'd been there! Of medium height, thin-faced, wiry build; his over-all appearance, his quick, sure moves, his instant appraisal of a situation, all combined to give him the general look of a bird of prey – a hawk, maybe.

As usual, our train terminated in Roseville's Antelope Yard miles from the catch-out yard at the north end. We geared up and silently started the long walk, filling our water jugs at the repair shop, then angling over to the city streets, hoping to find a convenience store open at this time of night. Roseville was one of SP's giant classification yards and repair points. Trains were dispatched out of here in five or six different directions. El Paso intended to go north, while I favored heading east through Salt Lake.

It was way past midnight when we finally bedded down under some bushes just a few feet from where the Northbound and Eastbound lines diverge. This way we could grab the first one out, no matter. We lay there quietly taking hits on our orange juice. The Kid neither smoked nor drank.

Before drifting off to sleep I asked him about his personal history, and, of course, <u>that</u> was a mistake. So many of the drifters don't like to explain their past, or account for anything, for that matter. But I gently explored, "Were you ever married?"

He shook his head. "Never in my life."

"How did you come by your moniker – are you originally from El Paso?" No reply, just a shake of his head. "Did you ever work at a trade?" I didn't give up easily.

"I went to Barber's School. Got my certificate."

"Did you work as a barber?"

"No, never did."

"What sort of work do you try for now?"

One word, "Gardening."

"Where's your home base . . . I mean where do you get your mail – El Paso?"

"Minnie."

The more I bored in, the more taciturn he became. End of conversation. We drifted off to sleep.

A diesel horn woke me up; a train was coming. El Paso was already up watching it; he looked like a Mexican in a serape standing there in the misty dawn. I saw that his sleeping gear was two army blankets stitched together at one end, leaving a hole large enough to stick his head through.

"I'm gonna catch me one of those empties, Whitey; if you're coming you better get a wiggle on." He had his blankets off and stuffed in his pack so fast, grabbed his water jug, hoisted his pack and was off – all in a matter of half a minute. I didn't even budge; knew I could never get rolled up and ready in time. I wished him well. "See you in Britt, El Paso, bet I beat you there by two days!"

I watched and marveled as he scrambled aboard effortlessly – all his moves were lithe and cat-like. I'd never met a better freight hopper.

I leisurely got my stuff together and strolled uptown looking for that first cup of black coffee. Who'd ever want to start out on a long ride at five o'clock in the morning without first having a good breakfast washed down with about three cups of the stuff? I realized I was an addict and had been hooked on coffee since age 16. A day wasn't ever going to be any good without it. It was just another of those minor dependencies we all seem to get saddled with and then can't do without. Ho hum, another day.

I was shown to my train by a helpful switchman later that morning, enjoying a premier ride over the Sierras, barreling through Reno, hiding in the hole of the grainer in Sparks, then off across the gray, elephant-eared deserts of Nevada. "Let's see, now," I mused. "By taking this more direct route through Salt Lake, Grand Junction, Pueblo, and across Kansas, then on into Kansas City, switching up North through Des Moines to Mason City – why, I can get there at least two days ahead of El Paso, and still be able to stop off at night to sleep a night or two." Sounded good. Britt was only 30 miles from Mason City. A piece of cake.

Seven days later I walked into camp in Britt to enjoy the 89th Annual National Hobo Convention. It was nine o'clock in the morning. It had taken only two hours to thumb in from Mason City. That might sound like awful slow traveling – covering thirty miles in two hours, but in Iowa that's considered damn fine! Those drivers eyeball a hitcher like he's the very first and the only one they've ever seen!

After washing up and BSing with various characters, I was enjoying a cup of coffee when a Westbound Soo grain train pulled in. I looked it over, noticing a familiar shape come hoofing it up from the rear of the train.

I squinted and waited; yep, sure was! It was him! It was the El Paso Kid!

I trotted over to shake his hand, checked my watch, it was straight up 11 o'clock. I'd beat him by . . . two hours!

Riding the Rails 1993 Style

On October 20, 1993 Roadhog USA and I left Dunsuir, CA on a Northbound SP freight train headed for Seattle. We figured we had time for one more ride before the weather got too cold. Roadhog locked up the familiar brown cabin, hugged Ruger one last time, and together we hiked down to the lower yards feeling excited and bubbly like a couple of kids. We were both at the age where we needed a companion, someone to watch our back and to help each other into a boxcar.

There were several trains already made up, so we combed the various cars for cardboard and airbags, selecting a nice clean wooden-floored boxcar, called it home and settled down to wait. Along about 2:00 pm we heard air hissing, then soon after, with a tremendous jerk, we were off. We kept out of sight till we were past the yard office. Then, standing near the open door we enjoyed the scenery, such as Mossbrae Falls, Cantara Loop and the headwaters of the Sacramento River – off again on another of those delightful rides so dear to a wanderer's heart.

Just twenty-one miles up the line at a place called Black Butte the train ground to a halt. What!? Not again?

Sure enough, we got backed down into a long siding; the power uncoupled and departed back down the mountain to Dunsmuir. Side-tracked again! As East Coast Charlie would say, "And so it goes!" We weren't too worried though, as one of the brakies had hollered that another train would be along to pick us back up later that evening.

Funny thing, I reflected, I had been side-tracked at this very spot twice before that year. Now, Black Butte is a lonely, isolated staging area nestled at the base of Mount Shasta, which was originally the place where trains were made up to go north on the Siskiyou line up to Ashland and Medford, but the SP had discontinued using that line and had it up for sale. It was now being used as a parking lot for low-priority mixed freight – overflow the tiny Dunsmuir yard could no longer handle.

So there we sat to wait it out. You do an awful lot of that on the road, waiting it out.

It had grown dark by then, so Roadhog decided to walk the mile or so down the little gravel road to South Weed to pick up some tailor-mades while I stayed in the car to watch the gear. Seems like I always had to stay behind and watch the gear.

He made the store okay and was hoofing back up the road when the darkness was broken by the lights of an overtaking car. A high-centered pickup carrying three guys passed him, went on a ways, then turned around and headed slowly back with a spotlight on, searching the shrubbery. Sensing possible danger, Roadhog scurried off the road, hiding behind a big tree. The probing spotlight poked everywhere as the Hawg layed low watching the scene. The pickup stopped.

He could hear voices inside arguing about just where that old guy could have disappeared to. Dressed in black jacket, black cap, dark jeans and black boots, the ex-King was pretty much invisible. It occurred to me a lot of younger rail-riders could take a tip from this old-timer about how to dress on the road. With dark, drab, inconspicuous clothing, it allowed you to pass through the cities, towns and railroad yards unknown, unseen and unnoticed. Just makes good sense to keep a low profile.

Roadhog waited a little while after the truck left, pondering a possible narrow escape. Who knows what the three young hot-bloods might have been up to. Who can say?

Sure enough, before midnight another train came by and picked up our string, taking us once more on our way snug in our sleeping bags and airbag mattresses, rattling along on a clear, cool night, "Riding Free on the old SP." Could anything be finer?

I slept the whole way, waking up about 5:30 am with everything quiet. Roadhog, already up, said we were in the K-Falls yards. We got rolled up, climbed stiffly down telling each other how these boxcar floors just don't seem as soft as we remembered and hit the grit for the lights of town, feeling real good and hoping to find a café open this early. We had to climb through several parked trains (something I dread to do while carrying a pack and groping around in the dark), but in about a half-hour's steady walking we arrived at the little all-night café right there by the depot, the one the rails patronize.

Stashing our gear in the corner we cleaned up a bit, then sat down to a delicious breakfast of bacon, eggs, hash browns, toast and coffee. We were ready for it. Why does train riding give you such an appetite? Why does a heavy, cholesterol-laden breakfast taste so good?

Coming out of the restaurant I could see several black locomotives waiting on #2 track, but couldn't see what they were pulling as the warehouses were in the way. She was apparently ready to go and just waiting for the highball. To me this had all the earmarks of a fast ride to the next Division. Just then a white Blazer pulled up to the freight office, and who should get out but good old "Roger the Dodger."

So the problem was; how to make that hot-shot without letting Roger see us? We had our packs strapped on, still standing by the café, when all of a sudden a miracle happened! The Northbound Coast Starlight, Amtrak's most popular train, glided into the station.

There was our answer! A golden opportunity! I said to the Hawg, "We've got about four minutes to nail our train! Let's go!"

Hustling rapidly past a warehouse then cutting across the mainline directly in front of the Amtrak head unit, we made it around the other side and down the length of the train with all the passengers staring at us from inside. Using the passenger train as a screen, we hurried past and over the adjacent track, crossing in front of the lead unit of our freight. The adrenalin was flowing, our hearts were pumping, it was a bold desperate move requiring daring energy and the gall of a burglar.

Looking up I saw the crew were already in the cab, air-tested, ready to go, awaiting the momentary departure of the Amtrak, when it would then be their turn. Stepping along the sharp ballast we hurried past all six units. Suddenly we heard the Starlight's two-toned chimed whistle as she pulled out of the station. Right on time – she'd stayed here only four minutes and now was gone – on her next leg to Eugene.

Looking briefly down the length of our train we saw it was double-stacks and single containers. We sensed we were not going to have time to walk the train looking for a rideable well. Departure was imminent. Our only chance was to grab the rear unit. It was now or never. We looked at one another and eyes locked – a wordless agreement. Roadhog nodded knowingly. It was the only way.

Without a word up the footboards we went, into the cab, down the steps and into the tiny head located in the very nose of the engine. I sat on the throne; Roadhog on the steps. We waited, not making a sound, not saying a word.

Within thirty seconds the mighty diesels roared, the generators whined to a high pitch, the throttle opened and with a tremendous surge of power we moved majestically forward. Had we been seen entering the cab? Would someone report us? Would Roger stop the train and pull us off? He was known to do just that.

We layed low for another ten minutes, grinning at each other like a pair of school kids who'd just played hookey, chortling with glee as the train picked up speed gliding along the Klamath Lake. We'd done it! We congratulated ourselves at our tremendous good fortune and audacity at having out-foxed the Bull, doing the impossible right under his nose. It was one of the most thrilling and most gratifying catch-outs either one of us had ever done.

I noticed I was trembling with relief. It was then that you recall all the people who have asked you, "Why in the world do you like to ride freight trains?"

Once in the clear we came out of hiding, taking our rightful places, settling comfortably in the big black leather seats, making sure to lean in while rounding the curves. No need to alert the crew to our presence. It was a fast, smooth trip, upgrade through the lovely pine forest to Cascade Summit, then down the mountains through the twenty-one tunnels into Springfield, and finally Eugene in just five hours. We stopped only once at Chemult to go in the hole for a Southbound stack train. Magnificent scenery, clear air, warm sunshine – everything ideal! One of those rides and one of those days you'll remember all your life!

Arriving in Eugene I figured she'd change crews on the main and continue north, but instead she took the siding and slowly moved past the arrival yard and clear on up to the departure yard before starting to back down. We left her there, very close to the place where we would be able to catch another Northbound. It had saved us about a two mile walk. Our luck was running high.

I questioned a carman on a four-wheeler who told us the first thing out going north would be leaving on track #6, so we waited around, rustled up some cardboard, found a clean boxcar and relaxed – hoping the power would be along soon.

There was a hobo resting in the shade of the highway overpass who looked interesting so I sauntered over to say hello. He was an old-timer dressed in remarkably clean-looking clothes with two big dogs on a leash. He didn't need much prompting to worm his story out of him.

Said a few days back he'd climbed off a Westbound MRL (Montana Rail Link) freight in Livingston, Montana early one morning with his two dogs and heavy pack. He was out of water. His dogs especially were thirsty.

Across from the tracks he spotted a water faucet at the corner of the office of an over-nighter trailer park. Taking his water pan and the dogs he headed for the spigot. There didn't seem to be anyone around, so, just as he was about to turn the handle, the office door opened and the manager came dashing out hollering, "Just what do you think you're doing?." At that moment a middle-aged lady rounded the corner in time to hear the hobo say, "Why, I just wanted to get a pan of water for my dogs, here, they're powerfully dry."

The manager growled, "We ain't got no water here for the likes of you, so keep moving!" The old-timer said he picked up the water pan and turned to go when the lady said, "Just a minute, Mister; I'll get you some damned water!" She had fire in her eyes as she cast a withering look at the manager, then turned, walked over to a long, shiny, aluminum trailer (one of those kind that looks like an airplane) and returned with a whole galvanized bucket full of cold water. "Give this to your dogs! Should be enough, right?"

The upshot of the story was she was driving clear to California, gave him and his dogs a lift all the way to Eugene, bought food for him and his dogs along the way and stopped at a Sears store in Portland where she outfitted him with all brand new clothes and boots. He could not get over it and kept telling this story over and over.

I fixed up two beds in the forward end of the car while the Hawg wedged a few spikes in the door-track. This time I made the run to the store for some food and grog. Satisfied, following a good meal, we layed around out of sight, relaxing and yarning about other days and other trips, wondering how our lives could possibly be any better.

This time we were late getting out. It was dark before we felt the nudge of the power coupling up, then the jerk and the jolt as this drag got slowly underway. I slept intermittently, waking from time to time, contentedly noting our steady progress and humming the familiar,

"Go to sleep you weary hobo, let the towns drift
  slowly by.
Can't you hear the steel rails humming?
  That's a hobo's lullabye."

Day Three broke cold, foggy, misty and miserable. All was quiet. It was evident we'd been side-tracked again somewhere. Looking out the door I could see nothing in the early morning fog. Roadhog, always cheerful, said, "Don't worry, Whitey, I'll get a fire going right away." He pulled a fuzee out of his pack (that he'd <u>found</u> in an empty caboose), took some of our precious cardboard and a few scraps of lumber and, true to his word, had a cozy fire going outside along the tracks in just a few minutes.

Meanwhile I walked up ahead where I discovered the Power had uncoupled and gone off and left us. Now, how much of the train had been left here? I decided to walk the length to find out. Visibility was down to just a few feet, so I started out through the fog, walking the entire train and discovering the FRED on the last car still blinking. So – the whole string was here – set-out by itself on some lonely rural siding, miles from any town.

The fog was starting to burn off, and as I retraced my steps to join Roadhog by the fire I saw a blacktop highway paralleling the track, found out later it was good old Highway 99E and this siding was called "Alford." But not a house or sign of civilization anywhere around.

By this time the big guy had a roaring fire going, so we warmed ourselves and breakfasted on stale sweet rolls, discussing our chances. Should we stay by the train and await the return of the power? What if they left this cut out here a day or more? No telling or predicting what the railroad will do.

By now a few cars were moving along the highway so we opted to try to hitch-hike. Which way? Where to? We had not a clue as to our whereabouts. Anywhere would be better than being stuck out here in the tules like this.

We gave it our best shot. Nobody stopped. They were mostly farm folks driving pickups who acted like we were the very first they'd ever seen out along a highway carrying heavy gear.

Roadhog, with his full beard and walking stick (the stick didn't help, either) looked for all the world like a big, good-natured pirate, so I really couldn't blame these people. They seemed flat out scared of us.

Anyway, no one stopped – no rides. We gave up thumbing, just turned our backs and kept up a steady pace, glad to see the fog dispersing and the sun breaking through. Ah, the sun, at last!

Along about mid-morning the Hawg hollers, "Hey, Whitey. I see a light!" Sure enough a train was approaching heading back south. At first we thought it was power sent out to retrieve our train. Instead it was a string of sealed-up boxcars pulled by two units painted green and yellow with the name "Willamette & Pacific." Neither of us had ever heard of that line. (I found out later from Choo Choo Johnson it was a new company that had taken over some of SP's branch lines in Western Oregon.).

Now, right in the middle of the consist was one, lone BN grainer, and, to our astonishment, as that hopper car came abreast of us, the train ground to a stop! It was as if that engineer had seen us, recognized us as rail-riders, knew we wanted a ride and had obligingly stopped his train with the only rideable car spotted exactly in front of us! I'm not saying that's why he stopped. In this case he probably got a red light, but I've had things happen just as amazing.

We made a run for it, crossed the highway, slopped through a muddy ditch, up a steep bank, climbed on the back porch of that grain car, and had no more then sat down on our gear, thanking our fates for our good fortune, than she jerked ahead and rolled us smoothly through the towns of Harrisburg, Junction City and finally the yards at Eugene where we piled off. We'd rode another New Railroad, had a twenty-four hour adventure and ended up right back where we'd started the day before. Welcome to life on the road!

Following a hot, tasty lunch at a place called the TURF and a two-hour nap, we found us yet another boxcar on yet another mixed freight and this time we picked a winner, holding her down all the way to Portland.

Next day we made Centralia, Washington, where Roadhog discovered a touching bit of old-time nostalgia. In the men's room of the old Northern Pacific Depot (still used to this day) he found where someone carved with a knife-point, a name and date in the marble partition. It read "A No. 1 - The Rambler - 1934." It looked authentic. Studying it while sitting on the throne, I realized that there is an invisible thread running through history tying all the hobo brothers together. The date 1934 could possibly have been A No. 1's last year on the road. I don't know. I do know that 1934 was my very first year on the road – and that my very first ride on a freight train was along this very track!

On the evening of the fifth day we arrived Seattle feeling strong, like a couple of conquering Pilgrims returning from a crusade. We made our way to the Publix Hotel where we sat in the lobby drinking thirty cent hot chocolate and swapping yarns with the legendary Fry-pan Jack, who lives there and is winding down a colorful career. At 77 he still moves around pretty good.

Listening to our stories I could tell he wished he could have been with us. You're never too old to wish. Five days, eight trains, no problems – just good clean hobo fun all the way. From such experiences are two buddies bonded for life. Roadhog USA – I salute you!

When Your Number Comes Up

I got to reminiscing about a young couple I'd met the summer of 1994 at the West Coast Hobo gathering. We were sitting in Roadhog's front yard, about thirty of us, nursing our beers and getting reacquainted, when into camp strolls a young couple, handsome and happy, introducing themselves all around. He said he was Gray Wolf and his girlfriend was called Trouble.

I shook hands, looking her over, as she was a real beauty, maybe age 22 or so, with a pretty face and a neat trim figure. "You call yourself Trouble?" I said. "Well, yes, you do look like Trouble all right. Maybe more like "Double Trouble!" She laughed, enjoying the compliment. Gray Wolf was a big, strapping, powerful built guy, maybe 25 or so. These were no first time out college kids. Oh no, they'd seen a lot of road miles by the looks of their clothes and packs. They both looked "experienced," even for their young age. They were a stand-out – a real good-looking couple.

I got a chance to know them a little as we were all together nearly four days. They said they had a tent-camp down along the Sacramento River, and each day they'd join us around the cemetery. They fit right in. Trouble had no problem keeping up with Gray Wolf, no matter what. She'd drink beer for beer right with him and roll Top Cigarettes as good as anyone. She didn't fall behind. It was easy seen they were deeply in love, absolutely inseparable.

On the fourth and last day of Railroad Days they walked into camp hurting. Gray Wolf was sick. It was something wrong with his arm and hand. We gathered around to hear his story. Something had bitten his right hand. It had started to swell and was beginning to look ugly. There were two tiny punctures about an inch apart on the heel of his hand. He didn't seem to know how it had happened, couldn't remember anything bothering him, but he was feeling weak and sick. Trouble looked worried.

Roadhog phoned the Sheriff's Department and they sent out a paramedic. This guy examined the hand and told Gray Wolf he'd better have medical attention. The nearest hospital was twenty miles north in Mount Shasta. The deputy called out on his car radio to check on the ambulance. Yes, they'd transport him but would have to charge four hundred dollars. Gray Wolf confessed he had no money and that he'd just take it easy and lay around for a day or so and that he'd be okay.

I recalled that "Dirtyface" Dan Dumont had told me the previous year that he'd seen a rattlesnake while camping up near Castle Crag. I got Roadhog to one side, asking him if there were any rattlers down by the river. "Yes, not too many, but a few. Why, Whitey, do you think he got bit by one?" I said, "Sure looks like it to me."

I sat down on the grass by Gray Wolf and Trouble. They were looking glum. I asked him, "Roll up your sleeve, let me see your arm." There was a faint, thin red line running all the way up. "Now, put your left hand under your right armpit and press down." He did. "Feel any pain?" He nodded, "Yeah, a little." He questioned me. "What do you think?" I said, "I think you've been bitten by a rattlesnake."

This guy was in pain, and lacking money, didn't know what to do. He said, "I'll be all right in a day or so. It's going to get better. I'll pull through okay."

I took hold of his shoulders, looking him straight in the eye. "Listen, don't try to tough it out, whatever you do. See some doctor and let him give you a shot. Don't try to tough it out on your own." He seemed convinced.

A hurried consultation started the wheels rolling. The Collinwood Kid, who had the only car in camp, volunteered to drive Gray Wolf and Trouble up to the hospital. Hobos take care of their own. He was treated, given some antibiotics and released. Collinwood said the doctor diagnosed the problem as spider bite! I wondered to myself how that could be?

I never saw either of these two great kids after that, as all this happened on getaway day when nearly all of the ninety or more assembled Bo's scattered to the four winds, but I heard that his hand and arm were fine from that day on.

Less than six months later I got the sad, sad story. When you hear about someone catching the westbound (dying), if they were up in years, you think maybe that's the way they would have wanted it. But when you hear about some beautiful, young girl in her early 20's meeting a violent death on a freight train, you feel stunned and hurt. Whether or not she was the victim of a freak accident or if she failed to hang on – it doesn't matter. Trouble was killed under the wheels of a freight car. It makes you shudder just to think about it.

Seems this girl with the pretty face and charming ways was riding with Gray Wolf on the back porch of a grain hopper car. Sometime in the night she crept out on the narrow, wire-mesh platform, just over the wheels to urinate. There is a single iron rod running across the rear of the platform which she possibly could have been hanging on to. It is so easy to get lulled into a sense of false security riding those trains day and night, and you take on the attitude that "Nothing can happen."

The details are sketchy and I can only conjecture what really happened, but probably she was balanced out there, in a squatting position, and possibly holding on with just one hand. It was probably that ever-present hazard – <u>slack</u> <u>action</u> – (the slingshot effect produced when the slack in the couplers and drawbars is taken up) – striking without warning and jerking that car so severely and instantaneously that her gentle handgrip was loosened. Over backwards she fell to her instant death – her young, vibrant, magical life snuffed out.

The wheel jolt was so severe that the crew in the lead unit felt it and stopped the train immediately. That's the story anyway. Collinwood Kid thinks what happened was that the wheel was raised high enough off the rail to throw the system into "emergency," which would lock all the wheels on the train.

Too late. Nothing could be done. It was over.

I felt especially sorrowful when I heard the story. I had met this beauty just a few months prior. I recall her offering her hand, smiling and saying, "It's so good to meet you!"

She obviously loved life and knew what she was doing. She wouldn't be the type to complain about the dirt and danger – the uncertainty and the insecurity of the hobo life she willingly shared with her boyfriend. She certainly knew the risks.

We all salute her memory.

Andy Ewanson - Hobo

I went up to Andy's room at the Otis Hotel in Spokane, an inside room on the third floor. He showed me a coil of heavy rope on the floor by the single window. "Know what that's for?" I shook my head, mystified. He pointed under the bed; I followed his lead. One end of the rope was tied around the entire frame of the steel bed. "In case this firetrap goes up in flames some night while sleeping," he said proudly, "all I got to do is open the window, toss the rope out and slide down to the ground!" He'd created his own fire-escape. Not a bad idea, either, knowing how quick these old wooden hotels could burn.

He was so resourceful, so adaptable, he thought of everything, as I'd found out after several trips on the road with him. Congenial, generous, not insisting on his own way, I'd enjoyed his company and knowhow. There was something a little strange about his thinking, but I overlooked that. Aren't we all a little crazy in our own way? Bit by bit his story began to emerge. Not pretty, mostly bitter, but it comes to me as an example of reasons why a middle-aged man takes to the road.

Living in one of those Chicago suburbs, Andy had worked twenty years for a meat packing company. Lived a quiet life with his wife in a little crackerbox house, a case of same-ness in suburbia. No dreams, no ambitions. One day on arriving at his job he was given a termination notice and check in full. Seems the company was cutting back. This without prior warning. Stunned and unable to think clearly, he returned home, arriving before noon, let himself quietly into the house to find . . . his wife in bed with the gardener.

This second shock left him speechless, he said, so he walked outside, not knowing what to do, unable to accept the meaning to all this. His mind refused to work, he was in a daze, so he started walking aimlessly, not knowing or caring where. "I found myself out on the highway, plodding along like a zombie. Sometimes somebody would stop and offer me a ride, but I didn't even answer them, just kept my head down and kept on a'walking. Went all day and all night, didn't care, didn't think, didn't give a damn what happened to me. After a couple of days of this, I got tired of having these cars stop and ask me if I wanted a ride, so I moved over where a railroad was, and started hiking down the tracks. At least I didn't have to talk to people." I was listening, saying nothing. I think he appreciated my interest.

"I don't know how long it was, or how many days; that's pretty much of a blur. But one day about dusk I stumbled onto a bunch of guys sitting on five-gallon cans around a fire. There was something cooking, I could smell it. Then it hit me! I hadn't had anything to eat – must have been days! I was starving hungry! These guys invited me to join them, one even loaned me his extra tin cup. I ate three servings of stew and could have scoffed more, but I felt ashamed to take more."

I interrupted, "Andy, how long ago was all this?"

"About fifteen years."

"Have you been on the road ever since?"

"Yeah, the whole time. Ya see, Whitey, these guys sort of saved my life. They brought me back to my senses. They gave me new hope, made me want to live again. If I hadn't found 'em when I did, I'd probably just kept a'going till I keeled over dead, or else stepped in front of a train. I'd thought about it. I had no more reason to live. When those two things happened the same day, I couldn't handle it. My mind got messed up. I went clear out of my head. Those tramps took me under their wing. They brought me around."

"What happened then? Did you stay with them?"

"Yes, I sort of buddied up with the oldest guy, and he let me travel with him for a while. I took to the life right from the first and picked up some of the tricks on how to keep alive without money and without working. That was the thing – people! I just couldn't stand to be around people. You know, the kind of people I'd lived with all my life. The thought of going back to a job and all that – the living in a town, and being what you might call respectable. Well, I was through with all that. I had a chip on my shoulder, a grudge against the world. I developed a hatred of authority – anybody who'd try to tell me what to do."

He stopped, looked over at me. "Whitey, you probably see me as a kind of easy-going guy, not uptight and not too worried about anything – and that's all right. That's how I am, now. But you should have known me back then. After I got over the shock, got myself together and began to start living again, I started to argue. Yeah, I'd argue with anybody over anything. Got pretty feisty, too. Wouldn't back down. If it came to a fight, believe me I was ready!"

Of medium height, Andy was built stocky and solid. I could picture him taking care of himself in a bare-knuckle skirmish. He was tough! "I got this all knocked out of me. It was mostly my own orneryness and I must have asked for it. Anyway, I really felt deep down that the world had treated me pretty shabbily and I was determined to get even. And I did get even, but sometimes I picked the wrong man. I started mouthing off at cops. That was a mistake. I had a close call."

I was listening attentively. This was a revelation to me. He'd never before mentioned any of his personal past.

"It was in a little sleepy town in Florida. I ran onto this city cop and wasn't about to take any shit off him. I was only mindin' my own business and when he got pushy I sassed him back, good. That did it.

"He got real mad, told me I was under arrest and told me to walk down the track toward his car. I told him to get fucked. That was too much. He took his foot, pushed me in the back, forcing me down the embankment; I had to run to keep my balance and when I got to the bottom I stopped and turned. There he was standing by the rails, had his gun held with both hands and aimed right at me.

"Before he could pull the trigger, a screen door slammed; a lady in an adjacent house had stepped out on the back porch to shake her dust mop. That interruption saved my life. He had his mind made up, he was going to shoot me! Instead, he holstered his gun, turned and went back to his car. I never saw him again."

I was puzzled. "Andy, why did the cop kick you and force you to run down the embankment?" Wise in the ways of the law, Andy chuckled, "Don't you get it Whitey? He was going to shoot me for TRYING TO ESCAPE!"

We were in the Havana Street Yards in Spokane one Sunday morning, hoping for a grain train to Pasco. Somehow, during the conversation over coffee (Andy would make coffee endlessly) the town of Winnemucca, Nevada came up. I knew that town well.

Andy, seemed to know it even better. "I was pickin' up aluminum cans there one day. Ya' see, Whitey, Nevada won't pay nothing for cans, but there's plenty layin' around. So I used to fill a bunch of onion sacks, as many as I could carry, and grab the Wobbly over to California. Sell 'em in Portola. They paid a fair price.

"One day a Winnemucca cop stopped to card me. I must have been on the prod and wised off at him. He stopped writing in his little book, ordered me into his car and drove me over to the town dump. I bitched to him about leaving all my gear and my cans, and that only made him madder. You won't believe what he made me do!" Andy looked at me like he DARED me to believe.

"Okay, what did he do?"

"Whitey, this guy made me take off my boots – and socks, too – then pointed across the dump. 'The railroad track out of town is right over there; now you head for it – make a beeline, right through the middle of that trash. Don't look back and don't you ever let me catch you in Winnemucca again!'

"Yes, that's what he made me do! I had to walk barefoot across five acres of garbage. It was one of those landfills, the kind they run big caterpillars over to cover up the junk. Only this wasn't covered yet! Lots of tin cans, broken glass, wire, everything you'd ever expect to see – and I had to pick my way through it. He was sitting in his patrol car watching me all the time, but I managed to slip behind a mountain of garbage and sit down. It was there I damn near stumbled over a pair of high-top tennies, all worn out, with the toes gone and about three sizes to big. But I grabbed them like they was gold, and managed to finish my walk without getting my feet cut to ribbons.

"That night I circled around to the jungle where I'd left my gear. The bedroll was still there but the cans were gone!" He looked sorrowful. I asked, "Have you ever been back to Winnemucca, Andy?"

"Been through it lots of times. But I never get off there."

Sunday was evidently a poor day for freight traffic. We waited all morning but only Eastbounds were coming through.

Andy said, "Whitey, rub your hand over the top of my head, right there." I felt with my fingers a slight raised ridge. "Yeah, that's it. Know what made that lump?" I shook my head, "What?"

"The butt of a .357 magnum, that's what!" He checked me closely. "Okay," I said. "Know where I got it? Well it was in West Colton, CA. The SP yards?" He nodded.

"It was a hot day. I crawled behind some little trees for shade. This SP Harness Bull came driving along and stopped. Said, "Don't you know you're trespassing on railroad property?" I was pissed off. I hollered back, "I'm not on railroad property, so get lost.""

"Well, I guess I still hadn't learned that the man with the gun and the badge and the radio and the car – well he's ALWAYS right! I'd shot off my mouth once more. He got out of his car, not saying a word, just a deadly serious look on his face, walked up to where I was sitting and asked for my I.D. I fished out my wallet, looked down to find my social security card, and before I could duck, this guy had pulled his big gun and brought it down full force on the top of my skull. I dropped like an anchor - out cold!"

It was hard to understand, for me, that Andy would provoke, or even fail to cooperate with any lawman, as I am docile as a puppy before any badge. But he had this lippy way and pugnacious attitude and it always ended up the same – he invariably took the brunt of the cop's wrath. Not a nice thing to contemplate.

"I don't really recall the ambulance ride or anything. I only remember waking up in the hospital in Riverside. The Doc told me he'd had to take seventeen stitches in my scalp. My head felt like it was coming off. There was a policeman in the room, guarding me. They told me I was under arrest." I asked Andy how long they held him.

"They moved me over to the County jail, I think that was in San Bernadino. And I was there three weeks. Nobody came to talk to me. Then one Monday morning, the jailer guy came around – and asked me if I wanted to be released that day? Hell yes, I wanted to get out. My head wound had pretty much healed up so I said YES!" Andy stopped, thought a minute, then, "Now here comes the screwy part, Whitey.

"This jailer brings back a piece of legal-looking paper, says "Just sign this paper and you're free to go." I read it real careful.

It was a CONFESSION. It read that on a certain day I deliberately sneaked up on a certain Special Agent, while his back was turned and attempted to strike him with a club. That this certain officer, sensing my approach, whirled around to protect himself and in his desperate attempt to save his own life, inadvertently struck his assailant with his gun butt. That I admit my own indiscretion, that it was all my own fault and that I will never do it again. Signed, Andrew Ewanson."

I looked at him in disbelief! "What did you do, then?"

"What could I do?" He challenged me with his eyes.

"I signed it and split."

I Met This Guy On the Empire Builder

I'd spotted this fellow for a Canadian. It's their clothes, or how they wear them that's just a tad different. You don't have to wait to hear them talk, and how everyone knows they say "aboot" and "aaeey." You can just sort of tell right off.

As we pulled out of Whitefish, MT, he was just behind me in the lounge car. We chatted for a few minutes, then, when the announcement for first call for breakfast came over the speaker, he got up and asked me to join him.

"Thanks, but I'm not having breakfast this morning."

He returned later, sat down next to me, introducing himself as Cal. Said he was a landscape gardener, lived in Vancouver and was going to Nashville to visit his brother.

"My brother took out American citizenship after the war. He's been working as a rhythm guitar player, you know, country western stuff. He hangs around Nashville, tries to write songs himself. I haven't seen him in years. It should be a good re-union." He lit up a cigarette, offered me one.

"No thanks, I don't smoke anymore." I told him I played guitar and tried to write songs, so we batted this around till noon, enjoying each other's company. Then the first call for lunch was announced.

Cal said, "Gee, I'm really hungry. It must be the train travel. Either that or all that delightful scenery coming through Glacier Park. Would you join me?"

"No thank you, I just don't feel hungry. You go ahead." He eyed me strangely, but said nothing.

Now, how do you tell a total stranger that you are not eating? And that the reason you are not eating is because you are FASTING? Fasting is a most misunderstood word, and it's been my experience that it's best if you don't even mention it. Young people, on hearing it, seem to be open and interested to learn the how and why, but most older or mature-aged people seem to be against it – without knowing why. It just doesn't seem quite right to them. Like you are doing something harmful or wrong, and that you had better not fool with it. So I had learned to keep it to myself. On past fasting trips I had tried to explain to people just what I was doing, but it turned out dismally every time, as it was plain to see folks couldn't understand why anyone would want to do a foolish thing like that! And didn't want to hear about it. They'd write you off as a freak and you could feel the REJECTION in their attitude.

Cal kept away all afternoon, but about (aboooot) four o'clock he stopped to invite me for a cocktail. Again I thanked him, but declined. He didn't argue, just went his way.

I'd been doing this for years now. January a lousy month to hobo, I'd go traveling anyway by passenger train. Ridership was usually down and lots of seats were available in coach. I'd ride on a thirty-day U.S.A. RAIL PASS for $255 and tour the country night and day, off one train and onto another until my month was up.

This was a great opportunity for undergoing a fast. I did it for weight loss – that is, it was the only way I'd ever found for eliminating the paunch. But the main reason was for discipline – to see how far I could go in a Spartan attempt at renewal of mind and body. I'd always shoot for the classic period – thirty days. Never once did make it, but I came close one year with twenty-seven days. My average was around eighteen days. This is no easy matter, but is well worth the effort. You come out of it with a triumphant attitude like a marching Pilgrim return-ing from a search for the Holy Grail! Fasting is the sole remedy em-ployed by all animals in the wild – and is used for any and all their ills. I looked forward every January to my fasting trip.

Now the first three days are the worst, as that is the time you are most hungry. After the third day your body shifts gears – changes from assimilating the food you eat to using up the body itself. At this time you lose all appetite, and keeping your physical activities to a minimum, you just hang in and wait it out.

This was where Cal came in. As you might expect, he once more invited me to have dinner with him. Once more I refused, thanking him.

He asked, "You sure don't eat much do you?"

"No, not this trip. I'm just not hungry, I guess."

There was that evasion again. Should I confide in him and ex-plain myself? I knew better.

Later that evening, seeing me again watching the scenery slide by in the dome car, he suggested, true to form, we have a nightcap together. No go. He avoided me like I had leprosy all the next day. On our arrival in Chicago I lost track of him. I had to walk the Loop for an hour or so before boarding the FLORIDIAN for Miami, which left out about midnight. I curled up in a seat in the dome car and slept till morning.

We were approaching Louisville at about 6:00 am when my dozing was interrupted by voices; two men sat just back of me and were evidently unaware of me there. I recognized a familiar voice. It was Cal.

"Yes, I'm like you, I love this train travel. But you sure meet some really weird people!"

"How do you mean?" It was the second person speaking.

"Well, I met this guy on the Empire Builder. Seemed a decent sort. I offered him a smoke, said he didn't smoke. I asked him to join me for a drink, said he didn't drink. Then, would you believe, I invited him to join me in the diner for three meals, breakfast, lunch and dinner? Each time he said he wasn't eating. I couldn't figure him out!"

The second man puzzled over this, but he didn't say anything.

As if talking to himself, Cal muttered, "For all I know his cock didn't work either."

Night Train to Veracruz

What was the matter with me? Never had I felt this sense of re-luctance. Twice now I'd walked the length of the coach cars asking per-mission to share seats with single occupants. My questioning voice "¿PERMISSO, POR FAVOR?" was met with vigorous shakes of the head, or a gruff "NO, NO VAMOSE!."

There were no seats to be had. I stepped off the train onto the concrete landing here in the mammoth Monte Vista Railroad Station of Mexico City to ponder my fate. It was 9:30 at night, the Veracruz Express would be leaving in a few minutes, yet something was trying to tell me not to board this train. But why? Since when did it matter that I had a seat? I'd rode many times on the floor, in the vestibule, curled up in a linen locker, in the luggage rack; so why the big deal about no seats?

I'd already bought my ticket – PRIMERA CLASSE (coach). I'd asked for a compartment or sleeper berth, but they were all sold out. Too late to look for a place to sleep in this giant city of twelve million people – the prospect of being lost and alone and knowing only about a dozen words of the language was frightening. I HAD to catch this train!

So, defying my hunch, my premonition, my gut feeling, I picked up my carrying bag and strode back into the train – now jammed – no place to sit down anywhere. I kept on from car to car – nothing.

Finally, in the very last car of the train, I came upon a blonde-haired girl sitting by herself. I wondered how it was I hadn't seen her the first times I'd been through. No matter, it was my last chance.

I stood by the empty seat, "¿SENORITA?" She looked up; I repeated my shaky request, "¿PERMISSO, FOR FAVOR?" pointing to the seat. She nodded, "SI." I murmured, "GRACIAS." At last – a place to sit down!

I eye-balled her covertly. She was a most attractive girl, maybe 25 or 30 years old. She looked me over, "¿HABLA USTED INGLES?"

"Yes, I do!" My interest came alive.

She turned and looked at me with new enthusiasm, "ARE YOU AMERICAN?"

I grinned delightedly, "SURE AM. HOW ABOUT YOU?"

"OF COURSE!"

We shook hands jubilantly. She went on, "I WAS HOPING TO MEET SOMEONE I COULD TALK TO. YOU'RE THE FIRST PERSON I'VE SPOKEN TO FROM UP NORTH IN A WEEK!"

Seems she was a school teacher, working in Florida, on a winter vacation to sharpen up her Spanish, and heading for Veracruz, same as me. We chattered like a pair of magpies till nearly midnight, enjoying the sight of a full moon floating over a high mountain peak to the north of us. I finally drifted off.

A strange sound broke my sleep – like a high-pitched scream. I was quite awhile coming awake. Then, when I did, I felt myself being propelled forward. Sensing alarm, I sat bolt upright; the screaming sound was deafening; I came to all at once; this was an emergency; the sound was made by the brakes locking the wheels tight – we were still traveling at a high rate of speed, but all the wheels locked and dragging. The engineer was surely trying for a last-ditch, panic stop! It all happened in a few seconds; the train was coming to an abrupt stop. I looked behind at the other passengers; their momentum was pushing them towards the front of the car where the girl, Joanie, and I were sitting. Making a splintering sound, the seats themselves were moving forward, tearing the screws or fastenings loose from the wooden floor, sending the seats and the horrified occupants all to the front – unable to do a thing to prevent it. Just as we came to a sickening halt, Joanie went flying out of her seat headed for a wall; I braced my feet and legs against the partition, reached out and grabbed her with both arms, as the rest of the seats behind us ground to a crumbling, rumbling stop.

Kids were crying, the shouts and screams were suddenly audible. We were now stopped. Surprisingly, there was nobody hurt – just scared and shaken up. We couldn't believe our luck!

I told the girl to sit tight, that I'd see what was the matter and be right back. I climbed over the pile of wrecked seats, opened the car door and stepped down to the ground. It was still dark, but the moon was bright. It shone down on the strangest sight I've ever seen! A train wreck! Not just a derailment; not just our train colliding with something on the track; not just a rear-ender – bad as all these things can often be, this was something else.

I had just experienced . . . "A CLASSIC TRAIN WRECK!" An extremely rare occurrence! "TWO PASSENGER TRAINS COL-LIDING HEAD-ON!"

In disbelief I walked forward to survey the scene. Only two cars of our train were still standing on the track, all others jack-knifed, strewn every which way, some still upright, some laying on their sides, people clambering out of and over the windows and standing around dazed, trying to gather their families and children, some hollering and screaming, but mostly just quiet – in a state of shock.

I kept on up to the head end. What a tangled pile of twisted steel! It was plain to see what had happened. The opposing diesel locomotives striking head on had telescoped each other, turning end up and over, falling back down – all of a piece – so you couldn't distinguish one from the other; just a smoking, twisted pile of metal. There were three guys crawling up to what was left of the cab of our engine; they poked around, then called out for assistance. They needed one more person. I looked around; quite a crowd of men stood there looking up, but no one volunteered; just wrapped themselves in their serapes and blankets and didn't move.

It was obvious someone had to help in this attempted rescue. I waited, not wanting to appear as the ugly American, the loud-mouthed know-it-all – after all this was Their country and Their train! But when no one budged, I reluctantly began the climb. Up the oil-covered tangle I went, hand over hand, till, reaching the top, I saw the three guys had a hold of a man's body, and needed someone to pick up on his other leg. I grabbed the foot and we slowly dragged this lifeless form back down to the ground where a blanket was mercifully draped over him. The leg and foot I had a hold of was crushed to a pulp. It was a gruesome sight. Nobody said a word.

Walking down along the OTHER train, or what was left of it, I saw that most of its cars had climbed the rails, too, with two or three at the back end still on the tracks. This train had several express cars up front. I heard this sound of bellowing and groaning, so I came closer. A cattle car full of bulls (we later read that these were high-priced, hot-blooded fighting bulls destined for the Mexico City Bull-Ring) had landed on its side, killing several, pinning some underneath, and allowing one to run loose. This one was still standing nearby, snorting and pawing the ground. I saw one animal pinned down underneath the wreck, unable to get its head free, whose back legs kept thrashing and moving and making pitiful sounds.

Another express car, lying crosswise over the rails, had broken open, disgorging its contents over a couple hundred feet of track. Books! All the same book! Thousand of copies of a children's illustrated book entitled "JOSE Y MARIA," the equivalent of "THE ADVENTURES OF DICK AND JANE." People were picking them up.

It began to grow lighter. The first person to arrive was a man riding a burro! No ambulances with screaming sirens, no police, no reporters, no excited, curious throngs. Just an old Mexican riding a burro! I never did know exactly where this accident happened, but it was not too far from a fairly large town called Puebla. After a while farmers in wagons pulled by horses, a few cars and one flatbed truck arrived.

Meanwhile, I had returned to our car, where my school-teacher friend, Joanie, still waited. I said, "If you brought a camera, now is the chance to get some pictures of a lifetime."

The sun was out by now; she exhausted all the film she had. It looked like no official from either the N de M, Nacional de Mexico, or the local law was going to show, so we decided to head for Veracruz on our own.

We paid the man of the flatbed truck to take us to the nearest village, where we caught the local "chicken" bus to the city of Puebla. From there, after a long wait, we boarded a deluxe auto-bus that took us on into Veracruz, arriving there in early evening. What a day!

Joanie made a good companion as she could speak the lingo. We sat at a table in an outdoor sidewalk café in the town plaza, talking over the day's adventure and our miraculous escape.

It had been another clear case of "DELIVERANCE." We ate a delicious dinner, watching the parade of humanity circling the plaza side-walk. It was a scene right out of Hollywood. All that was missing was Humphrey Bogart and Peter Lorre.

I told Joanie I had all I could take of Trains in Mexico and was going to catch the bus up to Matamoros the next morning and head on home for Christmas. She said she'd meet me at the Centro De Auto Bus for a farewell cup of coffee. She showed up right on time with a copy of the local paper. Yes, the Express from Veracruz had failed to heed a signal and had run into the night train from Mexico City. Both engine drivers had been killed, and it was believed the Eastbound engineer had been drinking and had ignored the red light. Nine passengers had lost their lives – all aboard the sleepers – on my train! I thought about my nagging reluctance to even make the trip, my unexplained feelings of impending doom, of my futile argument with the ticket clerk who refused to sell me a Pullman space, of my unheard-of problem in finding a seat, and of the uncanny coincidence of finally GETTING a place to sit in the VERY LAST CAR!

Was this another verification that I did indeed have a Guardian Angel?

At least it was my last time on the NIGHT TRAIN TO VERACRUZ.

Out In the West Texas Town of Del Rio

Someone was in the caboose. I called out, "In the caboose."
A tall lanky young guy mosey'd out, "Yeah?"
"Will you be leaving out soon?"
"Uh huh, in just a few minutes."
"Going all the way to Sanderson (Texas)?"
"Yep."
"Mind if I find me an empty and ride along?"
"No, that would be okay."
I walked up the train, found a fairly clean car, but look as I might, could find no cardboard, no paper, nothing. I could tell already we were in for a cold night and me with no gear.

I'd just come out of Old Mexico from a month of riding their passenger trains; I carried just a small handbag, nothing else. In Mexico you don't really need a bedroll. It's decently warm even in mid-December. You never carry a pack and you NEVER ride freight trains. Especially if you are a small-built person with white hair, blue eyes who can't speak Spanish – you don't go near their freights and you try to always stay in hotels. You learn how important it is to stay strictly out of trouble, mind the laws and don't attract attention to the fact that you are a Norte-Americano. I had seen one or two of their prisons on my travels before, high-walled stone structures with guards patrolling, machine-guns at the ready. They made a somber and thought-provoking picture. It made you more than willing to walk the straight-and-narrow.

So here I was in Del Rio, Texas, standing in the door of my very own side-door-Pullman, watching the pale, warm sun going down and waiting for the highball. As a kid I'd heard of Del Rio from listening on our battery-set radio in our cabin in the backwoods of Oregon to "cowboy" stations on which they played old-time music – guitars and fiddles and such – sponsored by the CRAZY WATER CRYSTALS company and coming to you on KRIO, the forty-thousand watt station from DEL RIO, TEXAS.

I heard voices and the sound of footsteps crunching the track side ballast. I ducked quickly back into the dark corner of the boxcar; pretty soon four teenage boys passed my car, but didn't look in. I didn't make a sound. They were town kids, not road kids. I gave a sigh of relief when they passed out of sight. Had they spotted me it could have been a hairy situation – one lone free-rider against four good-sized boys armed with sharp rocks.

Kids all over America recognize the obvious; the Dirty Old "Bum" (that's their word for any guy on a train) has NO clout, and so, won't usually chase them – so the kids have themselves a good old time honing their throwing skills and never mind if they draw blood.

Ask any tramp who's been along the tracks any length of time. He'll tell you this very predicament is one of the most dangerous and most-feared things that can befall you. It's also the main reason the auto racks on today's trains are sealed up so a mouse couldn't squeeze in. Before, when the tri-frames were open sided, the kids of various towns would each get a chance at pelting the new cars with rocks or ballast till the breakage was massive. Oh, yeah, the kids of America are indeed talented! Excellent throwing arms!

It turned out to be a rough ride. I couldn't figure why we bumped and jerked and whipped around like we did. Then, at a brief stop, the same brakeman came walking up to my car to check me out. He seemed interested, and I wondered how many riders they saw. This was on the SP's Sunset Route from New Orleans to El Paso.

"How you makin' out?"

"Oh, I'm surviving. Sure is a rough ridin' train!"

"Real bad. It's cause we're so long."

"How many cars?"

"Oh, we got nearly one hundred fifty cars, mostly empties, very few loads." The longer the train, the more pronounced is the SLACK ACTION – that's the whipping snap, or sling-shot jolt that occurs when the coupling mechanisms stretch out and then push back to normal. The push-together is call BUFF, while the pull-apart action is called DRAFT. You have to be careful how you stand and how you move around in or on the car, as this extreme jerking can throw you down right off your feet – suddenly – when you're not expecting it.

No sleep and no rest, just hunker down, try to keep your balance; I thought of Woody's song, "Talkin' Dust Bowl."

> We was goin' pretty fast, and wasn't even stoppin',
> Bouncin' up and down like popcorn a-poppin'.

At long last I felt her slowing down. Thank God! I couldn't take no more of THIS train.

Sanderson doesn't have much to offer, but at least it's a crew change, and I'd be able to get me another train tomorrow. It was nearing midnight and I remembered I had no bedroll with me. Now what? The head end was up near the depot about a mile or more away, but directly across from the end of the train I was on, I could make out the highway and a neon sign blinking – I could just barely read it. Said "Motel."

I checked my pockets. I could afford it this one time. (That's what I always say when I want to pamper myself; JUST THIS ONE TIME!) There didn't seem to be any roads leading away from the right-of-way, and I couldn't see walking the length of the train and then have to double back, so I just cut straight across, through the sagebrush, greasewood and chaparral, keeping that Motel sign in sight, like a sailor trying to make a lighthouse.

What had looked to be a level field turned out instead to be a series of gullies and washes. I was having tough sledding trying to navigate it in the dark, slipping, sliding, falling down, but after about a half hour I came out onto the road and there was the good old Motel – right across the street.

As usual the night clerk lady was surprised to see me, she hadn't heard a car stop and I guess pedestrians are rare. But, yes, she had a single room and it was mine for $6.00. Cold and sleepy as I was, I didn't argue the price, nor object to the room which wasn't much but as least it was warm.

I passed a quick night, dreaming about SNAKES, of all things. Normally I seldom dream at all, but here I was foot-slogging through rooms full of big old snakes of all sizes and shapes, till when I finally woke up, I was tired instead of rested.

I got dressed, stepped outside, took a breath of good West Texas air, bowed five times towards Mecca, then looked around for an early-opening café. I walked into the Motel office to return my key and asked where a restaurant might be.

The lady says, "Well, let's see now; there's one back down the highway about a mile, and there's one up towards town . . . which way did you come in from last night?"

I told her I hadn't arrived by highway at all.

"I cut straight across from the railroad through that big gully."

"You mean this one right out here in front?"

"Yes, this one right here." She looked at me strangely.

"Did you have any – trouble?"

I shook my head, "No, it was tough walking but I had no trouble."

"Didn't see or hear anything?"

"No. Why, what's the matter, did I do something wrong?"

"No, but folks around here don't walk in that gully. It's full of snakes!"

"Snakes?" I remembered my dream. "What kind of snakes?"

"Rattlers. It's just crawling with great big Texas Diamond-backs!"

Definition Of a Hobo

A television reporter once asked Roadhog, USA, what it took for a person to be a hobo. I'll never forget his reply. He said, "You've got to have the heart, mind and soul of a drifter."

I've never heard a better answer. Seems that a hobo, or vagabond of any sort, wants a temporary connection. Temporary job, temporary residence, temporary relationships with people – always a short-time situation. There must always be light at the end of the tunnel. He's willing to put forth an effort and get it together for a day, a week or a month, but avoids, at all costs, a serious, long-term commitment. He can't stand to be faced with a situation from which he can't withdraw. He's always looking for an out, a loophole, an escape hatch. He considers any entangling relationship as a threat to his freedom. His freedom, to him, means nobody having a claim or hold on him or his time. He has no long-range plans; instead makes his own plans daily, or even hourly, and reserves himself the right to change these plans at will – without the necessity to explain, apologize or defend.

This is not necessarily a weakness, a flaw. No, this is an integral part of the make-up, the personality, or character of the drifter. In our society, these qualities or traits are frowned upon, looked down on – considered hindrances to becoming an integrated member of our culture – but they have always been a part of our American heritage.

A vagabond needs to have all his options open and available. Even though he may have no immediate plans to leave, to move on, he still likes to reserve himself the right to make that move – at a moment's notice. And without consulting or asking permission of anyone. He especially hates to allow anyone to put a hold or lay a claim on him. Is this part of the pioneer urge felt by generations of malcontents in their mostly westward migrations from Europe and across the Americas – or is this rather a form of aberration, a sickness, sort of, that grabs a hold of a person and makes him do strange and irresponsible acts, and makes him turn his back on convention and family to float aimlessly about the world? What makes a person want to hop a freight train? Why pass up on comfort, cleanliness and security to opt for a life on the road, where danger and uncertainty are the norms? Why do so many prefer riding freight trains to hitching rides on the highway in comparative comfort? Yes, the drifter is a strange breed, all right. But not to one another.

When you are looking for a job (I've looked plenty) and must complete an employment application (I've filled them out by the hundreds) in the job-history section after noting, name of co., the description of job or duties, the amount of your remuneration, then the length of time on job – then the Coup D' Grace – "Reason for Leaving?" Well! Now comes the rub!

The fact that you left at all is already a minor blot on your record. In this land we are all expected to accept a job, any job, and stay with it come hell or high water and never complain, but rather to feel grateful and give our best till gold-watch ceremony or pension arrives. So, if you indicate that you QUIT (oh, my God, what a damning confession), you are straight-away labeled an irresponsible dilettante and are probably made of inferior stuff – and probably harboring an ungrateful attitude.

Now, if you have the temerity to put down that you were Fired, let go or laid off! – that is an even worse admission than quitting. That, no doubt, indicates that YOU behaved in some offensive manner – or were performing your duties incompetently, thereby giving your employer no option but to Can Your Ass.

A drifter is not interested in retirement; nor is a pension an inducement for him to stay with a job. A lifetime occupation stretching across his future into infinity, with no end in sight is, to him, like a stranglehold around his throat. Money is not necessarily motivating.

The average hobo would just as soon do without the money rather than accept a demeaning task to earn it. This is true, mostly of so-called steady jobs. He'll find a way to get by, and it'll be his way. He often doesn't mind a temp job at spot labor, or fruit picking or harvesting. This he understands. He can accept a few days' or weeks' work if the understanding is he can get his pay and split – no questions asked!

He asks one thing only – don't tie him down; don't ask him to behave according to YOUR expectations. Don't look for miracles, don't expect gratitude and don't let him know you feel sorry for him. Let him go on his way.

The hobo loves the open road stretching away off into the distance. He wants to be outside in the open air with the sun beating down and with no worries beyond the next meal, the next cup of coffee, the next train, the next town or the next drink. He wants to be surprised! Each day must hold forth new adventures, new roads, new vistas. Roadmaps, employee timetables, scanners, radios – all kinds of aids – only serve to confuse him and mess up his mind. He does not want to know what tomorrow may bring. Sufficient unto the day . . . etc. He is not saving up for the future, nor is he concerned about what will happen to him when he gets old and feeble.

Sounds like a giant cop-out, doesn't it? But is it?

Go To School

How do you learn to be a hobo? Study the letter, do the thing, and imbibe the spirit! That's how! The same as anything else. If you wanted to learn a trade or master an art or become proficient in some area, you would – what? Why, you'd GO TO SCHOOL, of course.

What school? School of hard knocks. The first thing is to find a teacher. Put yourself in the hands of an expert. Seek out one of the itinerant gentlemen. Most any respectable tramp will listen to your request. Many will take you under their wing – for a short time at least. Don't come looking for a long-range commitment.

Look for some dude who gives you the impression he can take care of himself, who seems to know how to pack his gear and is dressed utilitarian. Pick a guy who wears sturdy LEATHER boots. No tennis shoes. Don't travel with a man who carries nothing. It's pretty important to join forces with an experienced traveler who can show you the ropes and show you how to avoid getting killed on your very first ride!

When you've found such a one – then pay attention, follow his leading and LEARN. You can pick up more road-smarts in a week from an all-weather hobo than you could possibly find out by yourself in a year. The guys who've been out living like wild animals on America's right-of-ways have developed ways and means of survival and getting by – with next to nothing – that would astonish the uninitiated.

This is your chance to get it – and get it for free! All you have to do is to be a friend; to share; to trust, to be willing to believe in and listen to this guy – and then – do it! What he tells you.

We're all different. After one ride, or one week, or one season, you might be so disenchanted you can't WAIT to return to the land of hot baths. Or, you may discover, as quite a few do – that HEY, there's something TO this thing after all! Many a home-guard has found his life's calling after only one ride. So, don't ever think that you couldn't possibly catch the FEVER!

Why the Freight Train?

Why the freight train? The freight train is the ESSENCE of hoboing. Take away the train and you've eliminated most of the attraction. Here you have the secret of the vagabond life. Motion, movements, escape, travel – in a word, AMBIENCE! The rail-riding fraternity is a loose-knit family of sorts – drifters who come and go using the freights as their convenience – their utility – their main theme! These people become bored with a staid life of respectability and long to cut their ties, dump their encumbrances and take off – where? Well, anywhere they want to go – where the four winds blow. The constant changing panorama, something new every day, is the very meat and drink of the nomadic way of life. The vast distances, enormous areas, variations in climate and elevation of the United States all combine to offer a lifetime's adventure for the desperate wanderers of today who have been bitten by the same bug as the Mountain Men of a hundred and seventy years ago. They shun the cities and suburbia just as they shun the farms and factories. They are a restless, searching, disenchanted lot – looking to see beyond the mountain, to some never-never land which they'll admit does not exist.

But the trains keep on rolling, providing a partial escape, a temporary resolving of their immediate needs. Towards a check, towards a home, a warmer climate or to escape an intolerable situation. The freight train is all things to all hobos. It's their home, their connection with other hobos and it's a tremendous comfort to know that the train is ALWAYS THERE! If you need it, it's there. The freight train is the ever-present ANSWER!

The old-time hobo was so bonded to the railroad, that he almost never strayed. If he couldn't ride a freight to some destination – he wouldn't go. He was married to the tie-trail; lived and often died along the tracks.

Study the Letter and Imbibe the Spirit

The quickest way to grasp the FEEL of the world of hobo-dom is to get yourself primed by doing a lot of reading. To appreciate what you're getting yourself into, you just MUST get a handle on the basic history of the species and how it all came about, and why, in this land of jet planes and computers, it still exists, and what's more, is still viable.

All sorts of books are out there, especially books written many years back by some of the legendary travelers such as A No. 1. In fact, most of the available work on this subject is way out of date, there being a preponderance of published information on hobo-ing from, say Jack London's "The Road," written in 1890 (still one of the best), to Jack Black's classic, "You Can't Win" (1926), on up to Fishbone's "Hobo-ing in the 1930's." The libraries will mostly stock these old-time hobo classics. Up to date works are rare indeed. I mean – anything from about 1960 on. I know of only five. Today's young railrider is not so much curious to hear about the days of "steam" and how to steal a chicken as he is to learn all about how it's done here in the Twenty-First Century. Sure, there were a million and a half men on the bum during the depression days, but their problems and their solutions are pretty meaningless to today's young, red-blooded adventurers. What they are looking for is a damn good book addressed to them, their age group, their ideology.

These books are out there. One of my favorites is Michael Mathers, "RIDING THE RAILS." The photos and verbatim dialogue are priceless. Michael rode the trains, took all his own shots and assembled them in one of the most readable and enjoyable pieces of work I've seen.

THE FREIGHTHOPPER'S MANUAL for North America, by Daniel Leen. This is a classy little volume put out about 1980 full of timely tips, good humor, done with a wry homespun philosophy and not too much instruction. Daniel works his own experiences in with the information. He apparently rode quite extensively in the 60's and 70's, so his book is current and up to date. The photos are excellent. His advice is true. He has revised his first book, "Revised and Updated for the 21st century," and still calls it "The Freighthopper's Manual for North America."

Ted Conover's ROLLING NOWHERE, written in the early 80's, is an interesting job of reporting. As a young man still in college he took several months off to record his own thoughts and experiences traveling with America's hobos. Makes a pretty gritty story. He spares the reader nothing. To me, he leans a bit too heavy on the seamy side of hobo life. Maybe he didn't experience much of the other side. He sounds like he is telling it like it is. His title, "Rolling Nowhere," sort of gives me the impression that he felt his freight train travel was simply "going nowhere."

Now I believe that freight train travel is no different in essence than ANY kind of travel – in that the destination is of only secondary importance – whereas the TRIP, ITSELF is the whole thing!

The fourth recent book on hobo-ing is HOPPING FREIGHT TRAINS IN AMERICA, by Duffy Littlejohn. Obviously a labor of love by someone who's been there plenty – this is your definitive piece on the whole spectrum of freight trains: how to catch them, how they "work," the history of the railroads, how the hobo arrived on the scene, plus every conceivable fact of "How to" information you could ever think to ask. Encyclopedic in scope, a world of in-depth technical lore and complete. Not an easy book to read, but worth digging into and a "must" if you want to learn how to stay alive on the rails. This is easily the most complete and comprehensive book yet to appear. One word describes the handling of the material – AUTHORITATIVE.

"GOOD COMPANY," by Douglas A. Harper, published by The University of Chicago Press in the 80's, is the detailed account (with photos) of a neophyte reporter making a trip via freight train across the country, accompanied by an old-time hobo. They catch the trains, sleep out, and find work in the Wenatchee Valley Apple Harvest. This book could be used as a working text for a college course on the lore and philosophy of tramp-dom. Scholarly written with careful attention to dialogue and an eye to reporting the TRUTH. Unfortunately the characters in this work come out not too lovable. I've been through it twice and it is definitely not easy to read. It seems to be a chore for me to get through it. It smacks of college campus attitudes while trying to portray the workingman and his plight.

This book is beautifully printed and bound, and is different.

Where Did She Get the Idea I Wanted to Get Married?

I thought I knew him at first. He looked so familiar standing in the boxcar door. When I asked him if I could share his car he seemed agreeable – even helped me in. As we rolled up the Royal Gorge I kept eye-balling him, then, suddenly it came to me.

Of course! He was a Henry Fonda look-alike! No wonder he seemed familiar. Not as tall, nor as rugged, but had a striking resemblance to Henry when he played Tom Joad in "The Grapes of Wrath."

I commented on this. He smiled wryly. "Yeah, I guess I do. I've been told that lots of times."

Then, wistfully, "I wish I had his money."

I'd guessed him at around 40 and something of an enigma. He had a whipped-dog look about him, like he was accustomed to being taken advantage of, like he was almost asking for it. It was obvious he wasn't your standard working hobo. Had no gear, not even a coat, but wasn't a "streamliner" either and posed no threat. Harmless and inoffensive I decided.

It was a warm day and at each pull of my water jug I'd offer him some. He always drank. Carried neither food nor water with him.

To explain he offered, "I left the mission in Colorado Springs in a hurry and I didn't even bother to bring anything." He was another of those guys who trusted to "Providence" for his needs. That day I was "it."

The prospect of a cold night going over the Hump on a freight train didn't seem to faze him. About the middle of the afternoon we were approaching Leadville Junction, where the elevation is over ten thousand feet. I'd already slipped on a light jacket. Frankie said he didn't feel the cold much. Wish I could say that. I've over-packed in the Rockies as I was <u>always</u> cold!

He would stand staring out the door at the farthest mountain ranges, lost in thought for the longest periods, then come out with, " I was raised in New Jersey but I hang out mostly in L.A. now."

"What part of L.A.?"

"Oh, I got me a room in one of those older hotels."

"Would it be the Cecil Hotel?"

He eyed me sharply. "No, but it's not too far from there."

I got the impression Frankie wanted to be friends with me, but was somehow reluctant. Like he was afraid of me. Not knowing if he could trust me. I'm pretty used to that as I found out years ago that I kind of intimidate people without meaning to. It's not that I'm unfriendly or distant, but rather I'm so organized and self-disciplined that it turns people off.

He had this hang-dog look about him that indicated he'd been hurt a lot and didn't want any more of it. I did what I could to put him at ease and asked him his line of work?

"Well, I always get these nothing sort of jobs in electronics places assembling little gadgets. I guess I'm good with my hands. I can do the work but I don't really care for it, so it's always the same story – I work a few weeks, or sometimes all winter, then I give it up in disgust and walk away. It's been like that for years now. That's why I come out here on these trains – to get away and get my mind clear and always hoping to find inspiration."

"Inspiration? For what?"

"Well, I like to think I could be a writer. You know, stories and stuff?" He studied my face, looking for a reaction.

"That's great Frankie," I enthused. "What have you written?"

Our train was stopped at the high point of Tennessee Pass, waiting for something. The signal mast showed red. Evening was coming on and with it a cool breeze. I shivered. Frankie looked away, then gave me a wan smile. "Nothing."

"Nothing! Haven't you ever written anything?"

He shook his head apologetically. "No . . . nothing." He showed all the earmarks of the confirmed defeatist. "I sit there and stare at the blank piece of paper. I can never seem to get started!"

He saw me observing him with a mixture of disbelief and commiseration, "I know it sounds silly but I just have this . . . this . . . mental block."

I told him I'd heard an interesting story about that very problem. He brightened up right away like he wanted to hear more. As I remembered it, "Sterling Hayden, the movie-actor guy, was living on his boat tied up to the dock at Papeete, Tahiti. He'd been there a solid month trying every morning to begin the first page of his intended book. He'd get the paper in the typewriter, beat out the title, "Rebel," by Sterling Hayden, then sit for hours waiting for inspiration to release the story he was sure he could tell.

But nothing came out. Every day was the same. Writer's block, creative paralysis, procrastination – call it what you will. Frustration was eating him alive. How come he couldn't find himself? What was this accursed hang-up?"

Our train had started the downgrade. We agonized around the curves, flanges screaming at a greatly reduced speed. This was a treacherous piece of track on a severe grade. We'd be arriving in Minturn in an hour or so, where we'd stop long enough to get a bite to eat. Frankie had no grub with him at all. I continued the story.

"Right across the seawall from Sterling's boat was this swanky hotel, a stone's-throw away. One morning as he was fuming and stewing in front of the blank page one more time, he was interrupted by the furious, machine-gun clatter of another typewriter over on the hotel verandah. He could hardly believe what he was hearing. He jumped to his feet, walked down the dock and headed for this person like an arrow to the target.

"Thoughts seethed through his mind. 'Who is this guy? Who is this person who can type so fast? What is his secret?' He just had to find out and talk to him.

"Well, it turns out it was no less a personage than Herb Caen of the *San Francisco Chronicle*, who wrote a world-famous thousand-words-a-day By-line called, "Bhagdad by the Bay." He had arrived only the night before, was already out on the porch by 9:00 am, busily cranking out his column – and couldn't relax until he had fulfilled his everyday commitment. After an hour or so each morning he'd be through for the day and could go enjoy himself. He would be here on his vacation for two more weeks.

"Sterling Hayden was impressed! He was flabbergasted! He was so jolted by Herb's energy and drive that it broke his own block! He returned to his boat, buoyed by a new energy and enthusiasm, sat down once more to his typewriter, wrote several hours uninterrupted and finished his book in thirty days!"

Frankie was staring at me, his eyes in a sort of hypnotic fixation – like he was trying to picture himself breaking the spell, too, and wondering if it was possible.

"I could never do anything like that." He hung his head.

"Why do you say that, Frankie? You could do it if you really wanted to."

He smiled ruefully. "I know you're only trying to encourage me, Whitey, but it's no use. I'll never get it together. That's why I like it here out the rails – nobody bothers me or tries to get me to do something."

"That's just loser's talk, Frankie. Do people really bug you?"

"Yeah, they do. It's like they're always making plans for me and not letting me just slide along the way I like." His will-to-fail was simply overpowering. He wanted to talk.

"Instead of settling down and actually <u>writing</u> something – I'd got into the habit of dropping into the public library and reading books on <u>How</u> to write. I can still recall one book called, "How to Write for Money." Now, that was exactly what I wanted – to write for money – for a living, and not have to slave away in those factories. I thought it would be so neat to just stay home in my room and turn out stories and articles and get paid for doing it. It all seemed so right – so simple!" He gazed out the door at the encroaching darkness – reliving his memories, then shook his head sadly.

"I never was able to create a story, like this author said, but – " grinning now at some humorous bit, "I can still remember what he said about plots, you know, the plot of a novel.

He claimed there was only <u>one</u> real or basic plot, and that all other plots were just variations on this <u>one</u>."

"What <u>was</u> this plot?" I was curious to find out.

"The plot had three parts, and it was always the same:

1.   Boy meets girl.
2.   Girl gets boy into pickle.
3.   Boy gets pickle into girl"

We smiled at one another as the train groaned to a stop. Frankie seemed pleased with himself, was growing more animated, warming up to me, seeming to trust and want me to hear him out. He felt like pulling the string on his bag of troubles and spilling his guts.

It was about 9:00 pm, the Minturn yard was all quiet. The dispatcher, drinking coffee in the restaurant, told us our train wasn't called till midnight, so we had plenty of time to eat and lay around. We took a booth in the corner, continuing our discussion. I ordered ham and eggs for us both.

"Were you ever married, Frankie?" I'd apparently touched a nerve-center.

"That was how it all got started."

"You mean, how you got started on the road?" He nodded.

"I didn't have any idea of getting married, but anyway . . . ." He couldn't wait to tell me about it. I knew I'd struck oil.

"I was living with my folks in Trenton. Marie, that was my girl friend, she lived with her parents in Philly. I'd been going out with her for quite a while, nothing serious. Oh – I'd drive over a couple or three times a week and we'd go for a walk, or maybe go to the show. I just liked being around her but didn't have any plans or anything. I've never had any plans."

He looked at me seeking approval or understanding. I nodded, encouragingly. Our late-night breakfast arrived; we wolfed it down.

"Then, after a while, she sort of changed. We'd be driving in town and she'd see a real nice house and point to it, saying, 'I hope we can have a house like that when we get married.' Or maybe it would be, from out of the blue, 'Will I be able to quit my job, Frankie, when we get married?'

"This bothered me. I didn't know what to say to her. I'd never even mentioned getting married. Hell, Whitey, I could hardly support myself, much less her, too, and buy a house and all that! I paid my mom room and board and had an old car – couldn't afford a decent one. My electronics job didn't pay that kind of money, so how could she ever expect me to marry her? She was a real decent kid and I liked her a lot. Oh, don't get me wrong, I wasn't screwin' her or anything . . . ."

He paused, grinning that fetching Henry Fonda grin. "Not that I didn't try, you understand, but she was Catholic and she used to say,

'Frankie, I'm willing and I'm able – but I'm not <u>ready</u>.' So I didn't press it. Then it all started to come to a head when my older brother, Al, got married."

"What happened then?" I was being given a tiny little peek into the mind of a four-star loser! Now, I get along very well with losers – much better than with shakers and movers, as, I too, have been down that trail a ways. I felt for him. This guy was baring his soul to me.

"Well, as soon as my brother got married he went out and put down a payment on a house, bought a whole shit-pot of furniture and moved to the suburbs. He kept after me, 'Frankie, when are you and Marie gonna get married?' Then my mom and dad picked it up and kept asking me, 'Frankie, you and Marie have been going together a long time now. Isn't it about time you tied the knot?'

"I was starting to feel like a rat caught in a trap. Everywhere I turned people were <u>pressuring</u> me to <u>do</u> something! And all the time it was <u>my</u> life, not theirs!

"Then Marie's parents started in on me until I could hardly bear to walk into her house. I knew what was coming. Then, one night the whole thing blew up."

"It blew up? Tell me how?"

"I guess I didn't realize it, but I was almost to the breaking point. People were expecting <u>more</u> from me than I had to <u>give</u>! Do you understand?"

I nodded. My attention was all the assurance he needed. The words were coming faster now. He couldn't wait to finish the story. His face showed the anguish he felt. He was reliving the crisis as he was telling it.

"This one night when I came to call on Marie, her dad took me into the other room. 'Frankie, this has been going on just too long. I've been meaning to have a talk with you for quite a while. You're a nice fellow, we both think the world and all of you, but . . . what's the hold-up, Frankie? Marie's beginning to get worried, and . . . well . . . you know, this can't be going on forever. Frankie – what are your intentions toward my daughter?'

"I didn't <u>have</u> any intentions, Whitey! I never <u>did</u> have any intentions. Like I said before, I wasn't the sort to <u>ever</u> make plans, but now, well – I had to face up – I'd been backed into a serious corner."

"What did you do? What did you tell her old man?"

"I told him I didn't have any intentions, and boy did he get mad! By this time Marie was standing in the hall, all dressed and ready to go out, so he didn't say any more – just walked off in a huff.

"It was then that I knew the party was over. I told Marie to wait just a few minutes, that I had to run an errand and would be right back. I didn't know what to do – but I did know I had to do something <u>quick</u>!"

Frankie breathed in a big sigh, stuck his hands out, palms up, sort of pleading. I waited, saying nothing. Breakfast over, we sipped our coffee.

"I guess I panicked, Whitey! Only one thing was on my mind – escape! Yes, escape before it was too late. I felt like a wild animal and didn't want to be caught! Would you believe that not <u>once</u> did it ever cross my mind that maybe it would have been a good thing for me to just <u>give</u> <u>up</u> and go along with what everybody seemed to want – to go ahead and <u>marry</u> the girl and get it over with?"

He hesitated, then finished, lamely. "Anyway, I drove home, loaded all my stuff in the back seat of my Chevy Impala and headed for the freeway. Didn't even say goodbye to my folks. Just split!"

He searched my face for a reaction, for silent condemnation. All he wanted was understanding. He read the sympathy in my eyes.

I asked him, "Then what? Where did you go?"

"I got on the Pennsylvania Turnpike and ended up driving all the way to California! I never went back."

They Have Clubs

One summer I met some interesting guys out riding the trains across Montana. One in particular was the Kentuckian or "K.Y," as he called himself. Another was Randy, who was a "nipper" – always taking a bit off a bottle but never drunk. He was also an unrepentant thief who would steal shamelessly from grocery or convenience stores but wouldn't think of ever robbing a buddy.

On that same trip I ran on to Steve and John, who were that new breed of recreational rail riders know as Yuppie Hobos. Here is how we all came together.

Just as the sun came up I found myself hitchhiking at the eastbound onramp of Agronne Boulevard and I-90 in the Spokane Valley. I thought I'd drift on over to the Glacier Park area, one of my very favorite places in the whole world. I was hungry to see some wildlife; bear, elk, deer and assorted creatures found in abundance along the Flathead River. This time I would travel the clean way – I would ride my thumb.

Two hours later I was still standing there wondering if I'd lost my touch. Very, very seldom had I ever waited that long for a ride. Lots of drivers turning onto the freeway – so it wasn't a lack of traffic.

On an impulse I crossed over to the westbound ramp, stuck out my hand and was picked up by the very first car. This was more like it. Only thing was, this driver was going only three miles, dropping me off at Sprague and Havana.

Never one to resist fate, I quickly saw I was only six blocks from the Burlington Northern freight yard known as Yardley, and without a moment's hesitation started walking. So much for my plans for riding in style and keeping clean. I accepted this change in plans, hoping there would be something leaving soon. I hate those long delays.

What it really amounts to is that the true vagabond (I'm a charter member) craves to be on the move. Once his mind is set, he wants to go, and it doesn't make any big difference which way or how – just as long as he's traveling. He chafes at long waits, delays or postponements – he wants to get moving right now.

Arriving at the tracks, I was rewarded with the sight of two trains all set and ready, power on and cabooses manned – both Eastbounds. A "rail" was lounging on the back platform of one caboose, observing me as I approached.

"Good morning! Is your train bound for Missoula or Whitefish?"

He smiled. "We're going to Whitefish!"

"How about that one? Where is he headed?"

"He's Whitefish, too."

"Well, thank you. Looks like you'll be leaving soon, right?"

"We sure are. If you're going with us, you'd best get on."

All the cars from the caboose forward were auto racks and tri-frames loaded with foreign pickups. I started to walk the train hoping to find some other place to ride but she started pulling before I'd gone a hundred yards. I swung on to the front end of the third car and started to walk forward. In those days the ends of the auto racks were all open, allowing you to move through the train like it was a long tunnel.

First thing I saw was two hippy-type hobos sitting on the HOOD of a red pickup with their backs reclining against the wind-shield. They had their packs up there too and had two large police-type dogs lying down in the bed of the truck.

I kept on walking fast, giving them a short "Howdy" as I went past. I noticed that their combined weight had bent a slight hollow in the hood of the truck. They appeared not to care that they were severely damaging the shiny new vehicle. I made a mental note never to do this.

In my book it was okay to hop a train but never damage or van-dalize the equipment or cargo. I attributed this callous mistreatment to the mind-set of some of the new breed and their prevalent "What the Hell!" and "Who gives a Damn!" mentality. Too bad, as it spoiled the game for everyone. This type of vandalism plus the constant "rocking" of the auto trains by kids in numerous railroad towns is what led to the now method of protecting this kind of precious merchandise, closed and sealed up so nothing can get in – and the genteel (that's me) rail rider has lost yet another dandy fine place to ride. "And so it goes."

Looking back, I see these two bearded hippies coming my way, leading their dogs on leashes, jumping across the open spaces between cars. I noticed another rather strange thing; they both were wearing rubber boots. For a minute I got a little scared; were they coming to get at me? I thought about climbing up to the third deck, but decided instead to keep the cool attitude. Not to worry, these young guys meant me no harm, and just smiled and nodded as they went past on up the train.

I got my heartbeat slowed down to a comfortable pace and be-gan to enjoy the scenery. We had just crossed the Idaho state line and pulled into the town of Rathdrum, where the BN had recently built a staging yard of perhaps a dozen sets of tracks – using it as a temporary holding area for low-priority freight, to take the load off the over-worked Spokane yards. Our train stopped. Three Special Agents boarded at the head end and methodically worked their way down the length of the train; one on top, one on the second deck and one on the lower level, rousting out all the free-riders – of which there was a bunch. I was near the tail-end and so was the last to be kicked off. When he got to me the bull said, "Okay you – get the Hell off!" Saying nothing, I slipped on my pack and prepared to climb down the ladder on the right-hand side. He said, "Not that side! Get off on the other side." I complied. Then he seemed to relent, "There's a blacktop highway right over there. You can probably hitch a ride."

I said, "Okay, thanks" and started hoofing it. I'd gone maybe a quarter mile up the road when the train got underway. I watched it out of sight. Inside of fifteen minutes another train pulled up and stopped. I guessed this was the train on the adjacent track back in Spokane. This one was a mixed freight and had an open doored boxcar near the head end. It said, "Southern Railway – Southern Gives A Green Light to Innovation." Almost as silly as General Electric's, "Progress Is Our Most Important Product." Another stupid company slogan.

Never mind – if I hustled I might catch it. I hurried over, slowed having to crawl through a couple of fences, but made it, swinging aboard and finding a really nice, clean, wooden-floored boxcar. I made a place up forward and in no time we were on our way, turning north through the lovely timber country of the Idaho Panhandle on the old Northern Pacific Mainline.

Scenery-wise this is one of the most rewarding rides in the whole Northwest – from Spokane to East Glacier. It's got everything an itchy-footed tramp could ever ask for – rivers, forests, wild animals, glaciers, and range after range of snow-capped mountains. I nibbled apples and carrots and feasted my eyes on the incomparable countryside. What a ride. Would I ever get tired of it? On this run I seldom sleep or even nap, as I don't want to miss anything. I've ridden it dozens of times, loving it more each time.

There used to be a crew-change at Troy, Montana, where many of the Bo's would get off to go camp and fish along Callahan Creek, a truly pretty and restful place where you could jungle up along the creek with only a ten minute walk down to a small Mom and Pop Grocery. Hobo Heaven. Now the trains don't stop at Troy or Libby; they just barrel on through to Whitefish.

Travelers have discovered a new camping and fishing place that's even better than Troy – it's called Essex, and it's where they hook on the helpers to get the trains over Marais Pass. It's just past the historic Isaac Walton Hotel (a flag stop on Amtrak), and there're lots of neat hideaway places along the Flathead River – and so convenient, as most all the mixed freights stop there.

The following morning after a night run through Glacier Park I'd had enough riding for a while, so I bailed out at Shelby, hoping to catch the early morning local down to Great Falls. I missed it by thirty minutes, so hiked on over to the truck stop for a leisurely breakfast, then hit the onramp, where I got a ride with a BN employee, a clerk, clear down to the yards in Great Falls. I told him I was wanting to make the run from there on down to Laurel, an old Great Northern route that I'd never been on. He told me that train usually left around late afternoon. I thanked him and walked along the edge of the yard to wait it out. I found me a nice shady place, stretched out and tried to get some sleep.

A couple of hours later I see this green BN Suburban creeping slowly along the frontage road. I'm immediately alerted to the possible presence of a Bull. Then the driver, spotting me, turns and drives over to where I'm sitting, stops and rolls down the window.

To my surprise it's the clerk I rode down with. He says, "I just got word on your train. They've got to wait for some lumber loads coming up from Butte, so it won't be called till after midnight. Thought you'd like to know."

Can you imagine this guy going to all this trouble to inform me so I wouldn't have to wait around? We chatted awhile as I thanked him, telling him I'd decided to hitchhike down to Helena and that I appreciated his helpfulness. These rail employees are such neat guys.

It was in the Helena yards the next day that I ran into "K.Y.," who was huddling around a fire under the freeway overpass. He seemed glad of some company. Said he was a Paratrooper who'd made one too many jumps over in Korea. He'd landed wrong, messed up his right leg and hip and had to spend eighteen months in a body cast in some big VA hospital back East.

His prognosis was that he'd likely never walk again, but he fooled them – not only learning to walk all over again, but resuming his freight-hopping life – and what's more, he had a pension to back him up. Like so many others, he still made the monthly run to Minnie to collect his GA (General Assistance) check every month. Said he really didn't need the money but he liked the ride.

A few minutes later another tramp sauntered up to the fire, told us his name was Randy, and so there were the three of us, all heading West, yapping and yarning like three congenial magpies. We had plenty of time, as a car-knocker said noon was the earliest scheduled Westbound.

K.Y. mentioned something about some hobos he'd seen who had clubs. "Yeah, there's guys out here now who have clubs."

I said, "You mean they carry clubs right with them – in with their gear?"

"Oh no, Whitey, not that kind of clubs. I mean they have clubs that they belong to."

"Is that so? What do they call themselves?"

"I'm not real sure, but I think its something about Freight Train Riders."

Randy broke in with, "You must be talkin' about the F.T.R.A. – right?"

K.Y. asks, "What does F.T.R.A. stand for?"

Randy replies, "'Freight Train Riders of America.'" He grinned. "Some people call them other things too, like, 'Fraid To Ride Alone,' and I've also heard, 'Fuck The Railroad Authorities.'"

I was curious. "Where have you seen these guys, K.Y.?"

"Right up here in Montana. They like to ride the Highline. I've run onto several of them coming back from Minnie. One guy told me that they even put out a little paper or newsletter, so I guess they're pretty well organized."

Randy took off for the IGA Grocery Store, returning with all kinds of goodies under his extra-large shirt. I wondered how he'd been able to carry all that stuff so he showed me a large, wide, web belt under his shirt that held all these food items, such as cans of sardines, cookies, and even a package of rolls. He was a booster. He'd bought and paid for a quart of beer – the rest he'd stolen. You meet all kinds.

Randy was the type who lived by his wits. Years ago this kind were called tramps as opposed to hobos, who carried bindles and worked for their living. The tramps carried no gear and did not work. Randy told me he'd been scheming around, filling out government applications, hoping to persuade the authorities that he was disabled so he could draw a pension. His mind just naturally ran to "Con and Scam" and all kinds of trickery. A nicer guy you'd seldom ever meet. Con men are nearly always charming.

Randy got his mail at a post office box in Wishram. Said he always buried his belongings, like heavy winter gear, wrapped in plastic sacks along the tracks or down by the Columbia River. He was a strange one.

We three shared out of our chuck sacks and had a great lunch, enjoying each other's company there in Helena under the bridge. We could care less if a train came by or not. This was too much fun.

K.Y. had a pound can of "Top" and inside the can he had one of those clever little cigarette rolling machines – the kind everybody used during the depression when tailor-mades at fifteen cents a pack were out of reach price-wise. He'd keep a constant supply of these neatly constructed ciggies appearing as he talked. And talk he did.

"I took a temporary job in Seattle one time doing maintenance work – you know, like keeping the city parks picked up and the leaves raked and stuff like that. There was four of us got hired the same day; a black gal and three of us white guys. On the third day on the job the foreman, who'd been in charge of us, came over and made the black gal the "straw-boss," and told the rest of us that she'd be in charge from now on. We'd all gotten along real good up till then. Pretty soon this gal says to the other two guys, 'Now you two start raking those leaves, and you' – she pointed to me. 'You start picking up the papers and stuff off the grass.'"

I said, "I quit." Just like that.

She says, "Quit? Why do you want to quit?"

I says, "Lady, I'm from the South – and I don't take no orders from niggers."

Her mouth flew open. "You callin' me a nigger?"

"I sure am."

"What's the matter with you? I ain't never been called that before!"

"Well, you have now!"

"You must be one of them racists, right?"

"One hundred percent."

That was the end of the story. He added lamely, "I caught me a train out of Interbay that evening. Didn't even wait for my check."

The three of us held down a boxcar from Helena to Missoula, arriving there mid-afternoon. That's when we met the two Yuppies, Steve and John. Both in their late twenties, I'd guess, they were a well set-up pair of red-blooded adventurers out for a good time, riding the rails and seeing the county. They said they made a trip like this every summer. We invited them to join us in our car. I took careful note of their equipment. Not cheap or hand-me-down, like out of a Sally or a Willie, but really good, expensive, state-of-the-art boots and packs. They were well equipped – had those red Swiss Army knives and all. Nice friendly kids, too, said they were from California. They appeared able to take care of themselves, too.

Sitting around in the boxcar in Missoula waiting for the bell, we got to discussing all the different ideas people had of what to bring along on a freight train. It started to get hilarious. I started in on them.

"You know, when the El Paso Kid was King, he said the Yuppie Hobos had ten or twelve tee-shirts, folding buck knives and Eddie Bauer sleeping bags, but didn't carry any food or water. Had plenty of money with them too, but said that it would be useless in case of an emergency like a derailment."

Steve grinned good-naturedly, "Yeah, Whitey, I've seen those kind too, but that's nothing to what some of them bring along." He saw I was waiting for him to continue, "We know this one guy calls himself 'California Kid,' he's a high-powered account-executive out of L.A. Likes to take train rides to sort of relax and get away from the office. You wouldn't believe what he takes along." He glanced at his buddy, John, for confirmation.

John said, "Well, for starters, he's got an employees' timetable. Knows someone who works for the Santa Fe – keeps him supplied."

Randy asks, "What does he need one of them for? Can't he just ask one of the rails when and where the trains are leaving?"

Steve answered, "He's also got a scanner with him."

K.Y. was getting curious by now. "I've heard of them but never seen a guy with one. What does he do with one of these scanners?"

This time it was John's turn. "This lets you eavesdrop and listen in on the conversation between the dispatcher and the engine crew. You keep it monitored in on the right frequency and you get the orders and information as quick as the engineer."

K.Y. was not impressed. "Sounds too complicated to me."

Steve was enjoying this trend in the conversation. "Hell, you three old-timers might not even believe this" – he glanced around to see if we just might believe him – "but besides an employees' timetable and a scanner, old California Kid sometimes carries a lap-top <u>computer</u> and a <u>cellular</u> <u>phone</u>!" He looked at us as if challenging us to believe him.

We felt a nudge as the power coupled up, then in a few minutes we heard the air hissing through the lines. We'd be leaving soon.

Randy was skeptical. "Sounds like a crock to me. What does anybody <u>do</u> with a – what did you call it – a lap-top computer?"

John patiently explained. "It's just a small, portable, battery-powered computer, the same as any other." He looked around, realizing none of us even knew what one of them gadgets was. "Well, he handles his accounts business and keeps up his correspondence with this machine – only out riding the train, he gets to clear his head and breathe some fresh air."

I still was unconvinced. "Okay, you've told us about the time-table, the scanner and the computer. Just tell me what in Jesus name is he going to use the telephone for?"

John and Steve looked at each other, shrugged their shoulders helplessly. "Well, Whitey, I'm not sure who they call or why, but the California Kid takes it along, I suppose, so he can call in to check with his office – or maybe to call home to let his wife know he's okay."

"Why would he call his wife. He only left home that morning?"

Our two good-natured Yuppies had done their best to smarten up three dusty and dirty old train riders. We just couldn't see it. They realized it was just another case of generation gap.

Nobody said anything for a few minutes. Randy dug around in his pack, coming up with a half-pint of Old GrandDad which he starts nipping on. He didn't offer it around, either. He'd share his food willingly – but his booze he kept for himself. Not being a drinker I didn't give it a thought.

The old Kentuckian had kept pretty much silent through all this gab about high-tech equipment. Finally he lit up yet another of his machine-rolled cigs. "Now about this telephone you talk about. Can a person really call up someone – most anybody – from a moving train and talk?"

John says, "Yes, they sure can."

K.Y. looked real serious. "In that case I can understand just how important and how valuable that phone could be."

Steve and John were listening. K.Y. goes on.

"Now if this guy you call California Kid is riding the Santa Fe out of L.A., why then, when he gets somewhere close to Barstow, he can ring up Domino's and order a pizza delivered to train-side. As you're riding by – you get 'Pizza on the Fly!'"

Nobody said a word. We all sat there grinning, picturing in our minds the ridiculous situation. Then we all began to chuckle. The tension was broken. We howled. The yuppies, realizing how it must had looked, laughed just as hard. All five of us were now one happy family. We got up to stretch and watch Missoula slip behind us out of sight.

It Was My Own Damn Fault

I'd been used to seeing the Preacher and the little guy who walked with a limp, who they called Spaceman, at Britt. They'd be camped down along the Soo track, away from the hobo camp, where they could drink their beer in peace and not be bothered.

Traveling with NY Ron west from Minnie, he said, "Whitey, let's stop over in Staples and rest up at the Preacher's place." That was fine with me.

Now directly across from the Staples yard and about half a mile west of town was their house. So, when you piled off your train, or were ready to catch out, all you did was walk out the door and cross the tracks and you were there!

There were three or four guys calling this place home, Preacher, Spaceman, Mickey and one other I can't recall. No friendlier, open-hearted, open-handed bunch of Viet veterans and assorted freight train riders could you ever hope to meet. They took care of me like I was their DAD! Fed me ham dinners, fixed me up with a new plastic coffee mug (the kind the truckers use that has the tight lid with a hole in it), and when we left to find our train and they saw me shivering like the warm-blooded hot-house flower from California that I am, Preacher ran back to the house and GAVE me an extra goon-suit they had laying around. A goon-suit was what they called insulated coveralls. It saved my bacon and I wore it all across the country till we reached California.

Spaceman wore a plastic foot (his real foot was missing) when he'd go out, but in the privacy of his home he'd take the fake foot off and go clumping around on the bare stump! He told me he'd had his foot cut off in a train accident. Said it happened in Vancouver, WA (one of my favorite places). He was running for a grain car, grabbed the ladder all right, but his foot missed the stirrup and slid over the rail and between the wheels. Said he watched the "Salami Slicer" remove his foot from his leg in one terrifying instant. Found himself lying out on the ballast while people tried to stop the bleeding, and was fully conscious through the ordeal, including ambulance ride and surgery.

He was eventually fitted with the plastic foot and – believe this – still goes out and rides the occasional train! I asked him if he had ever thought about suing the Burlington? A lot of people do, and the railroads are so vulnerable. Spaceman said "Hell no, Whitey, why would I want to sue them? It was my own damn fault!"

The Preacher's story was similar but not so devastating. He, too, was guilty of a mistake in judgment, missed the stirrup on another train, but, luckily, only the toe of his boot was grabbed under the wheel and all five toes were crushed. He lost the toes all right but no discernible limp. These guys accept these inconveniences as part of the price they pay for messing around on the trains. You never hear them complain.

The Genuine Article

It was a comical and revealing sight to sit back and watch the tourists roam the campsite at the National Hobo Convention in Britt, Iowa. They had their camcorders at the ready, their cameras poised, their tape-recorders set to go. Now all they needed was a "Hobo" who would sit quietly and allow them to conduct an "interview." They'd be milling around from early morning on – all seeking to capture on film or tape a real, in-the-flesh hobo to take home to show to their friends and families – a souvenir to prove they'd rubbed shoulders with some of the few remaining – and larger-than-life – "Knights of the Road."

There were always plenty of posers; friendly, accommodating fellows rigged up in bandannas, long hair and beards, "funny" clothes covered with pins, buttons and sewn-on patches showing logos and names of railroads and train motifs of all kinds. Some carried "walking sticks," some had books of stories and poems that were "for sale." All in all they were a colorful bunch.

I'd noticed one old man who sort of sat by himself, not taking much part in the frivolities, just quietly looking on. He was a mild mannered, soft-spoken and retiring sort, but who would gladly chat and answer questions amiably. Generally, though, he was overlooked and passed over. Tall, gaunt, slightly hunched over, sporting a wispy gray beard, wearing drab clothes, a floppy straw hat and often wrapping himself in an old, gray blanket – he wasn't the most colorful guy there, so most of the celebrity-stalkers simply ignored this old man and passed him by. Frankly, he didn't look like a hobo (whatever that is); no, he resembled more an elderly, senior citizen you might see in a city park – just putting in his time. He was nearly 80 years old, still smoked Marlboros and carried a manila envelope stuffed with photos of hobos he'd known dating back to the 30's.

He admitted he couldn't ride freights anymore – too stiff and creaky to get on and off, but did ride the Greyhound bus each summer from George, Washington (near his home) to Britt and back. To me, the Greydog was more punishing than most freights. He did what he could.

When asked about his own history, I noticed he had some stock stories. He'd often open up with, "I blinded my first passenger train when I was eight. I didn't get very far. They took me off, but that did give me a start. I'd had a taste and from then on for over fifty years I rode trains all over the country. My mother didn't take very good care of me so I lit out. Never went past the sixth grade – was never inside a school room again till I turned 50. I went to night school to learn to be a 'Political Activist.'

"I was a road kid on the streets of Tulsa, living by my wits and stealing mostly. Growing up on the streets and in the jungles of the 1920's, we had only four priorities to stay alive: a safe place to sleep, something to eat, something to drink and a package of smoking tobacco. We sometimes lived on nothing but coffee and Bull Durham cigarettes. Now there's no food value at all in coffee and cigs, but we got by.

"The cops were always chasing us, figuring we'd just stolen something – or were just about to. They were mostly right, too.

"Yes, I was married. My wife divorced me. Can't say I blame her – I was never home. Had three kids. No, they won't have anything to do with me anymore. They seemed to be embarrassed by the way I was dressed, and by my outspoken opinions. They haven't written to me in years. I built this little shack along the Columbia River in a place called Beverly – used to be a crew-change point on the Milwaukee. I stay pretty close to home now. This is the only gathering I attend – oh, this and Roadhog's thing in California."

I found him irresistible – a fascinating and uncompromisingly truthful-speaking person. He made not the slightest effort to impress anyone. So sweet and mild! He was the ultimate non-aggressive, non-assertive, self-effacing – the kindliest person I guess I've ever known!

Visiting him once at his place in Beverly, I saw he had three vehicles; an Old Chevy van that hardly ran, an Escort sedan, and an ancient Kawasaki Motorcycle.

"Do you ride that?" I asked. He grinned like a little kid, "Yes, up until last year, when I layed it down and wrecked my leg. Haven't been on it since."

Unbelievable, I thought, riding a cycle at age 78. His main occupation these part years was publishing a little fold-over newsletter called "Hobo," which he put out all by himself, including the writing, typing, photo-copying and mailing. His spelling was hilarious! All phonetic but he didn't care – he got his message over. He accepted no money from anyone for subscriptions – just mailed it out free to anyone he considered deserving. His articles came out pretty gritty. He didn't mince around with his words but you instinctively knew this man was speaking the truth!

Oklahoma Slim had one unmistakable quality that out-shone all he did; that was integrity. His total income consisted of a Social Security check of around $500 a month. It arrived on the first day of each month. On the last day of each month he would drive up to Wenatchee and buy groceries with whatever remaining dollars he hadn't used for his own Spartan-like existence, delivering this food to the three missions and food give-away places, and then return home flat broke – not one cent did he hold out for himself. Said that when he died he wanted to go out the same way he came in – with nothing.

He'd already taken care of his burial arrangements. Typical of Slim to do it all himself, not wanting to bother anyone else, by buying a cemetery plot and headstone in advance in the town of Quincy, Washington. This Memorial Park was located across the highway from the

Burlington Northern mainline. At the time of purchasing the plot he told the man he wanted one at the end of the cemetery.

"Oh, Slim," the guy remonstrated – "not down there . . . you see, that's where all the Mexicans are planted. You'd be better off getting a plot up at this end, okay?"

Slim didn't tell the man <u>why</u> he preferred the lower end, but he did tell me. "Whitey, I held out for this spot – this one right here – the closest one to the tracks. This way, when these freights come roaring by, the old-timers who knew me can wave as they pass – 'Hi-ya Slim!,' I'd like that!"

His grave-marker was already set in place and carved. Just a plain slab of marble engraved with "OKLA SLIM. BORN 1913 DIED _____ followed by his motto; "PLAY THE HAND THAT'S DEALT YOU."

It was easy seen he'd lived by that sage advice. It bothered me a little that this soft-spoken pioneer didn't receive more recognition at the Britt Convention. I'd seen him sitting quietly at the picnic table at three separate year's gatherings. It seemed to me that Slim had more experience – that is, road experience – than possibly any man there. Because of his shy, retiring nature and his dislike of spectacle, he always was overlooked. No one ever called him to the microphone to speak. He was not recognized or saluted by the chair-person, was not invited to sit with the hobo kings and queen on the celebrity wagon during the parade. He was just plain ignored. Maybe that's how he preferred it. I never heard him complain.

You couldn't blame the visitors and tourists for not spotting or appreciating this gent – but it did seem strange that none of the old-timers recognized him either.

After all, the whole celebration – publicized nationwide – and attracting up to thirty thousand people to this tiny town of Britt, was ostensibly to honor and pay tribute to a fast-fading-away image of the Great American Hobo – and, there he was, sitting unobtrusively, uncom-plainingly silent . . . OKLAHOMA SLIM . . . the genuine article!

One Word Tells It All

Fred pointed. "There, you can see it plain."

I followed his hand, way off to the left of the train was a smoke-stack. I'd been noticing it every time I'd been this way. This was the route of the Northern Pacific from Butte to Missoula. It was a landmark of the region. "They say it's the biggest stack in the world," Fred went on. "Not the tallest, but the biggest in diameter. You ought to see what it looks like when you're standing right next to it."

He gazed out the boxcar door in a reverie for a long time, like he was recalling his past. "It's my own damn fault I'm out here riding these filthy trains. I blew it. But then, so did everybody else; we all thought it would go on forever. One word says it all."

I waited for him to continue. It was clear he wanted to talk. Fred had boarded in Butte. I'd been riding in this same car from Livingston. When he came passing by I liked his looks, and when he asked could he ride with me, I was glad for some company. In his 30's, dressed better than most, and carrying a large aluminum frame pack, I was curious as to what he was doing out here. He said he was looking for a job. Grinning at that statement, "Seems I'm always looking for a job, but I don't stay long; my attitude shows through."

"You mean you really don't want a job?"

"I always think I do, but when I'm offered one I no sooner get started than I start thinking back on my time with Anaconda, and the big money and all, and then I look at the piddling wage I'm getting and my heart all at once just ain't in it. My work suffers, and I just don't give a damn, then I either quit or get fired. Always ends up the same. I'm spoiled, I guess!"

"So, you worked at Anaconda?"

He nodded, "It was my one and only job. In fact I was second generation; my dad worked there too. I started right out of high school as an apprentice electrician. Great job. We had it made." He was reliving his past, and it hadn't been that long ago either.

"You should have seen Anaconda when it was booming. No unemployment, everybody doing fine, buying their houses, keeping them painted up so neat and pretty.

"Not like Butte. That's an ugly, dirty place – all the buildings made of red brick. Gives it the appearance of an old, real old town.

"Anaconda ain't that old. They only cared about one thing. Copper. The Anaconda Copper Company's open pit mine right there in the heart of Butte was the largest mine of its kind in the world."

Now I had always like Butte as it was admittedly a working-man's town, and I loved workingman's towns, like Tacoma, WA, Everett, WA, Yakima, WA, Astoria, OR – places like that. My favorite place in Butte was L & M Café and Bar. Restaurant on one side, bar on the other, and card tables in the rear. A warm, friendly and busy place.

Fred was right about the brick buildings though. I remembered the Milwaukee Depot was all red brick. The Northern Pacific Depot was part brick and part gray stone. I think they're both gone now. I asked Fred, "What happened to your good job?"

He shook his head slowly back and forth. "How stupid can people get? Here we all were sailing along on a lifetime job, with easy work and real good pay. My part was electrical maintenance – trouble-shooting around the smelter – keeping the conveyor motors running.

"Most of the time I had nothing to do. Just put in my shift. If no breakdown happened, sometimes I'd drink coffee and sit around the whole eight hours. I'd even take naps on company time. The whole place was union – heavy union.

"They'd bring ore from Butte over to the smelter in Anaconda, about thirty-five miles. There'd be smoke pouring out of that giant stack twenty-four hours a day for years and years. We got too comfort-able. We wanted more money. Every time our contract came up we'd demand about twice as much of a raise as the company offered. We'd threaten to strike if we couldn't get it. That went on for several years.

"We never had to go out on strike – the company always knuck-led under and met our demands. Oh, it was beautiful, I tell you! Each year we'd blossom out with something new. A hefty pay raise would mean a new car or boat and trailer, or maybe a vacation somewhere. It was all coming so easy, we lived in new houses – in Anaconda, it was all wood siding – painted up so neat. Nobody wanted brick. We didn't want to look like Butte!

"Oh yeah, I had a car and a pickup, and was buying a place at the lake. Living high on the hog was the way to go. Talk about the ME generation. I was it! My wife and I kept postponing having a family – we were just too damn selfish – we were living for US."

He stopped and looked quietly out the door. We were passing the State prison in Deerlodge – one of the most chilling, depressing sights I've ever seen from a freight train. We both shuddered.

I marveled at the number of mountain ranges you could see up here in Montana. They were everywhere – surrounded by mountains. Winter it was pretty rugged country to 'bo in. Summers were gorgeous.

"If you could see Anaconda now," Fred resumed, "you'd find that every other house is up for sale. All the younger people have moved away. There is nothing happening. No way to make a living. Climate's way too cold for the seniors to move in, so the place is just wasting away. That's what happens when the economy is based on just one industry – smelting."

"What happened to the smelter then, the copper industry?" I was curious.

"We killed it. We asked for too much. We thought there was no end in sight. Nobody seemed to realize that what the company had been trying to tell us for years was true! That there was only so much PIE to go around."

"So what did they do?"

"Our contract expired and we did the usual – what we'd been doing all along. We made a whopping big demand. Oh, not just a pay raise, oh no, we asked for all kinds of fringe benefits – you wouldn't believe the goodies we insisted on. The Anaconda Copper came out flat-footed with 'No way.' They not only refused our benefit package but they turned down our pay raise, too. So, like a pack of damn fools we all went out on strike – all the different unions. The hand writing was on the wall, but we were so pig-headed we couldn't see it. Now, I've got nothing." He looked grim faced and solemn.

"What do you mean, nothing?"

"Well, I've got no home, no car, no pickup, no boat, no job and my wife divorced me. How's that for having nothing?"

He had a faraway look in his eyes for the end of the story, "Would you believe, instead of fighting the strike, or negotiating a new contract – guess what they did?" I told him I couldn't guess.

"They closed down the largest copper smelter in the world – shut her down cold!" His eyes penetrated mine. "Then, they started shipping trainloads of ore clear to Seattle, loaded it on the monster ore-boats and sent it all the way to Japan!

"Now, get this. The company's excuse was that they could send it all the way across the Pacific, have it smeltered in Japan, and then bring the finished copper back here to Montana – for considerably less than they'd been paying to have it done right here!" He paused to let that sink in. "What does that tell you? Couldn't blame the Anaconda Copper Co. They were just trying to work the best deal they could – same as we'd been doing. Now they're still going strong – and we're all out of a job! We killed it ourselves!"

"Killed what?"

"What? Why, Hell, we killed the GOOSE THAT LAYED THE GOLDEN EGGS!"

I nodded. It was all too plain. It didn't have to happen.

Fred concluded, "One word tells it all – GREED!"

He piled off at Garrison Junction. I never saw him again.

You're the Only One Still Riding

I got this phone call from Michael in New York. Yes, I remembered him and his lady, "Lexie." They were the film-maker team I met two years earlier at the first annual Pennsburg Hobo Gathering. They were doing some video interviews of some of us "characters" and mentioned that they planned a documentary concerning persons, still living, who had ridden the country on freight trains back in the thirties Depression days, part of an American history project to be worked in with existing WPA footage still available from that time. They were waiting on a government grant to finance the film. They discovered during the interview that I had started riding the rails back in the thirties, and asked if I would be willing to take part in the documentary – and would I be willing to take the camera crew out on the rails for a ride? I said I would, them promptly forgot all about it for nearly two years.

Over the phone now Michael said that they had run a single ad in the Sunday supplement of Modern Maturity and had received a staggering two thousand five hundred replies from people all over America who had actually rode freights as youngsters back then. It took months of phone calls and letter writing to sift them all out and then work out an itinerary and interview schedule. They had received the grant and were now ready to travel. Finally, out of all the persons he had contacted – I was the only one still riding!

So on the appointed day, April 8, 1994, the five of us in a rented van set out for the San Luis Obispo, California, freight yards – considered one of the friendliest and easiest catch-out places in the nation. We arrived early but found out the Northbound had already left. As we stood there wondering how to handle the disappointment, we could hear the throbbing of the diesels as the train labored up Cuesta Grade. The helper units were not around, so I figured they had joined the train and would be returning from Santa Margarita after they'd helped push the drag over the summit. I realized we still had time to overtake and nail our man up the hill in Santa Margarita, where she would stop to disengage the helper.

We piled back into the van and headed up the grade, overtaking the Northbound just past the town. We were in luck. She was stopped to disengage the three-unit helper. We cruised up along the train, selecting two back-to-back grainers with adjoining porches and scrambled aboard, just in time to get underway immediately.

Lexie rode with me while "Sam the Cam" and "No-sound Neil" boarded the opposite car. Michael, the co-producer and co-director (Lexie was the other half) drove the chase car intending to pace the train to the first convenient stop, then pick us all back up. Weather was cold with rain forecast.

This happy film crew, having the absolute time of their lives, had stopped at some Goodwill store where they outfitted themselves in old clothes, plus Sam and Neil had each bought old yellow suitcases for carrying their extremely high-tech equipment – real honest-to-God – 16mm camera and super-sensitive sound-recording machine. Oh, yes, they had some pretty sophisticated stuff – enough to intimidate me at first – what with covered mike, mike boom, circular light-reflectors, an $80,000 camera and even one of those little gadgets they stick in front of the camera to commence each "take" – they called it a "clap-board."

Picture the four of us jolting our way down the tracks at about forty five miles an hour in the cold wind and rain on an SP mixed freight trying to take moving shots of me, the train and the passing scenery and recording the sound too. This was Lexie's very first time out. Sam and Neil had ridden just once before. It wasn't your standard, ideal filming situation, but we did our best.

Just past Soledad our train went into the hole to accommodate a stack train and the Southbound Amtrak Coast Starlight. It looked like a good place to get off the train, and Michael was there alongside with the van. We all piled back in, congratulating ourselves on our one hundred mile ride. End of day one.

The next day, wanting to go the other way, we arrived at the San Luis Obispo depot extra early and had to wait three hours for the Southbound. This time was spent getting an interview of me telling my story of how I got started at age 13 and some of my rides as a boy. They also recorded me singing five of my songs. This time the weather was back to normal – bright sunshine and clear skies.

The Southbound arrived about 9:30 and, to my surprise, it was an all-container or stack train. This was not exactly what we were hoping for, as most of these new style five-cars-in-one jobbers have no bottoms – nowhere to ride. I spotted one a few cars back that had the metal ribs (stiffeners) along the side, that had a four-foot well complete with metal floor, and we made a dash for it with the heavily-laden film crew puffing and panting behind me.

We were in luck. I climbed up first, then the others handed me all their mountain of gear and then clambered up the ladder and dropped into the cubicle. At that moment the train lurched forward. We had just barely made it! It had been a three-minute crew change. These hotshots don't hang around and when they clear the yards, they are <u>moving</u>!

The ride south from SLO-town is spectacular, one of the premier rail jaunts of this country. The right-of-way follows the ocean for nearly one hundred miles, passing the beaches, flashing along on top of the bluffs affording an unobstructed view of the surf, the fishing boats, the kelp-beds and the surfers lazing offshore, waiting for the seventh wave – the big one. I know of nowhere in North America where a railroad parallels an ocean beach the way this one does.

These fun-loving yuppie film-makers shot the whole sequence, enjoying the ride and displaying the tell-tale signs of euphoria so common to first-time rail-riders. It was over all too soon. Our train stopped in a siding at Santa Barbara where we bailed off. Michael and the van were waiting. Our return to San Luis Obispo was uneventful, at least for me, as I slept most of the way.

Michael told me that they were interspersing a few rolls of black and white film to sort of make it blend in with the thirties WPA footage, and not shooting everything in color. His interviews with people along the route so far had shown a wide disparity of attitude, some recalling with shuddering distaste the "Dirty Thirties," whereas my remembrances were fondly nostalgic and for the most part I had enjoyed and even reveled in whatever hardship I'd seen. It was similar to my experiences of four years in the Navy during WW II – I loved most of it and wouldn't have missed it.

I found out that the actual mechanics of shooting a film amount to one interruption after another. You might spend three hours trying to get one ten–minute on-camera interview. You no sooner start to roll than an airplane flies over, causing an immediate stoppage. You start again and this time a dog barks. Another interruption. The sun disappears behind a cloud momentarily, making the light wrong. Another stop. At one point we set up in the barnyard of a small farm out in the country, hoping for stillness and quiet. This time someone started up a pump, shattering the silence. More airplanes flew overhead. Frustrating and extremely time-consuming. The color film cost $100 per ten-minute reel. It all looks so simple, but the technical problems are astounding.

The three-day session was apparently successful, as they had captured on film, with sound, a real, honest-to-God freight train ride with an old-time depression-era rail rider, plus had gotten his story of his days on the fruit-tramp trying to earn a living while riding from job to job on the trains, along with the vast army of disenfranchised and restless men out searching for the rainbow's end and mostly not finding it. From 1929 to 1941 it was estimated that a million and a half men or more were rambling this country on the railroads. Michael had heard an official estimate that perhaps a hundred thousand or so are still living.

The tall and willowy Lexie, she of the reddish-blonde hair (and a graduate of Yale University, I might add) said the editing of the film, surprisingly, would require a year or more! They had another thirty days of travel, interviewing and shooting left to do, which would take them into May, 1994, so, the final finished project, to be entitled, tentatively, "Riding the Rails," was expected to be premiered possibly in the summer of 1995 – with luck.

Actually, the film, entitled "Riding the Rails," aired over national TV on PBS in April, 1998 to rave reviews.

So farewell and future good luck – my dauntless film-makers from Brooklyn!

The Streaker

Riding the Coast Starlight along the shore of the Pacific near the tiny place called SURF, I had gone down below to the vestibule where I opened the top half of the door, the better to see out and feast my eyes on the near-deserted hard-packed sandy beach where the breakers roll and crash. I was joined by four burly railroad men who told me they were deadheading back to San Luis Obispo and had come down to see if they could spot this beautiful, blonde girl who liked to take off her swimsuit and run like mad alongside the engines of their freight trains, laughing and waving and having a wonderful time giving the engine crew a thrill and seeming to enjoy it every bit as much herself. The guys said they always waved and hollered and tooted the whistle and did everything except stop the train in appreciation of her enthusiastic high-jinx.

They said all the freight crews were hip to this gal and eagerly awaited her appearance. Here they were, laughing, talking and crowding around the window I'd opened, hoping to be the first to spot her. They told me that as their train approached they could see her slip out of her already scant bikini and angle over towards the locomotive until she was right alongside, then with a burst of speed she'd sprint with it, giving it her all and showing her all until being finally overtaken. They said they didn't know if she also streaked for the passenger trains, but they were here to find out.

I was looking forward to this treat same as the rail crew, but look hard as we did, she failed to show. We concluded that she chose not to perform for the passenger trains. So that was the story of the Southern Pacific STREAKER.

On being questioned, they affirmed, that yes, she was indeed a real blonde.

The Nude Sunbathers

Riding the rear end of a Northern Pacific grain car through Northern Idaho one August day, I was privileged to behold four well-proportioned young ladies taking a sun bath in the buff. The track crosses part of Lake Pend Oreille on a long causeway before skirting a public beach just on the east part of the town of Sandpoint, a pretty little resort area. The girls evidently leave the beach area and walk out on the rail right-of-way till they are well out of sight, then stretch out, bare-ass naked, like so many sticks of cordwood on the sand, right smack along the track. Apparently they don't seem to mind – even though they are in full view of the crews on the trains. They may even enjoy this surveillance.

The train slowed as it approached the town limits and I stood up to check out all the beach action. To my knowledge I was the only free-rider on that train. As we trundled along, not knowing what to look for, but noting the train whistle had given off a few short toots, I saw something at the water's edge and to my total astonishment and no small delight, I was confronted by these well-tanned and voluptuous mermaids staring back up at me. Their looks told me they were as surprised as I, but they didn't seem to be put out any. They weren't ten feet away and all too quickly passed from view. They made my day.

The things you can see from a train, and you don't even need a ticket!

The Exhibitionists

The Amtrak Coast Starlight, America's most popular passenger train, on her Southbound passage leaves Eugene, Oregon at about 4:30 every afternoon, and begins her ascent up the Cascade Mountains over the summit, through twenty-one tunnels, on down to Klamath Falls and into California.

The summer of 1995 I was sitting in the high-level dome car sipping a glass of Chablis, gazing out and glorying in the fantastic scenery of which I never seem to tire. The entire train was packed. The lounge car was abuzz with happy travelers as we passed the little mill town of Oakridge and started the steep, winding grade up the mountains along the East Fork of the Willamette River.

It is about 6:00 pm on a warm August day, and as we approach a bridge I hear a succession of short toots on the two-tone chime whistle. As our car crosses the bridge, all eyes are alerted to something going on down below in the river.

As the river makes a wide band, we see five people standing in shallow water, all dressed alike, and lined up in full view not over two hundred feet away. They all have on a floppy sort of fishing hat and each is holding a fishing rod. All five are smiling-faced young girls.

And all are completely naked.

The fifty or so people in the car started whooping and exclaiming at this totally unexpected treat, while the girls, enjoying it hugely, waved and hollered back. We had about a ten-second peep-show before the train moved on into the greenery, but it gave us all something to talk about for hours.

I figured they probably put on this act every day. I haven't been along that route since, but you can bet next time I'll be on the lookout.

Adventures Down Under the Equator

For years I'd wanted to visit South Africa, to see their enormous country and ride their trains. I'd read reports a person could even find a steam train or two still operating. The opportunity came in January of 1995 and I grabbed it, flying from San Luis Obispo to San Francisco, Washington DC, then across the Atlantic to Cape Verde Island where we refueled, and finally the last leg to Capetown – all told required two days and a night. Long distance flying is, to me, a mild form of torture. I'd prefer a boxcar any day, but I endured it as there was no other way there.

Three days in sunny, sparkling Capetown gave me a chance to check out the train situation and to discover that a couple of shipping companies offered coast-wide voyages on board their freight ships. I hadn't taken a trip on a freighter in nearly thirty years, so I jumped at the chance and booked myself a passage on the motor vessel, "HELDER-BERG," of Safmarine Lines, from Capetown to Durban. Cost was 950 rand or about $300. She would be sailing that coming Friday, which gave me a couple of days' waiting time, so I immediately bought a third class ticket on the morning train to De Aar, about a thirteen hour run. I'd heard this was a busy rail crossroads with a "diamond," or cross-ing, where the mainline trains to Johannesburg crossed the main steam-train route from De Aar to Windhoek ("Veenduke"), in Namibia, miles across the Kalahari Desert in what was once South West Africa.

The third class coach was just a row of double seats with a table between, and was fine until so many people (all black except me) had crowded on at the various stops that there was no room to sit down. I later learned that I had committed a minor blunder of sorts by travelling third class; "It just isn't done, you know." Then out came the ghetto-blasters, three or more playing tapes of electronic music, synthesizers with high-pitched female voices screeching out idiotic lyrics repeated endlessly. On the trains, earplugs were not required, and so what might have been quietly modulated music turned out to be a bedlam of noise, with each player cranking up louder and louder in an attempt to drown out the others. It became an ordeal, a form of torture almost, producing a near-frenzy among the passengers who, unlike me, seemed to enjoy it – and the louder the better. Right there I made up my mind to upgrade to second class on the return trip, as I was scheduled to go the other way that same night, allowing me about an hour to look around De Aar and check out the train action.

As I stepped off the train, I was surprised to note a chill wind blowing. It was nearly midnight and the night had turned cold. I found the ticket office and requested an upgrade ticket in a second class coach, where I could have a bunk and hope for some sleep. I'd come to this country without a bedroll of any kind, thinking in January – the warmest month – I wouldn't need blankets. Wrong again.

The agent, a stocky, non-committal Afrikaans gentlemen sold me a berth in a second class carriage plus a bedding ticket (thirteen rand – or about $4.50) which entitled me to a single sheet, two blankets and two pillows. This bedding package was optional, so if you elected not to buy it, you could still stretch out on the bunk – but with nothing to put over you. I discovered later that night it was well worth the extra money, as I wrapped up and slept like a baby.

The agent asked me where I was from and when I replied, California, he reflected a moment, then looked up interested, asking, "You mean the place where they make all those cowboy flicks?" I nodded, "Yeah, John Wayne, Gary Cooper, Clint Eastwood stuff." He must have been a Western movie buff because, hearing that, he brightened up and seemed suddenly to become my friend. He offered me a cup of tea, whereupon we settled down to a steady question and answer session; me plying him with questions about South African trains and him wanting to know all about cowboys and horses and were there any real cowboys still left, and where did they live. The agent informed me that the once-popular steam train operating from De Aar on up to Windhoek had been closed down just the year before, and he didn't know of any other steam trains still running – except for one special tourist job running between Bulawayo and Victoria Falls in Zimbabwe.

Our gab was interrupted by the appearance of a tall black man who drifted in out of the night, wanting to book a berth in a second class coach on the Capetown train. (The same train I'd just moments before bought a ticket for). The agent, without blinking, told him gruffly that all first and second class coaches were full, but that there was still room in third class. The man didn't seem too happy about being turned down, but accepted his third class stub silently and strode out. I made no comment either but knew in my heart this was a case of pure intimidation, there being still plenty of second class compartments empty.

I learned later, after having ridden several trains and talking with the Train Managers (conductors) that, since Nelson Mandela was elected President of South Africa after having been confined as a prisoner on Robben Island (in Capetown's outer harbor) – he'd done twenty-seven years as a convict – the native Africans had suddenly started demanding space in second and first class cars on the trains – something that had never happened before. The Managers were hard-pressed as to how to accommodate these people, as it was unthinkable (in their eyes) to mix black and white in the same compartment – and often there were just not enough compartments available to house them separately. Therefore the simplest solution was to refuse to sell them (natives) space with the excuse that the train was "full." The Apartheid policy had only been lifted in the past two years, and there were still some pretty touchy situations arising.

Lying in my bunk that night I did a lot of serious thinking about race relations. As a boy raised in Seattle, I had never come across any prejudice or discrimination that I can recall, but further reflected that as a white boy, how could I possibly know? At that time in Seattle the only minorities I'd ever seen were Japanese, Chinese, Indians, and an occasional Negro. In twelve years attending public school, never once was there a minority child in any of my classrooms. In Queen Anne High School the most popular boy in school was a Japanese American who was elected class president. At the time this subject never entered our minds.

It seemed to me that South Africa was having to face up to more or less the same situation we Americans had been having as an ongoing experience – except we had more than a one hundred year head-start. The only conclusion I arrived at was that I knew of no easy answer.

Steam Trains: What's the Big Deal?

There is a perception that the old time steam locomotive of story and song is a near-sacrosanct institution of mythical proportions, an entity unto itself, sort of, and to be worshipped with religious devotion. That it served our transportation needs heroically for generations and that it was a mistake to ever replace it with today's diesel-electric units. This is a myth, but the myth persists.

On February 3rd, 1995, at about noon, I boarded the Trans-Caroo – South Africa's daily express from Johannesburg to Capetown, making twelve hundred kilometers in twenty-six hours. My seat was in the very first coach.

Seat? Yes, I somewhat guiltily confess I was riding the cushions instead of in my usual style. I had already checked out the possibilities of riding freight trains in this land down under only to learn that it's next to impossible. The security is just too tight as you find train guards at every station and in all the yards; big, husky black men carrying shot-guns. Instead of being asked for ID and ordered out of the yards, I had a strange feeling that if discovered on a train or around the yards, a person might well find himself being shot at and never mind the questions afterwards.

I was early, the power was not yet hooked on. I sat quietly, wondering who my fellow passengers might be. There were four bunks in each compartment, which on this train were usually full.

I felt a nudge as the power coupled up, then heard a strange and different sound, like compressed air escaping, making a definite hissing sound. Almost at the same time I detected an odor wafting in through the open window (South African Railways passenger trains are not air-conditioned and in summer the windows are left open). These sounds and smells took me back many years, as they reminded me of trains I'd ridden as a boy. It was unmistakable, the delicious smell of coal-smoke, while the sound could be nothing less than escaping steam.

How could it be? This country had converted to electrified rail some years back. They had held on to their steam loco's right on up to the 1980s before surrendering to the inevitable, and I had seen dozens of these marvelous old work-horses parked in various yards rusting away and fading into oblivion on deserted sidings. If there was any doubt, our departure cleared that up, as, promptly, at 12:30, we got under way with a mighty jerk that told me that, yes, indeed, we <u>did</u> have a real, honest-to-God steam engine pulling this train.

At the first curve I stuck my head out the window and saw not one, but <u>two</u> giant steam locomotives hooked up in tandem. We were double-headed, a rare sight. Leaving the station and accelerating rapidly, these two monsters were unable to synchronize their drive-wheels, which resulted in their fighting each other, producing a jerky, spasmodic ride, bouncing and jolting the entire twenty-car train and likely upsetting the water glasses in the dining car. Then as they reached their stride at about fifty-five, they leveled off, delivering power in a smooth surge.

I leaned back, enjoying myself immensely, thrilling to the magic of the whistle's high-pitched scream, reveling once more at the thought of steam railroading. Then I found I had to close the window, as the thick, black smoke poured back along the train, while the cinders came sifting by, striking my face. I held my hand out the window and it was like grains of sand in a windstorm.

At each stop all us old men came boiling out of the cars, running up ahead to gawk at the engines and ask all sorts of questions from the driver and the driver's assistant (Engineer and Fireman). Each engine had a crew, genial happy guys who loved their jobs and kept their engines shined and polished with the gauges and brass fittings gleaming. They seemed to relish all the attention and excitement, and loved to answer questions or brag about their iron horses.

They told me the two steam locomotives were only used once a week, on Fridays, as an added tourist attraction, and would be replaced with the regular electric units at the first Division Point, about two hundred miles down the line.

I noticed that the engines displayed names as well as numbers. The lead engine was called "Pamyra." They were identical 4–8–4's and their shining appearance testified to the tender loving care they got. Crowds collected at each stop to stare and photograph these gleaming reminders of a by-gone age, when railroading was filled with pride and romance and when the arrival of a train was an exciting event, not to be missed. This reverence, bordering on awe, was still visible, as I noticed that several schools in towns along the way let their kids out to line the tracks and scream and shout and wave as the Trans-Caroo went snorting by. It was quite a sight.

Later that afternoon, when the steamers were replaced by the dual electric units, we reverted back to the status of "just another train." We glided smoothly out of the station, back once more in the care of these noticeably clean and quiet engines. No smoke, no cinders, no jerky starts. Rather an almost imperceptible start, gathering speed smoothly, and rapidly achieving road speed. The steam engines were quickly forgotten. It was a minor marvel to realize how superior and efficient the electric and diesel power were in the hauling of trains. All that remained was a touch of nostalgia among the older passengers. The younger people hadn't been _that_ impressed.

Now I have always been loyal in the appreciation of steam railroading. Born and raised in that era, I considered steam almost sacred, but never went overboard about it. At the time it was the only kind around – nothing special. Here's what one had to put up with sometimes.

During WW II about twenty of us sailors dressed in summer white uniforms were detached from a ship in the Charleston Navy Yard and sent, by train, for reassignment to the Armed Guard Center in New Orleans. It was a thirty-six hour run, first on the Seaboard Air Line (SAL), then switching to the Southern Railway (Sou).

We were loaded into an old dilapidated day-coach made of wood. The weather was intolerably hot and muggy, so we opened the windows for some air and tried to settle down and sleep. By the time we arrived in New Orleans our snow white sailor suits had turned to a dirty, blackish gray color. The coal-smoke and cinders from those steam locomotives had filtered unobstructed into our car, blackening not only our clothes, but our hands and faces as well, and as we marched down Canal Street from the train station to the ferry we were a sorry yet still hilarious bunch of gobs, causing quite a spectacle. We didn't mind the stares and sympathetic grins from the people. That was all a part of the hazards of train travel back in the glorious days of steam.

About 1965, while camping with my family up in the mountains of Northern California, I heard about a steam train excursion to be held on July 4th, the next day. The town of Mount Shasta was chartering a train from the McCloud River Railroad for a trip up along the base of fabulous Mount Shasta, one of the pristinely lovely forest areas of our country. A four hour ride plus a picnic lunch – just the ticket.

My kids would simply love it. None of them had ever been on a train – much less an open air excursion pulled by a snorting steam engine. Boy, what a thrill. I was sure they'd all be as excited as I as we drove up to the siding the next morning, all primed and ready for a great day. Were they ever smiling-faced and eager as they saw the consist of three old wooden flatcars that had wooden benches nailed to the deck, plus two tired day-coaches, all pulled by an ancient 2–6–2 that had probably hauled logs for fifty years and had been taken out of retirement and fired up for this one occasion. Were they bubbling with enthusiasm? Did they exclaim joyfully, "Oh, daddy, how wonderful of you to surprise us on the Fourth of July with a neat-o ride on a real, back-in-your-day steam train?" Well . . . not quite.

I could tell by their faces they considered the whole concept a bit gross, but they glumly climbed aboard, taking their places on the bench seat with an air of injured innocence, like, "What will our dad make us do next?" sort of thing.

We were soon on our way chugging through the forested greenery and toiling up the grade at about fifteen mph. At the summit we stopped for water at an old wooden water tank that evidently hadn't been used for years, as it was leaking from every joint. At noon we all got off for a picnic lunch then returned slowly down the mountain and back to Mt. Shasta City, where the kids were only too happy to get off. End of excursion.

I was a bit disappointed that the trip wasn't all I'd hoped for. The children seemed totally unimpressed, tolerating the trip only for my pleasure. They thought the train was too slow; that there was nothing to see – just trees; the smoke had irritated their eyes and made them cough. Plus the unspoken disapproval on their faces as they watched their parents unabashed enjoyment.

My big Fourth of July surprise had been a bust. They didn't say it in so many words, but I could tell by their expressions they had this one big question uppermost in mind.

"What's the big deal about steam engines, anyway?"

Hobo Rap

My name's not Hammer
I wrote this little poem
No need to clap
Take it nice and slow
If I had my way
It's no pity
Celebrate Mayday
Or turn some pages
Mind in a fog?
If you ride Amtrak
If you're a high liver
Want a real pain?
Turn your face
C & O
Stop and dally
Pay a fine
Hit the track
Travel light
Hop a freight?
Ride the Rods?
Grass is green?
Headin' West?
Goin' East?
There's no sauna
Got the fever?
Ridin' free
Santa Fe?
Heavy load?
Feelin' blue?
Dodge a cop?
Be specific
Lots of time?
Fire-ball mail?
Runnin' late?
See the sign?
What to do?
Not too full?
Want to melt
Need a friend?
Miss home base?
See the view?
Where owners are crew
Ride with the jerks

I'm not on a map
I call Hobo Rap
Just give it the snap
Now here we go
I'd leave old L.A.
Leavin' Shaky City
Up in the Gay Bay
Over in Lost Wages
Take the Grey Dog
You might not get back
Ride the McCloud River
Boston & Maine
To the Natchez Trace
Is the way to go
On the Lehigh Valley
On the Rummy Dummy Line
Don't look back
Keep outta sight
Learn to wait
Time with Gods
Make the scene
Highline's best
Lowline's least
On the Lackawanna
Time to leave her
On the old S.P.
No way
Milwaukee Road
Ride the Soo
Catch the MOP
Union Pacific
Frisco Line
Try Conrail
Catch the Nickle Plate
Rock Island Line
Catch the "Q"
Dodge the Bull
Try Cotton Belt
That's BN
Ride old dirty face
D & RGW
C N W
The Cheap & Nothing Works

Billy Goat Verse
Lord, Lord
Have a good time
Baltimore & Ohio
No where to hide
You can't go
Got no ticket?
You got a pass?
If you got a pass
Yes, you can ride
Feelin' fine
Hoist your pack
Headin' home?
Wave your hand
Travel in style
Catch me if you can
Hey, hey
Sign on a Milwaukee
Cheap Material
Atchison, Topeka
All tramps
Denver & Rio Grande
Damn Rough
Dirty Rotten
The Big "G"
Those were my
Hit the grit
Last time around?

See America first
Get on board
Don't cost you a dime
That's a route I want to go
No place to ride
On the B & O
You'll have to kick it
Bet your ass
You ride first class
And ride inside
Get down the line
Climb a double-stack
No more to roam
All over this land
Mile after mile
On the California Man
What you say
Boxcar Door
And Service Poor
And Santa Fe
And Soldiers free
Western
Goin' West
Greasy & Wet
And the N.P.
University
Head for Britt
Catch the WESTBOUND

I Knew About Mexicans

(Editor's Note: This is a 1993 re-print from "THE HOBO" Magazine, written by its founder – Oklahoma Slim – who played his final hand and caught the Westbound in February, 2000)

The rain that falls on the just and the unjust alike, falls just a little bit more on the hobo.

I was cold, tired and hungry. This isn't unusual in the life I lived, but ever so often you have to do something about it and the time was now.

All I had in the line of food was large bag of coffee beans and about fifty sacks of Bull Durham I had boosted (stolen) from the Great A and P Tea Company. Now I know there ain't no food value in caffeine and nicotine, but we lived on the stuff for months.

It was a dinky little town but I thought I might squeeze a handout from it, but the town clown caught me right away. I stood in the rain while he sat in a warm squad car and told me what would happen to me if I was not on the next freight out. Of course I done the proper thing. I went back to the yards. Who wants to go to jail?

I found a little shack where, if I stood up straight with my back to the wall, I could stay out of the rain – well, almost out of the rain. The next freight had no empties. When the next train came I didn't go to the tracks as I couldn't see an empty until close to the rear.

There is protocol in the hobo world. You don't jump into an empty if there is someone in the car. You ask permission to share their car.

I see an empty coming up and had to run like Hell to catch it; threw my bedroll in the door and climbed in. Then I see the two Mexicans in the south end of the car. I went to the north end of the car, spread my bedroll out, crawled in and stuck my switchblade by my ear. I knew about Mexicans.

After a train gets its speed up it hits a smooth rhythm so that anything that moves will change the rhythm, and then you come up swinging your switchblade. The train hits its rhythm, I shut my eyes, and slept like a babe in arms.

Came the dawn and the rain stopped. It was a dreary day. I gathered up a few scraps of wood that was laying around and hit the grit as we pulled into the jungle. I see the Mexicans gather up a little wood as I bailed out. I got a small fire going, put on some coffee water and ground up some of my coffee beans on a rock. That coffee sure smelled good; with a smoke, nothing is better, especially when you have nothing else.

A short way off I see the Mexicans had a fire going and was cooking something that smelled damn good. In every life there are times you come up with a good idea and this was the time I came up with a brilliant one. I ground up some coffee, made a half gallon and walked over to their jungle – not too close, and said, "Amigo" (the only word I knew in Spanish).

They were somewhat startled at my approach and offer of coffee. I could tell they knew about white men, but the smell of coffee got to them. I went back to my jungle and waited to see if the bread I had cast on the waters would come back soggy, or would it gain me something.

I see the Mexicans cooking up something. After a while one of them came over to my jungle with a can. "Amigo," he says, and held out the can.

Turned out it was full of mush. Now there is nothing better than corn-meal mush, coffee and Bull Durham, I always say, especially when you ain't got anything else.

When the train high-balled I whistled at the Mexicans and ran for the same boxcar – and they followed. We was in for a long, slow drag. During the day I tried to talk to the boys, and one had an address he showed me. It was south of Pueblo, Colorado. I nodded that I knew where, and when the train stopped for water, I ran over to a gas station and got a free road map for them.

After a long, tiresome journey we pulled into Pueblo. I talked to a brakie and found out we had a couple of hours till the Southbound local was due, so we jungled up on cornmeal mush, coffee and Bull Durham.

As we set and smoked, I fix up a little packet of coffee and Bull Durham for the boys. When they saw what I was doing, they fix up a small pack of corn-meal for me.

The local came in and I took them over to a boxcar. When the train high-balled, I gave them a wave.

I guess I don't know about Mexicans, and I think they realized they didn't know about Gringos.

* * * * *

ABOUT THE AUTHOR

Robert J. Symmonds, aka Guitar Whitey, was born in Seattle in 1921. He attended John Hay Grade School and Queen Anne Highschool, dropping out his junior year of 1938 to help support the family when his father's business failed. He traveled the Western States, mainly by freight train, working as a "fruit tramp" until joining the U.S. Navy soon after Pearl Harbor, in 1942. Four years of touring the world on Navy ships gave him a taste for globe-trotting. At war's end he joined the U.S. Merchant Marine for another two-year stint at sea.

Settling in California with his English wife, Joyce (now together 55 years), they raised four children while he worked at dozens of unrewarding, low-paying jobs – a proper career always eluding him. Whitey tried his hand in many unrelated fields, such as deckhand on tugboats, door-to-door selling, construction laborer, tour-boat operator and store-keeping. He was seven years at Knott's Berry Farm Amusement Park in Southern California, as a combination bartender and folksinger.

Whitey states that he was, "an impractical dreamer, a rebel, a malcontent and a lifelong wanderer." He admits he was a hopeless romantic and adventurer, always a financial failure. He figures he was born fifty years too late; he was the guy Robert Service had in mind when he wrote "The Men Who Don't Fit In." That was Whitey. Seems he resisted all attempts by friends and family to make him settle down, fly right, wear a suit and tie and be an upstanding citizen. He preferred to run free, do his own thing. He was like a wild animal – not wanting to be caught.

Whitey has had a lifelong love affair with guitar playing, though he claims to be not a very good player. He bought his first guitar at age 12, and hopped his first freight train at age 13, riding for pleasure off-and-on for some sixty-one years. He quit riding the rails regularly at age 74, realizing he no longer had the upper-body strength to hoist himself into a boxcar. He still plays guitar and sings hobo songs. His only public performances of late have been at high schools, where he tells students about the Depression Era and sings a few old-timey songs.

Now in his eighties, Whitey and Joyce, retired on Social Security, live contently in a modest mobile home near the ocean in San Luis Obispo, California, enjoying the excellent weather. Whitey doesn't travel much anymore, but still likes to look back and reminisce on his near-incredible adventures. In surprising good health, he considers himself the most fortunate man alive.